CHILDHOOD WRITINGS

The Cambridge
JANE AUSTEN

VOLUMES IN THIS SERIES

1. Childhood Writings
2. Northanger Abbey
3. Sense and Sensibility
4. Pride and Prejudice
5. Mansfield Park
6. Emma
7. Persuasion
8. Later Manuscripts

With prefaces and notes by Janet Todd

JANE AUSTEN

Childhood Writings

The Collector's Edition

With preface and notes by
JANET TODD

Shaftesbury Road, Cambridge CB2 8EA, United Kingdom

One Liberty Plaza, 20th Floor, New York, NY 10006, USA

477 Williamstown Road, Port Melbourne, VIC 3207, Australia

314–321, 3rd Floor, Plot 3, Splendor Forum, Jasola District Centre, New Delhi – 110025, India

103 Penang Road, #05–06/07, Visioncrest Commercial, Singapore 238467

Cambridge University Press is part of Cambridge University Press & Assessment, a department of the University of Cambridge.

We share the University's mission to contribute to society through the pursuit of education, learning and research at the highest international levels of excellence.

www.cambridge.org
Information on this title: www.cambridge.org/9781009432382

DOI: 10.1017/9781009432375

© Cambridge University Press & Assessment 2025

This publication is in copyright. Subject to statutory exception and to the provisions of relevant collective licensing agreements, no reproduction of any part may take place without the written permission of Cambridge University Press & Assessment.

When citing this work, please include a reference to the DOI 10.1017/9781009432375

First published 2025

Cover design, illustration and frontispieces by Lauren Downing
Text design by Lyn Davies Design

Printed in the United Kingdom by CPI Group Ltd, Croydon CR0 4YY

A catalogue record for this publication is available from the British Library

Library of Congress Cataloging-in-Publication Data
Names: Austen, Jane, 1775–1817, author. | Todd, Janet, 1942– editor.
Title: Childhood writings / Jane Austen ; with preface and notes by Janet Todd.
Description: The collector's edition. | Cambridge ; New York, NY : Cambridge University Press, 2025. | Series: CCJA the Cambridge Jane Austen | Includes bibliographical references and index.
Identifiers: LCCN 2024045996 | ISBN 9781009432382 (hardback) | ISBN 9781009432375 (ebook)
Subjects: LCSH: Austen, Jane, 1775–1817 – Literary collections. | Austen, Jane, 1775–1817 – Manuscripts.
Classification: LCC PR4032 .T57 2025 | DDC 828/.709–dc23/eng/20241007
LC record available at https://lccn.loc.gov/2024045996

ISBN 978-1-009-43238-2 Hardback

Cambridge University Press & Assessment has no responsibility for the persistence or accuracy of URLs for external or third-party internet websites referred to in this publication and does not guarantee that any content on such websites is, or will remain,

The texts in this edition are based on
The Cambridge Edition of the Works of Jane
Austen (2005–8), with grateful acknowledgement. Readers
interested in a more detailed textual account and in further
exploration of the novels and their publication history should
consult those volumes. The present edition contains explanatory
endnotes: under thematic headings, they provide information
on a cultural, historical and literary context that might be
unfamiliar to a modern reader. A few footnotes indicate
words that have changed meaning between
Austen's time and our own.

CONTENTS

Preface	*ix*
Volume the First	
Frederic and Elfrida	*3*
Jack and Alice	*11*
Edgar and Emma	*27*
Henry and Eliza	*31*
The adventures of Mr Harley	*37*
Sir William Mountague	*38*
Memoirs of Mr Clifford	*40*
The beautifull Cassandra	*42*
Amelia Webster	*45*
The Visit	*49*
The Mystery	*55*
The Three Sisters	*58*
A fragment—written to inculcate the practise of Virtue	*72*
A beautiful description of the different effects of Sensibility on different Minds	*73*
The Generous Curate	*75*
Ode to Pity	*77*

Volume the Second

Love and Freindship	*81*
Lesley Castle	*113*
The History of England	*141*
EXPLANATORY NOTES TO 'THE HISTORY OF ENGLAND'	*155*
A Collection of Letters	*158*
The female philosopher	*177*
The first Act of a Comedy	*179*
A Letter from a Young Lady	*182*
A Tour through Wales	*184*
A Tale	*185*

Volume the Third

Evelyn	*189*
Catharine, or the Bower	*198*
General Notes	*239*

PREFACE

On her fifteenth birthday, the future novelist Frances Burney solemnly burnt her juvenilia. By contrast, her contemporary Jane Austen carefully preserved hers. Some of the twenty-seven items she wrote between the ages of eleven and seventeen are just a few lines long, but all are carefully copied out into three little notebooks. These are presented so as to mimic published works, with volume numbers and dedications. She kept the volumes beside her all her life.

Austen enjoyed her early writings, as did the family to whom most are dedicated. All are embedded in this family, with 'The History of England' being an extreme example. 'The History' is illustrated with medallion or coin-shaped portraits by Cassandra Austen, caricatures probably based on prints, but with the picture of Mary, Queen of Scots, just possibly a portrait of Jane herself. The bias towards the Stuarts which Jane proclaimed throughout 'The History' was derived from family tradition: the Leighs, her grandmaternal ancestors, had sheltered the Stuart king Charles I at Stoneleigh Abbey during the seventeenth-century Civil Wars.

The pieces Jane composed between the ages of eleven and fifteen are ebullient, anarchic, salacious and often surreal: they display self-indulgence and wickedness of all sorts: gluttony, drunkenness, matricide, theft and sexy excess, as well as total self-absorption. The cheery characters roar through transgressions, mostly without a shred of shame or responsibility. With gallows humour, criminal acts become a cartoonish form of liberation accompanied by blithe unconcern at consequence, the only exceptions being Charlotte in 'Frederic and Elfrida' who drowns herself after recollecting she has promised herself to two men, and Sukey Simpson in 'Jack and Alice' who is hanged for murder. Time and space are confounded; people in their fifties are young, toddlers prudent, and precocious babies give 'sprightly answers' from the cradle.

Unusually for childhood writings, Jane Austen's earliest pieces are literary: they mock adult reading. The Austens must have been so familiar with romantic novels of the 1780s that, by the time she was eleven, Jane was ready to explode their themes and apparatus in a series of comical skits. In one tale, a title character never appears, other tales lack conclusions, while haphazard details such as hair colour and lists of incongruous dishes replace conventional descriptions. Sentimental clichés are relentlessly burlesqued in coincidences of lost and found infants while overblown emotions are delivered in insistently superlative vocabulary. When introduced in romance, characters tell their life stories; here an interesting lady refuses to divulge hers however much she is asked. In 'Love and Freindship', the most accomplished and longest of the purely comic works, Jane Austen draws attention to her own absurdity when a father interrupts his son's sentimental posturing by observing that the young man has been reading too many novels.

More serious literature also gets short shrift. The rotund rhetorical flourishes of the austere moralist Samuel Johnson are wickedly parodied in Jane's absurd antithetical sentences, while the exemplary hero of Samuel Richardson's *Sir Charles Grandison* is transformed into the vain and haughty Charles Adams of 'Jack and Alice'. Richardson's novel runs to seven prosy volumes; young Jane comments on this prolixity by letting the twelve chapters of 'The Beautiful Cassandra' cover only four manuscript pages; 'The History of England' reduces Oliver Goldsmith's four-volume *The History of England, from the Earliest Times to the Death of George II* (1771) to a mere thirty-three pages of outrageous 'prejudice'.

Through all the mimicry and mockery runs the excitement of language and its imaginative possibilities. Meaning is destabilised by zeugma – when seven days and 'the lovely Charlotte' have both 'expired' – and by incongruous adverbs – theft becomes 'graceful' purloining – or adjectives – a host offers accommodation in a 'noble' tent of blankets and sticks. Precise, often ridiculous, numbers for money or ages pretend to realism, as do the asterisks and dashes supposedly hiding actual locations and characters. Even sillier is the romance habit of disguising names: 'The noble Youth informed us that his name was Lindsay—. for particular reasons, however I shall conceal it under that of Talbot.'

Jane Austen's characters are freed from the commonplace civility and restraint of actual eighteenth-century English life. In defiance of conventional manners, they mock ugliness and deformity and they openly display the usually hidden traits of 'Ambition, Envy, and Self-admiration'. Food and drink become obsessive, dominating other social concerns, and even life and death: in 'Lesley Castle' anxiety for the fate of the great wedding meal tops that provoked by a dying bridegroom. Houses exist solely for their owners' convenience, so there is no need for superfluous chairs and guests must sit on each other's laps. Society's institutions collapse: underage couples are wed without ritual or priest, and youths walk at will from prison.

For all the comic high jinks, real-life issues do emerge, as in the tensions between generations. Land and money are held by older men, thus frustrating the desires of youth, and girls must be marketed for marriage or market themselves. Several tales focus on the inevitable and ruthless rivalry of young women for scarce affluent partners. No wonder Alice in 'Jack and Alice' runs to the bottle when denied the only eligible man in Pammydiddle. As she moves from the purely comical to the more psychologically and socially realistic in 'Catharine, or the Bower' written at sixteen, Jane Austen draws attention to the restricted life of genteel girls and the difficulty they encounter in being both spirited and prudent. How is sexual desire to be controlled in young women but provoked in young men, then channelled into marriage? Like 'The Watsons', printed in *Later Manuscripts,* this unfinished tale is linked to Austen's published novels. For example, Catharine's severe aunt connects her flirtations to national disorder, declaring 'the welfare of every Nation depends upon the virtue of it's individuals'. This idea would be more subtly and seriously addressed in *Mansfield Park*, the novel Austen wrote twenty-one years later. Also like 'The Watsons', and less clearly in the published novels, 'Catharine' touches on the extreme expedients to which women were forced to resort in search of husbands.

Austen's niece Caroline reported that her aunt 'wished she had *read* more, and written less' before she was sixteen. If Jane had followed this advice, we would have lost some of the best childhood writings in the language. Although all the items in the three notebooks irrupt from a private world – much of which remains private – they nonetheless have the power to speak to us now, delivering across the centuries a precocious, alarmingly assured young girl.

The childhood writings may be usefully read as preface to or alongside Austen's six great novels, setting out in spoof and burlesque themes later addressed seriously. Or they can be scrutinised for their subtext of social and psychological critique. Or they may be enjoyed simply for their raw energy and ruthless joie de vivre, for their portrait of a young author intoxicated by her own powers, bent above all on entertaining her family and making them laugh. In 'The first Act of a Comedy', a chorus of ploughboys gleefully echo the heroine: 'be fun, be fun, be fun'.

VOLUME THE FIRST

FREDERIC AND ELFRIDA
A novel.

To Miss Lloyd

My dear Martha

As a small testimony of the gratitude I feel for your late generosity to me in finishing my muslin Cloak, I beg leave to offer you this little production of your sincere Freind

The Author

CHAPTER THE FIRST.

The Uncle of Elfrida was the Father of Frederic; in other words, they were first cousins by the Father's side.

Being both born in one day and both brought up at one school, it was not wonderfull that they should look on each other with something more than bare politeness. They loved with mutual sincerity but were both determined not to transgress the rules of Propriety by owning their attachment, either to the object beloved, or to any one else.

They were exceedingly handsome and so much alike, that it was not every one who knew them apart. Nay even their most intimate freinds had nothing to distinguish them by, but the shape of the face, the colour of the Eye, the length of the Nose and the difference of the complexion.

Elfrida had an intimate freind to whom, being on a visit to an Aunt, she wrote the following Letter.

To Miss Drummond
"Dear Charlotte"
"I should be obliged to you, if you would buy me, during your stay with Mrs Williamson, a new and fashionable Bonnet, to suit the Complexion of your"
"E. Falknor."

Charlotte, whose character was a willingness to oblige every one, when she returned into the Country, brought her Freind the wished-for Bonnet, and so ended this little adventure, much to the satisfaction of all parties.

On her return to Crankhumdunberry (of which sweet village her father was Rector) Charlotte was received with the greatest Joy by Frederic and Elfrida, who, after pressing her alternately to their Bosoms, proposed to her to take a walk in a Grove of Poplars which led from the Parsonage to a verdant Lawn enamelled with a variety of variegated flowers and watered by a purling Stream, brought from the Valley of Tempé by a passage under ground.

In this Grove they had scarcely remained above 9 hours, when they were suddenly agreably surprized by hearing a most delightfull voice warble the following stanza.

Song.
That Damon was in love with me
    I once thought and beleiv'd
But now that he is not I see,
    I fear I was deceiv'd.

No sooner were the lines finished than they beheld by a turning in the Grove 2 elegant young women leaning on each other's arm, who immediately on perceiving them, took a different path and disappeared from their sight.

CHAPTER THE SECOND.

As ELFRIDA AND her companions, had seen enough of them to know that they were neither the 2 Miss Greens, nor Mrs Jackson and her

Daughter, they could not help expressing their surprise at their appearance; till at length recollecting, that a new family had lately taken a House not far from the Grove, they hastened home, determined to lose no time in forming an acquaintance with 2 such amiable and worthy Girls, of which family they rightly imagined them to be a part.

Agreable to such a determination, they went that very evening to pay their respects to Mrs Fitzroy and her two Daughters. On being shewn into an elegant dressing room, ornamented with festoons of artificial flowers, they were struck with the engaging Exterior and beautifull outside of Jezalinda the eldest of the young Ladies; but e'er they had been many minutes seated, the Wit and Charms which shone resplendant in the conversation of the amiable Rebecca, enchanted them so much that they all with one accord jumped up and exclaimed.

"Lovely and too charming Fair one, notwithstanding your forbidding Squint, your greazy tresses and your swelling Back, which are more frightfull than imagination can paint or pen describe, I cannot refrain from expressing my raptures, at the engaging Qualities of your Mind, which so amply atone for the Horror, with which your first appearance must ever inspire the unwary visitor."

"Your Sentiments so nobly expressed on the different excellencies of Indian and English Muslins, and the judicious preference you give the former, have excited in me an admiration of which I can alone give an adequate idea, by assuring you it is nearly equal to what I feel for myself."

Then making a profound Curtesy to the amiable and abashed Rebecca, they left the room and hurried home.

From this period, the intimacy between the Families of Fitzroy, Drummond, and Falknor, daily encreased till at length it grew to such a pitch, that they did not scruple to kick one another out of the window on the slightest provocation.

During this happy state of Harmony, the eldest Miss Fitzroy ran off with the Coachman and the amiable Rebecca was asked in marriage by Captain Roger of Buckinghamshire.

Mrs Fitzroy did not approve of the match on account of the tender years of the young couple, Rebecca being but 36 and Captain Roger little more than 63. To remedy this objection, it was agreed that they should wait a little while till they were a good deal older.

CHAPTER THE THIRD

In the mean time the parents of Frederic proposed to those of Elfrida, an union between them, which being accepted with pleasure, the wedding cloathes were bought and nothing remained to be settled but the naming of the Day.

As to the lovely Charlotte, being importuned with eagerness to pay another visit to her Aunt, she determined to accept the invitation and in consequence of it walked to Mrs Fitzroys to take leave of the amiable Rebecca, whom she found surrounded by Patches, Powder, Pomatum and Paint with which she was vainly endeavouring to remedy the natural plainness of her face.

"I am come my amiable Rebecca, to take my leave of you for the fortnight I am destined to spend with my Aunt. Beleive me this separation is painfull to me, but it is as necessary as the labour which now engages you."

"Why to tell you the truth my Love, replied Rebecca, I have lately taken it into my head to think (perhaps with little reason) that my complexion is by no means equal to the rest of my face and have therefore taken, as you see, to white and red paint which I would scorn to use on any other occasion as I hate Art."

Charlotte, who perfectly understood the meaning of her freind's speech, was too goodtemper'd and obliging to refuse her, what she knew she wished,—a compliment; and they parted the best freinds in the world.

With a heavy heart and streaming Eyes did she ascend the lovely vehicle[a] which bore her from her freinds and home; but greived as she was, she little thought in what a strange and different manner she should return to it.

On her entrance into the city of London which was the place of Mrs Williamson's abode, the postilion, whose stupidity was

[a] a post chaise [JA's note].

amazing, declared and declared even without the least shame or Compunction, that having never been informed he was totally ignorant of what part of the Town, he was to drive to.

Charlotte, whose nature we have before intimated, was an earnest desire to oblige every one, with the greatest Condescension and Good humour informed him that he was to drive to Portland Place, which he accordingly did and Charlotte soon found herself in the arms of a fond Aunt.

Scarcely were they seated as usual, in the most affectionate manner in one chair, than the Door suddenly opened and an aged gentleman with a sallow face and old pink Coat, partly by intention and partly thro' weakness was at the feet of the lovely Charlotte, declaring his attachment to her and beseeching her pity in the most moving manner.

Not being able to resolve to make any one miserable, she consented to become his wife; where upon the Gentleman left the room and all was quiet.

Their quiet however continued but a short time, for on a second opening of the door a young and Handsome Gentleman with a new blue coat, entered and intreated from the lovely Charlotte, permission to pay to her, his addresses.

There was a something in the appearance of the second Stranger, that influenced Charlotte in his favour, to the full as much as the appearance of the first: she could not account for it, but so it was.

Having therefore agreable to that and the natural turn of her mind to make every one happy, promised to become his Wife the next morning, he took his leave and the two Ladies sat down to Supper on a young Leveret, a brace of Partridges, a leash of Pheasants and a Dozen of Pigeons.

CHAPTER THE FOURTH

IT WAS NOT TILL the next morning that Charlotte recollected the double engagement she had entered into; but when she did, the reflection of her past folly, operated so strongly on her mind, that she resolved to be guilty of a greater, and to that end threw herself into a deep stream which ran thro' her Aunts pleasure Grounds in Portland Place.

She floated to Crankhumdunberry where she was picked up and buried; the following epitaph, composed by Frederic Elfrida and Rebecca, was placed on her tomb.

Epitaph
    Here lies our freind who having promis-ed
That unto two she would be marri-ed
    Threw her sweet Body and her lovely face
Into the Stream that runs thro' Portland Place

These sweet lines, as pathetic as beautifull were never read by any one who passed that way, without a shower of tears, which if they should fail of exciting in you, Reader, your mind must be unworthy to peruse them.

Having performed the last sad office to their departed freind, Frederic and Elfrida together with Captain Roger and Rebecca returned to Mrs Fitzroy's at whose feet they threw themselves with one accord and addressed her in the following Manner.

"Madam"

"When the sweet Captain Roger first addressed the amiable Rebecca, you alone objected to their union on account of the tender years of the Parties. That plea can be no more, seven days being now expired, together with the lovely Charlotte, since the Captain first spoke to you on the subject."

"Consent then Madam to their union and as a reward, this smelling Bottle which I enclose in my right hand, shall be yours and yours forever; I never will claim it again. But if you refuse to join their hands in 3 days time, this dagger which I enclose in my left shall be steeped in your hearts blood."

"Speak then Madam and decide their fate and yours."

Such gentle and sweet persuasion could not fail of having the desired effect. The answer they received, was this.

"My dear young freinds"

"The arguments you have used are too just and too eloquent to be withstood; Rebecca in 3 days time, you shall be united to the Captain."

This speech, than which nothing could be more satisfactory, was received with Joy by all; and peace being once more restored on all sides, Captain Roger intreated Rebecca to favour them with a Song, in compliance with which request having first assured them that she had a terrible cold, she sung as follows.

Song
When Corydon went to the fair
    He bought a red ribbon for Bess,
With which she encircled her hair
    And made herself look very fess.

CHAPTER THE FIFTH

AT THE END OF 3 days Captain Roger and Rebecca were united and immediately after the Ceremony set off in the Stage Waggon for the Captains seat in Buckinghamshire.

The parents of Elfrida, alltho' they earnestly wished to see her married to Frederic before they died, yet knowing the delicate frame of her mind could ill bear the least excertion and rightly judging that naming her wedding day would be too great a one, forebore to press her on the subject.

Weeks and Fortnights flew away without gaining the least ground; the Cloathes grew out of fashion and at length Capt. Roger and his Lady arrived to pay a visit to their Mother and introduce to her their beautifull Daughter of eighteen.

Elfrida, who had found her former acquaintance were growing too old and too ugly to be any longer agreable, was rejoiced to hear of the arrival of so pretty a girl as Eleanor with whom she determined to form the strictest freindship.

But the Happiness she had expected from an acquaintance with Eleanor, she soon found was not to be received, for she had not only the mortification of finding herself treated by her as little less than an old woman, but had actually the horror of perceiving a growing passion in the Bosom of Frederic for the Daughter of the amiable Rebecca.

The instant she had the first idea of such an attachment, she flew to Frederic and in a manner truly heroick, spluttered out to him her intention of being married the next Day.

To one in his predicament who possessed less personal Courage than Frederic was master of, such a speech would have been Death; but he not being the least terrified boldly replied,

"Damme Elfrida—*you* may be married tomorrow but *I* won't."

This answer distressed her too much for her delicate Constitution. She accordingly fainted and was in such a hurry to have a succession of fainting fits, that she had scarcely patience enough to recover from one before she fell into another.

Tho', in any threatening Danger to his Life or Liberty, Frederic was as bold as brass yet in other respects his heart was as soft as cotton and immediately on hearing of the dangerous way Elfrida was in, he flew to her and finding her better than he had been taught to expect, was united to her Forever—.

FINIS.

JACK AND ALICE
a novel.

*Is respectfully inscribed to Francis William Austen Esqr
Midshipman on board his Majesty's Ship the Perseverance
by his obedient humble Servant
The Author*

CHAPTER THE FIRST

Mr Johnson was once upon atime about 53; in a twelve-month afterwards he was 54, which so much delighted him that he was determined to celebrate his next Birth day by giving a Masquerade to his Children and Freinds. Accordingly on the Day he attained his 55th year tickets were dispatched to all his Neighbours to that purpose. His acquaintance indeed in that part of the World were not very numerous as they consisted only of Lady Williams, Mr and Mrs Jones, Charles Adams and the 3 Miss Simpsons, who composed the neighbourhood of Pammydiddle and formed the Masquerade.

Before I proceed to give an account of the Evening, it will be proper to describe to my reader, the persons and Characters of the party introduced to his acquaintance.

Mr and Mrs Jones were both rather tall and very passionate, but were in other respects, good tempered, wellbehaved People. Charles Adams was an amiable, accomplished and bewitching young Man; of so dazzling a Beauty that none but Eagles could look him in the Face.

Miss Simpson was pleasing in her person, in her Manners and in her Disposition; an unbounded ambition was her only fault. Her second sister Sukey was Envious, Spitefull and Malicious. Her person was short, fat and disagreable. Cecilia (the youngest) was perfectly handsome but too affected to be pleasing.

In Lady Williams every virtue met. She was a widow with a handsome Jointure and the remains of a very handsome face. Tho' Benevolent and Candid, she was Generous and sincere; Tho' Pious and Good, she was Religious and amiable, and Tho' Elegant and Agreable, she was Polished and Entertaining.

The Johnsons were a family of Love, and though a little addicted to the Bottle and the Dice, had many good Qualities.

Such was the party assembled in the elegant Drawing Room of Johnson Court, amongst which the pleasing figure of a Sultana was the most remarkable of the female Masks. Of the Males a Mask representing the Sun, was the most universally admired. The Beams that darted from his Eyes were like those of that glorious Luminary tho' infinitely Superior. So strong were they that no one dared venture within half a mile of them; he had therefore the best part of the Room to himself, its size not amounting to more than 3 quarters of a mile in length and half a one in breadth. The Gentleman at last finding the feirceness of his beams to be very inconvenient to the concourse by obliging them to croud together in one corner of the room, half shut his eyes by which means, the Company discovered him to be Charles Adams in his plain green Coat, without any mask at all.

When their astonishment was a little subsided their attention was attracted by 2 Domino's who advanced in a horrible Passion; they were both very tall, but seemed in other respects to have many good qualities. "These said the witty Charles, these are Mr and Mrs Jones." and so indeed they were.

No one could imagine who was the Sultana! Till at length on her addressing a beautifull Flora who was reclining in a studied attitude on a couch, with "Oh Cecilia, I wish I was really what I pretend to be", she was discovered by the never failing genius of Charles Adams, to be the elegant but ambitious Caroline Simpson,

JACK AND ALICE

and the person to whom she addressed herself, he rightly imagined to be her lovely but affected sister Cecilia.

The Company now advanced to a Gaming Table where sat 3 Dominos (each with a bottle in their hand) deeply engaged, but a female in the character of Virtue fled with hasty footsteps from the shocking scene, whilst a little fat woman representing Envy, sate alternately on the foreheads of the 3 Gamesters. Charles Adams was still as bright as ever; he soon discovered the party at play to be the 3 Johnsons, Envy to be Sukey Simpson and Virtue to be Lady Williams.

The Masks were then all removed and the Company retired to another room, to partake of elegant and well managed Entertainment, after which the Bottle being pretty briskly pushed about by the 3 Johnsons, the whole party not excepting even Virtue were carried home, Dead Drunk.

CHAPTER THE SECOND

FOR THREE MONTHS did the Masquerade afford ample subject for conversation to the inhabitants of Pammydiddle; but no character at it was so fully expatiated on as Charles Adams. The singularity of his appearance, the beams which darted from his eyes, the brightness of his Wit, and the whole *tout ensemble* of his person had subdued the hearts of so many of the young Ladies, that of the six present at the Masquerade but five had returned uncaptivated. Alice Johnson was the unhappy sixth whose heart had not been able to withstand the power of his Charms. But as it may appear strange to my Readers, that so much worth and Excellence as he possessed should have conquered only hers, it will be necessary to inform them that the Miss Simpsons were defended from his Power by Ambition, Envy, and Self-admiration.

Every wish of Caroline was centered in a titled Husband; whilst in Sukey such superior excellence could only raise her Envy not her Love, and Cecilia was too tenderly attached to herself to be pleased with any one besides. As for Lady Williams and Mrs Jones, the former of them was too sensible, to fall in love with one so much her Junior and the latter, tho' very tall and very passionate was too fond of her Husband to think of such a thing.

Yet in spite of every endeavour on the part of Miss Johnson to discover any attachment to her in him; the cold and indifferent heart of Charles Adams still to all appearance, preserved its native freedom; polite to all but partial to none, he still remained the lovely, the lively, but insensible Charles Adams.

One evening, Alice finding herself somewhat heated by wine (no very uncommon case) determined to seek a releif for her disordered Head and Love-sick Heart in the Conversation of the intelligent Lady Williams.

She found her Ladyship at home as was in general the Case, for she was not fond of going out, and like the great Sir Charles Grandison scorned to deny herself when at Home, as she looked on that fashionable method of shutting out disagreable Visitors, as little less than downright Bigamy.

In spite of the wine she had been drinking, poor Alice was uncommonly out of spirits; she could think of nothing but Charles Adams, she could talk of nothing but him, and in short spoke so openly that Lady Williams soon discovered the unreturned affection she bore him, which excited her Pity and Compassion so strongly that she addressed her in the following Manner.

"I perceive but too plainly my dear Miss Johnson, that your Heart has not been able to withstand the fascinating Charms of this young Man and I pity you sincerely. Is it a first Love?"

"It is."

"I am still more greived to hear *that*; I am myself a sad example of the Miseries, in general attendant on a first Love and I am determined for the future to avoid the like Misfortune. I wish it may not be too late for you to do the same; if it is not endeavour my dear Girl to secure yourself from so great a Danger. A second attachment is seldom attended with any serious consequences; against *that* therefore I have nothing to say. Preserve yourself from a first Love and you need not fear a second."

"You mentioned Madam something of your having yourself been a sufferer by the misfortune you are so good as to wish me to avoid. Will you favour me with your Life and Adventures?"

"Willingly my Love."

CHAPTER THE THIRD

"My Father was a gentleman of considerable Fortune in Berkshire; myself and a few more his only Children. I was but six years old when I had the misfortune of losing my Mother and being at that time young and Tender, my father instead of sending me to School, procured an able handed Governess to superintend my Education at Home. My Brothers were placed at Schools suitable to their Ages and my Sisters being all younger than myself, remained still under the Care of their Nurse."

"Miss Dickins was an excellent Governess. She instructed me in the Paths of Virtue; under her tuition I daily became more amiable, and might perhaps by this time have nearly attained perfection, had not my worthy Preceptoress been torn from my arms e'er I had attained my seventeenth year. I never shall forget her last words. 'My dear Kitty' she said 'Good night t'ye.' I never saw her afterwards" continued Lady Williams wiping her eyes, "She eloped with the Butler the same night."

"I was invited the following year by a distant relation of my Father's to spend the Winter with her in town. Mrs Watkins was a Lady of Fashion, Family and fortune; she was in general esteemed a pretty Woman, but I never thought her very handsome, for my part. She had too high a forehead, Her eyes were too small and she had too much colour."

"How can *that* be?" interrupted Miss Johnson reddening with anger; "Do you think that any one can have too much colour?"

"Indeed I do, and I'll tell you why I do my dear Alice; when a person has too great a degree of red in their Complexion, it gives their face in my opinion, too red a look."

"But can a face my Lady have too red a look."?

"Certainly my dear Miss Johnson and I'll tell you why. When a face has too red a look it does not appear to so much advantage as it would were it paler."

"Pray Ma'am proceed in your story."

"Well, as I said before, I was invited by this Lady to spend some weeks with her in town. Many Gentlemen thought her Handsome but in my opinion, Her forehead was too high, her eyes too small and she had too much colour."

"In that Madam as I said before your Ladyship must have been mistaken. Mrs Watkins could not have too much colour since no one can have too much."

"Excuse me my Love if I do not agree with you in that particular. Let me explain myself clearly; my idea of the case is this. When a Woman has too great a proportion of red in her Cheeks, she must have too much colour."

"But Madam I deny that it is possible for any one to have too great a proportion of red in their Cheeks."

"What my Love not if they have too much colour?"

Miss Johnson was now out of all patience, the more so perhaps as Lady Williams still remained so inflexibly cool. It must be remembered however that her Ladyship had in one respect by far the advantage of Alice; I mean in not being drunk, for heated with wine and raised by Passion, she could have little command of her Temper.

The Dispute at length grew so hot on the part of Alice that "From Words she almost came to Blows"

When Mr Johnson luckily entered and with some difficulty forced her away from Lady Williams, Mrs Watkins and her red cheeks.

CHAPTER THE FOURTH

MY READERS MAY perhaps imagine that after such a fracas, no intimacy could longer subsist between the Johnsons and Lady

Williams, but in that they are mistaken for her Ladyship was too sensible to be angry at a conduct which she could not help perceiving to be the natural consequence of inebriety and Alice had too sincere a respect for Lady Williams and too great a relish for her Claret, not to make every concession in her power.

A few days after their reconciliation Lady Williams called on Miss Johnson to propose a walk in a Citron Grove which led from her Ladyship's pigstye to Charles Adams's Horsepond. Alice was too sensible of Lady Williams's kindness in proposing such a walk and too much pleased with the prospect of seeing at the end of it, a Horsepond of Charles's, not to accept it with visible delight. They had not proceeded far before she was roused from the reflection of the happiness she was going to enjoy, by Lady Williams's thus addressing her.

"I have as yet forborn my dear Alice to continue the narrative of my Life from an unwillingness of recalling to your Memory a scene which (since it reflects on you rather disgrace than credit) had better be forgot than remembered."

Alice had already begun to colour up and was beginning to speak, when her Ladyship perceiving her displeasure, continued thus.

"I am afraid my dear Girl that I have offended you by what I have just said; I assure you I do not mean to distress you by a retrospection of what cannot now be helped; considering all things I do not think you so much to blame as many People do; for when a person is in Liquor, there is no answering for what they may do."

"Madam, this is not to be borne, I insist—"

"My dear Girl dont vex yourself about the matter; I assure you I have entirely forgiven every thing respecting it; indeed I was not angry at the time, because as I saw all along, you were nearly dead drunk. I knew you could not help saying the strange things you did. But I see I distress you; so I will change the subject and desire it may never again be mentioned; remember it is all forgot—I will now pursue my story; but I must insist upon not giving you any description of Mrs. Watkins; it would only be reviving old stories and as you never saw her, it can be nothing to you, if her forehead was too high, her eyes were too small, or if she had too much colour."

"Again! Lady Williams: this is too much"—

So provoked was poor Alice at this renewal of the old story, that I know not what might have been the consequence of it, had not their attention been engaged by another object. A lovely young Woman lying apparently in great pain beneath a Citron tree, was an object too interesting not to attract their notice. Forgetting their own dispute they both with simpathizing Tenderness advanced towards her and accosted her in these terms.

"You seem fair Nymph to be labouring under some misfortune which we shall be happy to releive if you will inform us what it is. Will you favour us with your Life and adventures?"

"Willingly Ladies, if you will be so kind as to be seated." They took their places and she thus began.

CHAPTER THE FIFTH

"I AM A NATIVE of North Wales and my Father is one of the most capital Taylors in it. Having a numerous family, he was easily prevailed on by a sister of my Mother's who is a widow in good circumstances and keeps an alehouse in the next Village to ours, to let her take me and breed me up at her own expence. Accordingly I have lived with her for the last 8 years of my Life, during which time she provided me with some of the first rate Masters, who taught me all the accomplishments requisite for one of my sex and rank. Under their instructions I learned Dancing, Music, Drawing and various Languages, by which means I became more accomplished than any other Taylor's Daughter in Wales. Never was there a happier Creature than I was, till within the last half year—but I should have told you before that the principal Estate in our Neighbourhood belongs to Charles Adams, the owner of the brick House, you see yonder."

"Charles Adams!" exclaimed the astonished Alice; "are you acquainted with Charles Adams?"

"To my sorrow madam I am. He came about half a year ago to receive the rents of the Estate I have just mentioned. At that time I first saw him; as you seem ma'am acquainted with him, I need not describe to you how charming he is. I could not resist his attractions;"—

"Ah! who can," said Alice with a deep sigh.

"My Aunt being in terms of the greatest intimacy with his cook, determined, at my request, to try whether she could discover, by means of her freind if there were any chance of his returning my affection. For this purpose she went one evening to drink tea with Mrs Susan, who in the course of Conversation mentioned the goodness of her Place and the Goodness of her Master; upon which my Aunt began pumping her with so much dexterity that in a short time Susan owned, that she did not think her Master would ever marry, 'for (said she) he has often and often declared to me that his wife, whoever she might be, must possess, Youth, Beauty, Birth, Wit, Merit, and Money. I have many a time (she continued) endeavoured to reason him out of his resolution and to convince him of the improbability of his ever meeting with such a Lady; but my arguments have had no effect and he continues as firm in his determination as ever.' You may imagine Ladies my distress on hearing this; for I was fearfull that tho' possessed of Youth, Beauty, Wit and Merit, and tho' the probable Heiress of my Aunts House and business, he might think me deficient in Rank, and in being so, unworthy of his hand."

"However I was determined to make a bold push and therefore wrote him a very kind letter, offering him with great tenderness my hand and heart. To this I received an angry and peremptory refusal, but thinking it might be rather the effect of his modesty than any thing else, I pressed him again on the subject. But he never answered any more of my Letters and very soon afterwards left the Country. As soon as I heard of his departure I wrote to him here, informing him that I should shortly do myself the honour of waiting on him at Pammydiddle, to which I received no answer; therefore choosing to take, Silence for Consent, I left Wales, unknown to my Aunt, and arrived here after a tedious Journey this Morning. On enquiring for his House I was directed thro' this Wood, to the one you there see. With a heart elated by the expected happiness of beholding him I entered it and had proceeded thus far in my progress thro' it, when I found myself suddenly seized by the leg and on examining the cause of it, found that I was caught in one of the steel traps so common in gentlemen's grounds."

"Ah cried Lady Williams, how fortunate we are to meet with you; since we might otherwise perhaps have shared the like misfortune"—

"It is indeed happy for you Ladies, that I should have been a short time before you. I screamed as you may easily imagine till the woods resounded again and till one of the inhuman Wretch's servants came to my assistance and released me from my dreadfull prison, but not before one of my legs was entirely broken."

CHAPTER THE SIXTH

At this melancholy recital the fair eyes of Lady Williams, were suffused in tears and Alice could not help Exclaiming,

"Oh! cruel Charles to wound the hearts and legs of all the fair."

Lady Williams now interposed and observed that the young Lady's leg ought to be set without farther delay. After examining the fracture therefore, she immediately began and performed the operation with great skill which was the more wonderfull on account of her having never performed such a one before. Lucy, then arose from the ground and finding that she could walk with the greatest ease, accompanied them to Lady Williams's House at her Ladyship's particular request.

The perfect form, the beautifull face, and elegant manners of Lucy so won on the affections of Alice that when they parted, which was not till after Supper, she assured her that except her Father, Brother, Uncles, Aunts, Cousins and other relations, Lady Williams, Charles Adams and a few dozen more of particular freinds, she loved her better than almost any other person in the world.

Such a flattering assurance of her regard would justly have given much pleasure to the object of it, had she not plainly perceived that the amiable Alice had partaken too freely of Lady Williams's claret.

Her Ladyship (whose discernment was great) read in the intelligent countenance of Lucy her thoughts on the subject and as soon as Miss Johnson had taken her leave, thus addressed her.

"When you are more intimately acquainted with my Alice you will not be surprised, Lucy, to see the dear Creature drink a little too much; for such things happen every day. She has many rare and charming qualities, but Sobriety is not one of them. The whole Family are indeed a sad drunken set. I am sorry to say too that I never knew three such thorough Gamesters as they are, more particularly Alice. But she is a charming girl. I fancy not one of the sweetest tempers in the world; to be sure I have seen her in such passions! However she is a sweet young Woman. I am sure you'll like her. I scarcely know Any one so amiable.—Oh! that you could but have seen her the other Evening! How she raved! and on such a trifle too! She is indeed a most pleasing Girl! I shall always love her!"

"She appears by your ladyship's account to have many good qualities," replied Lucy. "Oh! a thousand," answered Lady Williams; "tho' I am very partial to her, and perhaps am blinded by my affection, to her real defects."

CHAPTER THE SEVENTH

THE NEXT MORNING brought the three Miss Simpsons to wait on Lady Williams; who received them with the utmost politeness and introduced to their acquaintance Lucy, with whom the eldest was so much pleased that at parting she declared her sole *ambition* was to have her accompany them the next morning to Bath, whither they were going for some weeks.

"Lucy, said Lady Williams, is quite at her own disposal and if she chooses to accept so kind an invitation, I hope she will not hesitate, from any motives of delicacy on my account. I know not indeed how I shall ever be able to part with her. She never was at Bath and I should think that it would be a most agreable Jaunt to her. Speak my Love," continued she, turning to Lucy, "what say you to accompanying these Ladies? I shall be miserable without you—t'will be a most pleasant tour to you—I hope you'll go; if you do I am sure t'will be the Death of me—pray be persuaded"—

Lucy begged leave to decline the honour of accompanying them, with many expressions of gratitude for the extream politeness of Miss Simpson in inviting her.

Miss Simpson appeared much disappointed by her refusal. Lady Williams insisted on her going—declared that she would never forgive her if she did not, and that she should never survive it if she did, and inshort used such persuasive arguments that it was at length resolved she was to go. The Miss Simpsons called for her at ten o'clock the next morning and Lady Williams had soon the satisfaction of receiving from her young freind, the pleasing intelligence of their safe arrival in Bath.

It may now be proper to return to the Hero of this Novel, the brother of Alice, of whom I beleive I have scarcely ever had occasion to speak; which may perhaps be partly owing to his unfortunate propensity to Liquor, which so compleatly deprived him of the use of those faculties Nature had endowed him with, that he never did anything worth mentioning. His Death happened a short time after Lucy's departure and was the natural Consequence of this pernicious practice. By his decease, his sister became the sole inheritress of a very large fortune, which as it gave her fresh Hopes of rendering herself acceptable as a wife to Charles Adams could not fail of being most pleasing to her—and as the effect was Joyfull the Cause could scarcely be lamented.

Finding the violence of her attachment to him daily augment, she at length disclosed it to her Father and desired him to propose a union between them to Charles. Her father consented and set out one morning to open the affair to the young Man. Mr Johnson being a man of few words his part was soon performed and the answer he received was as follows—

"Sir, I may perhaps be expected to appear pleased at and gratefull for the offer you have made me: but let me tell you that I consider it as an affront. I look upon myself to be Sir a perfect Beauty—where would you see a finer figure or a more charming face. Then, sir I imagine my Manners and Address to be of the most polished kind; there is a certain elegance a peculiar sweetness in them that I never saw equalled and cannot describe—. Partiality aside, I am certainly more accomplished in every Language, every Science, every Art and every thing than any other person in Europe. My temper is even, my virtues innumerable, my self unparalelled. Since such Sir is my character, what do you mean by wishing me to marry your Daughter? Let me give you a short sketch of yourself and of her. I look upon you Sir to be a very good sort of Man in the main; a drunken old Dog to be sure, but that's nothing to me. Your daughter sir, is neither sufficiently beautifull, sufficiently amiable, sufficiently witty, nor sufficiently rich for me—. I expect nothing more in my wife than my wife will find in me—Perfection. These sir, are my sentiments and I honour myself for having such. One freind I have and glory in having but one—. She is at present preparing my Dinner, but if you choose to see her, she shall come and she will inform you that these have ever been my sentiments."

Mr Johnson was satisfied; and expressing himself to be much obliged to Mr. Adams for the characters he had favoured him with of himself and his Daughter, took his leave.

The unfortunate Alice on receiving from her father the sad account of the ill success his visit had been attended with, could scarcely support the disappointment—She flew to her Bottle and it was soon forgot.

VOLUME THE FIRST

CHAPTER THE EIGHTH

WHILE THESE affairs were transacting at Pammydiddle, Lucy was conquering every Heart at Bath. A fortnight's residence there had nearly effaced from her remembrance the captivating form of Charles—The recollection of what her Heart had formerly suffered by his charms and her Leg by his trap, enabled her to forget him with tolerable Ease, which was what she determined to do; and for that purpose dedicated five minutes in every day to the employment of driving him from her remembrance.

Her second Letter to Lady Williams contained the pleasing intelligence of her having accomplished her undertaking to her entire satisfaction; she mentioned in it also an offer of marriage she had received from the Duke of —— an elderly Man of noble fortune whose ill health was the cheif inducement of his Journey to Bath. "I am distressed (she continued) to know whether I mean to accept him or not. There are a thousand advantages to be derived from a marriage with the Duke, for besides those more inferior ones of Rank and Fortune it will procure me a home, which of all other things is what I most desire. Your Ladyship's kind wish of my always remaining with you, is noble and generous but I cannot think of becoming so great a burden on one I so much love and esteem. That One should receive obligations only from those we despise, is a sentiment instilled into my mind by my worthy Aunt, in my early years, and cannot in my opinion be too strictly adhered to. The excellent woman of whom I now speak, is I hear too much incensed by my imprudent departure from Wales, to receive me again—. I most earnestly wish to leave the Ladies I am now with. Miss Simpson is indeed (setting aside ambition) very amiable, but her 2^d Sister the envious and malvolent Sukey is too disagreable to live with.—. I have reason to think that the admiration I have met with in the circles of the Great at this Place, has raised her Hatred and Envy; for often has she threatened, and sometimes endeavoured to cutt my throat.—Your Ladyship will therefore allow that I am not wrong in wishing to leave Bath, and in wishing to have a home to receive me, when I do. I shall expect with impatience your advice concerning the Duke and am your most obliged"

&c &c—"Lucy."

Lady Williams sent her, her opinion on the subject in the following Manner.

"Why do you hesitate my dearest Lucy, a moment with respect to the Duke? I have enquired into his Character and find him to be an unprincipaled, illiterate Man. Never shall my Lucy be united to such a one! He has a princely fortune, which is every day encreasing. How nobly will you spend it!, what credit will you give him in the eyes of all!, How much will he be respected on his Wife's account! But why my dearest Lucy, why will you not at once decide this affair by returning to me and never leaving me again? Altho' I admire your noble sentiments with respect to obligations, yet let me beg that they may not prevent your making me happy. It will to be sure be a great expence to me, to have you always with me—I shall not be able to support it—but what is that in comparison with the happiness I shall enjoy in your society?—t'will ruin me I know—you will not therefore surely, withstand these arguments, or refuse to return to yours most affectionately—&c &c"

"C. Williams"

CHAPTER THE NINTH

WHAT MIGHT HAVE been the effect of her Ladyship's advice, had it ever been received by Lucy, is uncertain, as it reached Bath a few Hours after she had breathed her last. She fell a sacrifice to the Envy and Malice of Sukey who jealous of her superior charms took her by poison from an admiring World at the age of seventeen.

Thus fell the amiable and lovely Lucy whose Life had been marked by no crime, and stained by no blemish but her imprudent departure from her Aunts, and whose death was sincerely lamented by every one who knew her. Among the most afflicted of her freinds were Lady Williams, Miss Johnson and the Duke; the 2 last of whom had a most sincere regard for her, more particularly Alice, who had spent a whole evening in her company and had never thought of her since. His Grace's affliction may likewise be easily accounted for, since he lost one for whom he had experienced during the last ten days, a tender affection and sincere regard. He mourned her loss with unshaken constancy for the next fortnight at the end of which time, he gratified the ambition of Caroline Simpson by raising her to the rank of a Dutchess. Thus was she at length rendered compleatly happy in the gratification of her favourite passion. Her sister the perfidious Sukey, was likewise shortly after exalted in a manner she truly deserved, and by her actions appeared to have always desired. Her barbarous Murder was discovered and in spite of every interceding freind she was speedily raised to the Gallows—. The beautifull but affected Cecilia was too sensible of her own superior charms, not to imagine that if Caroline could engage a Duke, she might without censure aspire to the affections of some Prince—and knowing that those of her native Country were cheifly engaged, she left England and I have since heard is at present the favourite Sultana of the great Mogul —.

In the mean time the inhabitants of Pammydiddle were in a state of the greatest astonishment and Wonder, a report being circulated of the intended marriage of Charles Adams. The Lady's name was still a secret. Mr and Mrs Jones imagined it to be, Miss Johnson; but *she* knew better; all *her* fears were centered in his Cook, when to the astonishment of every one, he was publicly united to Lady Williams—

FINIS

EDGAR AND EMMA
a tale.

CHAPTER THE FIRST.

"I cannot imagine," said Sir Godfrey to his Lady, "why we continue in such deplorable Lodgings as these, in a paltry Market-town, while we have 3 good Houses of our own situated in some of the finest parts of England, and perfectly ready to receive us!"

"I'm sure Sir Godfrey," replied Lady Marlow, "it has been much against my inclination that we have staid here so long; or why we should ever have come at all indeed, has been to me a wonder, as none of our Houses have been in the least want of repair."

"Nay my dear," answered Sir Godfrey, "you are the last person who ought to be displeased with what was always meant as a compliment to you; for you cannot but be sensible of the very great inconvenience your Daughters and I have been put to during the 2 years we have remained crowded in these Lodgings in order to give you pleasure."

"My dear," replied Lady Marlow, "How can you stand and tell such lies, when you very well know that it was merely to oblige the Girls and you, that I left a most commodious House situated in a most delightfull Country and surrounded by a most agreable Neighbourhood, to live 2 years cramped up in Lodgings three pair of stairs high, in a smokey and unwholesome town, which has given me a continual fever and almost thrown me into a Consumption."

As, after a few more speeches on both sides they could not determine which was the most to blame, they prudently laid aside the debate, and having packed up their Cloathes and paid their rent, they set out the next morning with their 2 Daughters for their seat in Sussex.

Sir Godfrey and Lady Marlow were indeed very sensible people and tho' (as in this instance) like many other sensible People, they sometimes did a foolish thing, yet in general their actions were guided by Prudence and regulated by discretion.

After a Journey of two Days and a half they arrived at Marlhurst in good health and high spirits; so overjoyed were they all to inhabit again a place, they had left with mutual regret for two years, that they ordered the bells to be rung and distributed ninepence among the Ringers.

CHAPTER THE SECOND

THE NEWS OF THEIR arrival being quickly spread throughout the Country, brought them in a few Days visits of congratulation from every family in it.

Amongst the rest came the inhabitants of Willmot Lodge a beautifull Villa not far from Marlhurst. Mr Willmot was the representative of a very ancient Family and possessed besides his paternal Estate, a considerable share in a Lead mine and a ticket in the Lottery. His Lady was an agreable Woman. Their Children were too numerous to be particularly described; it is sufficient to say that in general they were virtuously inclined and not given to any wicked ways. Their family being too large to accompany them in every visit, they took nine with them alternately. When their Coach stopped at Sir Godfrey's door, the Miss Marlow's Hearts throbbed in the eager expectation of once more beholding a family so dear to them. Emma the youngest (who was more particularly interested in their arrival, being attached to their eldest Son) continued at her Dressing-room window in anxious Hopes of seeing young Edgar descend from the Carriage.

Mr and Mrs Willmot with their three eldest Daughters first appeared—Emma began to tremble—. Robert, Richard, Ralph, and

Rodolphus followed—Emma turned pale—. Their two youngest Girls were lifted from the Coach—Emma sunk breathless on a Sopha. A footman came to announce to her the arrival of Company; her heart was too full to contain its afflictions. A confidante was necessary—In Thomas she hoped to experience a faithfull one—for one she must have and Thomas was the only one at Hand. To him she unbosomed herself without restraint and after owning her passion for young Willmot, requested his advice in what manner she should conduct herself in the melancholy Disappointment under which she laboured.

Thomas, who would gladly have been excused from listening to her complaint, begged leave to decline giving any advice concerning it, which much against her will, she was obliged to comply with.

Having dispatched him therefore with many injunctions of secrecy, she descended with a heavy heart into the Parlour, where she found the good Party seated in a social Manner round a blazing fire.

CHAPTER THE THIRD

EMMA HAD CONTINUED in the Parlour some time before she could summon up sufficient courage to ask Mrs Willmot after the rest of her family; and when she did, it was in so low, so faltering a voice that no one knew she spoke. Dejected by the ill success of her first attempt she made no other, till on Mrs Willmots desiring one of the little Girls to ring the bell for their Carriage, she stepped across the room and seizing the string said in a resolute manner.

"Mrs Willmot, you do not stir from this House till you let me know how all the rest of your family do, particularly your eldest son."

They were all greatly surprised by such an unexpected address and the more so, on account of the manner in which it was spoken; but Emma, who would not be again disappointed, requesting an answer, Mrs Willmot made the following eloquent oration.

"Our children are all extremely well but at present most of them from home. Amy is with my sister Clayton. Sam at Eton. David with his Uncle John. Jem and Will at Winchester. Kitty at Queens Square. Ned with his Grandmother. Hetty and Patty in a convent at Brussells. Edgar at college, Peter at Nurse, and all the rest (except the nine here) at home."

It was with difficulty that Emma could refrain from tears on hearing of the absence of Edgar; she remained however tolerably composed till the Willmot's were gone when having no check to the overflowings of her greif, she gave free vent to them, and retiring to her own room, continued in tears the remainder of her Life.

FINIS.

HENRY AND ELIZA
a novel.

*Is humbly dedicated to Miss Cooper by her obedient Humble Servant
The Author*

As Sir George and Lady Harcourt were superintending the Labours of their Haymakers, rewarding the industry of some by smiles of approbation, and punishing the idleness of others, by a cudgel, they perceived lying closely concealed beneath the thick foliage of a Haycock, a beautifull little Girl not more than 3 months old.

Touched with the enchanting Graces of her face and delighted with the infantine tho' sprightly answers she returned to their many questions, they resolved to take her home and, having no Children of their own, to educate her with care and cost.

Being good People themselves, their first and principal care was to incite in her a Love of Virtue and a Hatred of Vice, in which they so well succeeded (Eliza having a natural turn that way herself) that when she grew up, she was the delight of all who knew her.

Beloved by Lady Harcourt, adored by Sir George and admired by all the World, she lived in a continued course of uninterrupted Happiness, till she had attained her eighteenth year; when happening one day to be detected in stealing a banknote of 50£, she was turned out of doors by her inhuman Benefactors. Such a transition to one who did not possess so noble and exalted a mind as Eliza, would have been Death, but she, happy in the conscious knowledge of her own Excellence, amused herself, as she sate beneath a tree with making and singing the following Lines.

Song.
Though misfortunes my footsteps may ever attend
    I hope I shall never have need of a Freind
as an innocent Heart I will ever preserve
    and will never from Virtue's dear boundaries swerve.

Having amused herself some hours, with this song and her own pleasing reflections, she arose and took the road to M. a small market town of which place her most intimate freind kept the red Lion.

To this freind she immediately went, to whom having recounted her late misfortune, she communicated her wish of getting into some family in the capacity of Humble Companion.

Mrs Willson, who was the most amiable creature on earth, was no sooner acquainted with her Desire, than she sate down in the Bar and wrote the following Letter to the Dutchess of F, the woman whom of all others, she most Esteemed.

"To the Dutchess of F."
"Receive into your Family, at my request a young woman of unexceptionable Character, who is so good as to choose your Society in preference to going to Service. Hasten, and take her from the arms of your"
                                                                   "Sarah Wilson."

The Dutchess, whose freindship for Mrs Wilson would have carried her any lengths, was overjoyed at such an opportunity of obliging her and accordingly sate out immediately on the receipt of her letter for the red Lion, which she reached the same Evening. The Dutchess of F. was about 45 and a half; Her passions were strong, her freindships firm and her Enmities, unconquerable. She was a widow and had only one Daughter who was on the point of marriage with a young Man of considerable fortune.

The Dutchess no sooner beheld our Heroine than throwing her arms around her neck, she declared herself so much pleased with her, that she was resolved they never more should part. Eliza was delighted with such a protestation of freindship, and after taking a most affecting leave of her dear Mrs Wilson, accompanied her Grace the next morning to her seat in Surry.

With every expression of regard did the Dutchess introduce her to Lady Hariet, who was so much pleased with her appearance that she besought her, to consider her as her Sister, which Eliza with the greatest Condescension promised to do.

Mr Cecil, the Lover of Lady Harriet, being often with the family was often with Eliza. A mutual Love took place and Cecil having declared his first, prevailed on Eliza to consent to a private union, which was easy to be effected, as the dutchess's chaplain being very much in love with Eliza himself, would they were certain do anything to oblige her.

The Dutchess and Lady Harriet being engaged one evening to an assembly, they took the opportunity of their absence and were united by the enamoured Chaplain.

When the Ladies returned, their amazement was great at finding instead of Eliza the following Note.

"Madam"
   "We are married and gone."
"Henry and Eliza Cecil."

Her Grace as soon as she had read the letter, which sufficiently explained the whole affair, flew into the most violent passion and after having spent an agreable half hour, in calling them by all the shocking Names her rage could suggest to her, sent out after them 300 armed Men, with orders not to return without their Bodies, dead or alive; intending that if they should be brought to her in the latter condition to have them put to Death in some torturelike manner, after a few years Confinement.

In the mean time Cecil and Eliza continued their flight to the Continent, which they judged to be more secure than their native Land, from the dreadfull effects of the Dutchess's vengeance, which they had so much reason to apprehend.

In France they remained 3 years, during which time they became the parents of two Boys, and at the end of it Eliza became a widow without any thing to support either her or her Children. They had lived since their Marriage at the rate of 12,000£ a year, of which Mr Cecil's estate being rather less than the twentieth part, they had been able to save but a trifle, having lived to the utmost extent of their Income.

Eliza, being perfectly conscious of the derangement in their affairs, immediately on her Husband's death set sail for England, in a man of War of 55 Guns, which they had built in their more prosperous Days. But no sooner had she stepped on Shore at Dover, with a Child in each hand, than she was seized by the officers of the Dutchess, and conducted by them to a snug little Newgate of their Lady's, which she had erected for the reception of her own private Prisoners.

No sooner had Eliza entered her Dungeon than the first thought which occurred to her, was how to get out of it again.

She went to the Door; but it was locked. She looked at the Window; but it was barred with iron; disappointed in both her expectations, she dispaired of effecting her Escape, when she fortunately perceived in a Corner of her Cell, a small saw and a Ladder of ropes. With the saw she instantly went to work and in a few weeks had displaced every Bar but one to which she fastened the Ladder.

A difficulty then occurred which for some time, she knew not how to obviate. Her Children were too small to get down the Ladder by themselves, nor would it be possible for her to take them in her arms, when *she* did. At last she determined to fling down all her Cloathes, of which she had a large Quantity, and then having given them strict Charge not to hurt themselves, threw her Children after them. She herself with ease descended by the Ladder, at the bottom of which she had the pleasure of finding Her little boys in perfect Health and fast asleep.

Her wardrobe she now saw a fatal necessity of selling, both for the preservation of her Children and herself. With tears in her eyes, she parted with these last reliques of her former Glory, and with the money she got for them, bought others more usefull, some playthings for her Boys and a gold Watch for herself.

But scarcely was she provided with the above-mentioned necessaries, than she began to find herself rather hungry, and had reason to think, by their biting off two of her fingers, that her Children were much in the same situation.

To remedy these unavoidable misfortunes, she determined to return to her old freinds, Sir George and Lady Harcourt, whose generosity she had so often experienced and hoped to experience as often again.

She had about 40 miles to travel before she could reach their hospitable Mansion, of which having walked 30 without stopping, she found herself at the Entrance of a Town, where often in happier times, she had accompanied Sir George and Lady Harcourt to regale themselves with a cold collation at one of the Inns.

The reflections that her adventures since the last time she had partaken of these happy *Junketings*, afforded her, occupied her mind, for some time, as she sate on the steps at the door of a Gentleman's house. As soon as these reflections were ended, she arose and determined to take her station at the very inn, she remembered with so much delight, from the Company of which, as they went in and out, she hoped to receive some Charitable Gratuity.

She had but just taken her post at the Innyard before a Carriage drove out of it, and on turning the Corner at which she was stationed, stopped to give the Postilion an opportunity of admiring the beauty of the prospect. Eliza then advanced to the carriage and was going to request their Charity, when on fixing her Eyes on the Lady within it, she exclaimed, "Lady Harcourt!"

To which the lady replied:

"Eliza!"

"Yes Madam it is the wretched Eliza herself."

Sir George, who was also in the Carriage, but too much amazed to speek, was proceeding to demand an explanation from Eliza of the Situation she was then in, when Lady Harcourt in transports of Joy, exclaimed.

"Sir George, Sir George, she is not only Eliza our adopted Daughter, but our real Child."

"Our real Child! What Lady Harcourt, do you mean? You know you never even was with child. Explain yourself, I beseech you."

"You must remember Sir George that when you sailed for America, you left me breeding."

"I do, I do, go on dear Polly."

"Four months after you were gone, I was delivered of this Girl, but dreading your just resentment at her not proving the Boy you wished, I took her to a Haycock and laid her down. A few weeks afterwards, you returned, and fortunately for me, made no enquiries on the subject. Satisfied within myself of the wellfare of my Child, I soon forgot I had one, insomuch that when, we shortly after found her in the very Haycock, I had placed her, I had no more idea of her being my own, than you had, and nothing I will venture to say could have recalled the circumstance to my remembrance, but my thus accidentally hearing her voice which now strikes me as being the very counterpart of my own Child's."

"The rational and convincing Account you have given of the whole affair, said Sir George, leaves no doubt of her being our Daughter and as such I freely forgive the robbery she was guilty of."

A mutual Reconciliation then took place, and Eliza, ascending the Carriage with her two Children returned to that home from which she had been absent nearly four years.

No sooner was she reinstated in her accustomed power at Harcourt Hall, than she raised an Army, with which she entirely demolished the Dutchess's Newgate, snug as it was, and by that act, gained the Blessings of thousands, and the Applause of her own Heart.

FINIS

THE ADVENTURES OF MR HARLEY.

a short, but interesting Tale, is with all imaginable Respect inscribed to Mr Francis Willm Austen Midshipman on board his Majestys Ship the Perseverance by his Obedient Servant
The Author.

Mr Harley was one of many Children. Destined by his father for the Church and by his Mother for the Sea, desirous of pleasing both, he prevailed on Sir John to obtain for him a Chaplaincy on board a Man of War. He accordingly, cut his Hair and sailed.

In half a year he returned and sat-off in the Stage Coach for Hogsworth Green, the seat of Emma. His fellow travellers were, A man without a Hat, Another with two, An old maid and a young Wife.

This last appeared about 17 with fine dark Eyes and an elegant Shape; inshort Mr Harley soon found out, that she was his Emma and recollected he had married her a few weeks before he left England.

FINIS

SIR WILLIAM MOUNTAGUE
an unfinished performance

is humbly dedicated to Charles John Austen Esqre, by his most obedient humble Servant
The Author.

Sir William Mountague was the son of Sir Henry Mountague, who was the son of Sir John Mountague, a descendant of Sir Christopher Mountague, who was the nephew of Sir Edward Mountague, whose ancestor was Sir James Mountague a near relation of Sir Robert Mountague, who inherited the Title and Estate from Sir Frederic Mountague.

Sir William was about 17 when his Father died, and left him a handsome fortune, an ancient House and a Park well stocked with Deer. Sir William had not been long in the possession of his Estate before he fell in Love with the 3 Miss Cliftons of Kilhoobery Park. These young Ladies were all equally young, equally handsome, equally rich and equally amiable—Sir William was equally in Love with them all, and knowing not which to prefer, he left the Country and took Lodgings in a small Village near Dover.

In this retreat, to which he had retired in the hope of finding a shelter from the Pangs of Love, he became enamoured of a young Widow of Quality, who came for change of air to the same Village, after the death of a Husband, whom she had always tenderly loved and now sincerely lamented. Lady Percival was young, accomplished and lovely. Sir William adored her and she consented to become his Wife. Vehemently pressed by Sir William to name the Day in which he might conduct her to the Altar, she at length fixed on the following Monday, which was the first of September. Sir William was a Shot and could not support the idea of losing such a Day, even for such a Cause. He begged her to delay the Wedding a short time. Lady Percival was enraged and returned to London the next Morning.

Sir William was sorry to lose her, but as he knew that he should have been much more greived by the Loss of the 1st of September, his Sorrow was not without a mixture of Happiness, and his Affliction was considerably lessened by his Joy.

After staying at the Village a few weeks longer, he left it and went to a freind's House in Surry. Mr Brudenell was a sensible Man, and had a beautifull Neice with whom Sir William soon fell in love. But Miss Arundel was cruel; she preferred a Mr Stanhope: Sir William shot Mr Stanhope; the lady had then no reason to refuse him; she accepted him, and they were to be married on the 27th of October. But on the 25th Sir William received a visit from Emma Stanhope the sister of the unfortunate Victim of his rage. She begged some recompence, some atonement for the cruel Murder of her Brother. Sir William bade her name her price. She fixed on 14s. Sir William offered her himself and Fortune. They went to London the next day and were there privately married. For a fortnight Sir William was compleatly happy, but chancing one day to see a charming young Woman entering a Chariot in Brook Street, he became again most violently in love. On enquiring the name of this fair Unknown, he found that she was the Sister of his old freind Lady Percival, at which he was much rejoiced, as he hoped to have, by his acquaintance with her Ladyship, free access to Miss Wentworth........

FINIS

MEMOIRS OF MR CLIFFORD
an unfinished tale—

To Charles John Austen Esqre

Sir,
   Your generous patronage of the unfinished tale, I have already taken the Liberty of dedicating to you, encourages me to dedicate to you a second, as unfinished as the first.

I am Sir with every expression
of regard for you and y^r noble
Family, your most obed^t
&c &c . . . .
The Author

Mr Clifford lived at Bath; and having never seen London, set off one monday morning determined to feast his eyes with a sight of that great Metropolis. He travelled in his Coach and Four, for he was a very rich young Man and kept a great many Carriages of which I do not recollect half. I can only remember that he had a Coach, a Chariot, a Chaise, a Landeau, a Landeaulet, a Phaeton, a Gig, a Whisky, an italian Chair, a Buggy, a Curricle and a wheelbarrow. He had likewise an amazing fine stud of Horses. To my knowledge he had six Greys, 4 Bays, eight Blacks and a poney.

In his Coach and 4 Bays Mr Clifford sate forward about 5 o'clock on Monday Morning the 1st of May for London. He always travelled remarkably expeditiously and contrived therefore to get to Devizes from Bath, which is no less than nineteen miles, the first

Day. To be sure he did not get in till eleven at night and pretty tight work it was as you may imagine.

However when he was once got to Devizes he was determined to comfort himself with a good hot Supper and therefore ordered a whole Egg to be boiled for him and his Servants. The next morning he pursued his Journey and in the course of 3 days hard labour reached Overton, where he was seized with a dangerous fever the Consequence of too violent Exercise.

Five months did our Hero remain in this celebrated City under the care of its no less celebrated Physician, who at length compleatly cured him of his troublesome Desease.

As Mr Clifford still continued very weak, his first Day's Journey carried him only to Dean Gate, where he remained a few Days and found himself much benefited by the change of Air.

In easy Stages he proceeded to Basingstoke. One day Carrying him to Clarkengreen, the next to Worting, the 3^{d} to the bottom of Basingstoke Hill, and the fourth, to Mr Robins's....

FINIS

THE BEAUTIFULL CASSANDRA
a novel, in twelve Chapters.

dedicated by permission to Miss Austen.

Dedication.

Madam

You are a Phoenix. Your taste is refined, Your Sentiments are noble, and your Virtues innumerable. Your Person is lovely, your Figure, elegant, and your Form, magestic. Your Manners, are polished, your Conversation is rational and your appearance singular. If therefore the following Tale will afford one moment's amusement to you, every wish will be gratified of

your most obedient
humble Servant
The Author

CHAPTER THE FIRST

C ASSANDRA WAS the Daughter and the only Daughter of a celebrated Millener in Bond Street. Her father was of noble Birth, being the near relation of the Dutchess of ———'s Butler.

CHAPTER THE 2^{D}

WHEN CASSANDRA had attained her 16th year, she was lovely and amiable and chancing to fall in love with an elegant Bonnet, her Mother had just compleated bespoke by the Countess of ——— she placed it on her gentle Head and walked from her Mother's shop to make her Fortune.

CHAPTER THE 3ᴅ

THE FIRST PERSON she met, was the Viscount of —— a young man, no less celebrated for his Accomplishments and Virtues, than for his Elegance and Beauty. She curtseyed and walked on.

CHAPTER THE 4TH

SHE THEN PROCEEDED to a Pastry-cooks where she devoured six ices, refused to pay for them, knocked down the Pastry Cook and walked away.

CHAPTER THE 5TH

SHE NEXT ASCENDED a Hackney Coach and ordered it to Hampstead, where she was no sooner arrived than she ordered the Coachman to turn round and drive her back again.

CHAPTER THE 6TH

BEING RETURNED to the same spot of the same Street she had sate out from, the Coachman demanded his Pay.

CHAPTER THE 7TH

SHE SEARCHED her pockets over again and again; but every search was unsuccessfull. No money could she find. The man grew peremptory. She placed her bonnet on his head and ran away.

VOLUME THE FIRST

CHAPTER THE 8TH

Thro' many a Street she then proceeded and met in none the least Adventure till on turning a Corner of Bloomsbury Square, she met Maria.

CHAPTER THE 9TH

Cassandra started and Maria seemed surprised; they trembled, blushed, turned pale and passed each other in a mutual Silence.

CHAPTER THE 10TH

Cassandra was next accosted by her freind the Widow, who squeezing out her little Head thro' her less window, asked her how she did? Cassandra curtseyed and went on.

CHAPTER THE 11TH

A quarter of a mile brought her to her paternal roof in Bond Street from which she had now been absent nearly 7 hours.

CHAPTER THE 12TH

She entered it and was pressed to her Mother's bosom by that worthy Woman. Cassandra smiled and whispered to herself "This is a day well spent."

FINIS.

AMELIA WEBSTER

an interesting and well written Tale
is dedicated by Permission
to
Mrs Austen
by
Her humble Servant
The Author.

LETTER THE FIRST

To Miss Webster
My dear Amelia
 You will rejoice to hear of the return of my amiable Brother from abroad. He arrived on thursday, and never did I see a finer form, save that of your sincere freind
Matilda Hervey

LETTER THE 2^{D}

To H. Beverley Esqre
Dear Beverley
 I arrived here last thursday and met with a hearty reception from my Father, Mother and Sisters. The latter are both fine Girls—particularly Maud, who I think would suit you as a Wife

well enough. What say you to this? She will have two thousand Pounds and as much more as you can get. If you don't marry her you will mortally offend

George Hervey

LETTER THE 3^D

To Miss Hervey
Dear Maud
    Beleive me I'm happy to hear of your Brother's arrival. I have a thousand things to tell you, but my paper will only permit me to add that I am y^r affec^t Freind

Amelia Webster

LETTER THE 4TH

To Miss S. Hervey
Dear Sally
    I have found a very convenient old hollow oak to put our Letters in; for you know we have long maintained a private Correspondence. It is about a mile from my House and seven from Yours. You may perhaps imagine that I might have made choice of a tree which would have divided the Distance more equally—I was sensible of this at the time, but as I considered that the walk would be of benefit to you in your weak and uncertain state of Health, I preferred it to one nearer your House, and am y^r faithfull

Benjamin Bar

LETTER THE 5TH

To Miss Hervey
Dear Maud
 I write now to inform you that I did not stop at your house in my way to Bath last Monday.—. I have many things to inform you of, besides; but my Paper reminds me of concluding; and beleive me y^{rs} ever &c.
Amelia Webster.

LETTER THE 6TH

To Miss Webster
Madam   Saturday
 An humble Admirer now addresses you—I saw you lovely Fair one as you passed on Monday last, before our House in your way to Bath. I saw you thro' a telescope, and was so struck by your Charms that from that time to this I have not tasted human food.
George Hervey.

LETTER THE 7TH

To Jack
 As I was this morning at Breakfast the Newspaper was brought me, and in the list of Marriages I read the following.

[47]

"George Hervey Esqre to Miss Amelia Webster"
"Henry Beverley Esqre to Miss Hervey"
and
"Benjamin Bar Esqre to Miss Sarah Hervey."

yours, Tom.

FINIS—

THE VISIT
a comedy in 2 acts

Dedication.

To the Revd James Austen.

Sir,

The following Drama, which I humbly recommend to your Protection and Patronage, tho' inferior to those celebrated Comedies called "The school for Jealousy" and "The travelled Man," will I hope afford some amusement to so respectable a Curate as yourself; which was the end in veiw when it was first composed by your Humble Servant the Author.

DRAMATIS PERSONAE

Sir Arthur Hampton
Lord Fitzgerald
Stanly
Willoughby, Sir Arthur's nephew

Lady Hampton
Miss Fitzgerald
Sophy Hampton
Cloe Willoughby

*The scenes are laid in
Lord Fitzgerald's House.*

VOLUME THE FIRST

ACT THE FIRST

Scene the first. a Parlour—

> *enter Lord Fitzgerald and Stanly*

STANLY. Cousin your Servant.
FITZGERALD. Stanly, good morning to you. I hope you slept well last night.
STANLY. Remarkably well; I thank you.
FITZGERALD. I am afraid you found your Bed too short. It was bought in my Grandmother's time, who was herself a very short woman and made a point of suiting all her Beds to her own length, as she never wished to have any company in the House, on account of an unfortunate impediment in her speech, which she was sensible of being very disagreable to her inmates.
STANLY. Make no more excuses dear Fitzgerald.
FITZGERALD. I will not distress you by too much civility—I only beg you will consider yourself as much at home as in your Father's house. Remember, "The more free, the more Wellcome."

> *(exit Fitzgerald)*

STANLY. Amiable Youth!
 Your virtues could he imitate
 How happy would be Stanly's fate!

> *(exit Stanly.)*

Scene the 2ᵈ.

> *Stanly and Miss Fitzgerald, discovered.*

STANLY. What Company is it you expect to dine with you to Day, Cousin?
MISS F. Sir Arthur and Lady Hampton; their Daughter, Nephew and Neice.

[50]

THE VISIT

STANLY. Miss Hampton and her Cousin are both Handsome, are they not?

MISS F. Miss Willoughby is extreamly so. Miss Hampton is a fine Girl, but not equal to her.

STANLY. Is not your Brother attached to the Latter?

MISS F. He admires her I know, but I beleive nothing more. Indeed I have heard him say that she was the most beautifull, pleasing, and amiable Girl in the world, and that of all others he should prefer her for his Wife. But it never went any farther I'm certain.

STANLY. And yet my Cousin never says a thing he does not mean.

MISS F. Never. From his Cradle he has always been a strict adherent to Truth.

(Exeunt Severally)

END OF THE FIRST ACT.

ACT THE SECOND

Scene the first. The Drawing Room.

Chairs set round in a row. Lord Fitzgerald, Miss Fitzgerald and Stanly seated.
Enter a Servant.

SERVANT. Sir Arthur and Lady Hampton. Miss Hampton, Mr and Miss Willoughby.

(exit Servant)
Enter the Company.

MISS F. I hope I have the pleasure of seeing your Ladyship well. Sir Arthur your servant. Y^{rs} Mr Willoughby. Dear Sophy, Dear Cloe,—

(They pay their Compliments alternately.)

[*51*]

Miss F.—Pray be seated.

(They sit)

Bless me! there ought to be 8 Chairs and these are but 6. However, if your Ladyship will but take Sir Arthur in your Lap, and Sophy, my Brother in hers, I beleive we shall do pretty well.

Lady H. Oh! with pleasure....

Sophy. I beg his Lordship would be seated.

Miss F. I am really shocked at crouding you in such a manner, but my Grandmother (who bought all the furniture of this room) as she had never a very large Party, did not think it necessary to buy more Chairs than were sufficient for her own family and two of her particular freinds.

Sophy. I beg you will make no apologies. Your Brother is very light.

Stanly, *aside*) What a cherub is Cloe!

Cloe, *aside*) What a seraph is Stanly!

Enter a Servant.

Servant. Dinner is on table.

They all rise.

Miss F. Lady Hampton, Miss Hampton, Miss Willoughby.

Stanly. hands Cloe, Lord Fitzgerald, Sophy Willoughby, Miss Fitzgerald, and Sir Arthur, Lady Hampton.

(Exeunt.)

Scene the 2^d
The Dining Parlour.

> *Miss Fitzgerald at top. Lord Fitzgerald at bottom. Company ranged on each side.*
> *Servants waiting.*

Cloe. I shall trouble Mr Stanly for a Little of the fried Cowheel and Onion.

Stanly. Oh Madam, there is a secret pleasure in helping so amiable a Lady—.

Lady H. I assure you my Lord, Sir Arthur never touches wine; but Sophy will toss off a bumper I am sure to oblige your Lordship.

Lord F. Elder wine or Mead, Miss Hampton?

Sophy. If it is equal to you Sir, I should prefer some warm ale with a toast and nutmeg.

Lord F. Two glasses of warmed ale with a toast and nutmeg.

Miss F. I am afraid Mr Willoughby you take no care of yourself. I fear you dont meet with any thing to your liking.

Willoughby. Oh! Madam, I can want for nothing while there are red herrings on table.

Lord F. Sir Arthur taste that Tripe. I think you will not find it amiss.

Lady H. Sir Arthur never eats Tripe; 'tis too savoury for him, you know my Lord.

Miss F. Take away the Liver and Crow and bring in the Suet pudding.

(a short Pause.)

Miss F. Sir Arthur shant I send you a bit of pudding?

Lady H. Sir Arthur never eats suet pudding Ma'am. It is too high a Dish for him.

Miss F. Will no one allow me the honour of helping them? Then John take away the Pudding, and bring the Wine.

(Servants take away the things and bring in the Bottles and Glasses.)

Lord F. I wish we had any Desert to offer you. But my Grandmother in her Lifetime, destroyed the Hothouse in order to build a receptacle for the Turkies with its' materials; and we have never been able to raise another tolerable one.

Lady H. I beg you will make no apologies my Lord.

Willoughby. Come Girls, let us circulate the Bottle.

Sophy. A very good motion Cousin; and I will second it with all my Heart. Stanly you dont drink.

Stanly. Madam, I am drinking draughts of Love from Cloe's eyes.
Sophy. That's poor nourishment truly. Come, drink to her better acquaintance.

(Miss Fitzgerald goes to a Closet and brings out a bottle)

Miss F. This, Ladies and Gentlemen is some of my dear Grandmother's own manufacture. She excelled in Gooseberry Wine. Pray taste it Lady Hampton?
Lady H. How refreshing it is!
Miss F. I should think with your Ladyship's permission, that Sir Arthur might taste a little of it.
Lady H. Not for Worlds. Sir Arthur never drinks anything so high.
Lord F. And now my amiable Sophia condescend to marry me.

(He takes her hand and leads her to the front)

Stanly. Oh! Cloe could I but hope you would make me blessed—
Cloe. I will.

(They advance.)

Miss F. Since you Willoughby are the only one left, I cannot refuse your earnest solicitations—There is my Hand.—
Lady H. And may you all be Happy!

FINIS.

THE MYSTERY
An unfinished Comedy.

Dedication

To the Revd George Austen

Sir,
 I humbly solicit your Patronage to the following Comedy, which tho' an unfinished one, is I flatter myself as complete *a* Mystery *as any of its kind.*
                   I am Sir your most Hum^{le}
                              Servant
                                   The Author

DRAMATIS PERSONAE

Men.
Colonel Elliott
Sir Edward Spangle
Old Humbug
Young Humbug
and
Corydon.

Women.
Fanny Elliott
Mrs Humbug
and
Daphne

VOLUME THE FIRST

ACT THE FIRST

Scene the 1st
A Garden.

 Enter Corydon.

Cory.) But Hush! I am interrupted.

 (Exit Corydon.)
 Enter Old Humbug and his Son, talking.

Old Hum:) It is for that reason I wish you to follow my advice. Are you convinced of its propriety?
Young Hum:) I am Sir, and will certainly act in the manner you have pointed out to me.
Old Hum:) Then let us return to the House.

 (Exeunt)

Scene the 2nd
A Parlour in Humbug's house.

 Mrs Humbug and Fanny, discovered at work.

Mrs Hum:) You understand me my Love?
Fanny) Perfectly ma'am. Pray continue your narration.
Mrs. Hum:) Alas! It is nearly concluded, for I have nothing more to say on the Subject.
Fanny) Ah! here's Daphne.

 Enter Daphne.

Daphne) My dear Mrs Humbug how d'ye do? Oh! Fanny 'tis all over.
Fanny) Is it indeed!
Mrs Hum:) I'm very sorry to hear it.
Fanny) Then t'was to no purpose that I. . . .
Daphne) None upon Earth.
Mrs Hum:) And what is to become of?. . . .
Daphne) Oh! that's all settled. *(whispers Mrs Humbug)*

THE MYSTERY

Fanny) And how is it determined?
Daphne) I'll tell you. *(whispers Fanny)*
Mrs Hum:) And is he to? . . . .
Daphne) I'll tell you all I know of the matter.

(whispers Mrs Humbug and Fanny)

Fanny) Well! now I know everything about it, I'll go away.
Mrs Hum: ⎫
Daphne   ⎬ And so will I
          ⎭

(Exeunt)

Scene the 3*ᵈ*

> *The Curtain rises and discovers Sir Edward Spangle reclined in an elegant Attitude on a Sofa, fast asleep.*
> *Enter Colonel Elliott.*

Colonel) My Daughter is not here I see . . . there lies Sir Edward . . . Shall I tell him the secret? . . . No, he'll certainly blab it . . . But he is asleep and wont hear me . . . So I'll e'en venture.

(Goes up to Sir Edward, whispers him, and Exit)

END OF THE 1ST ACT.

FINIS.

THE THREE SISTERS
a novel.

To Edward Austen Esqre
The following unfinished Novel
is respectfully inscribed
by
His obedient Hum^{ble} Servt
The Author

LETTER 1ST

Miss Stanhope to Mrs ————
My dear Fanny

I am the happiest creature in the World, for I have just received an offer of marriage from Mr Watts. It is the first I have ever had and I hardly know how to value it enough. How I will triumph over the Duttons! I do not intend to accept it, at least I beleive not, but as I am not quite certain I gave him an equivocal answer and left him. And now my dear Fanny I want your Advice whether I should accept his offer or not, but that you may be able to judge of his merits and the situation of affairs I will give you an account of them. He is quite an old Man, about two and thirty, very plain *so* plain that I cannot bear to look at him. He is extremely disagreable and I hate him more than any body else in the world. He has a large fortune and will make great Settlements on me, but then he is very healthy. In short I do not know what to do. If I refuse him he as good as told me that he should offer himself to Sophia and if *she* refused him to

[58]

Georgiana, and I could not bear to have either of them married before me. If I accept him I know I shall be miserable all the rest of my Life, for he is very illtempered and peevish extremely jealous, and so stingy that there is no living in the house with him. He told me he should mention the affair to Mama, but I insisted upon it that he did not for very likely she would make me marry him whether I would or no; however probably he *has* before now, for he never does anything he is desired to do. I believe I shall have him. It will be such a triumph to be married before Sophy, Georgiana and the Duttons; And he promised to have a new Carriage on the occasion, but we almost quarrelled about the colour, for I insisted upon its being blue spotted with silver, and he declared it should be a plain Chocolate; and to provoke me more said it should be just as low as his old one. I wont have him I declare. He said he should come again tomorrow and take my final Answer, so I believe I must get him while I can. I know the Duttons will envy me and I shall be able to chaprone Sophy and Georgiana to all the Winter Balls. But then what will be the use of that when very likely he wont let me go myself, for I know he hates dancing and what he hates himself he has no idea of any other person's liking; and besides he talks a great deal of Women's always Staying at home and such stuff. I believe I shant have him; I would refuse him at once if I were certain that neither of my Sisters would accept him, and that if they did not, he would not offer to the Duttons. I cannot run such a risk, so, if he will promise to have the Carriage ordered as I like, I will have him, if not he may ride in it by himself for me. I hope you like my determination; I can think of nothing better;

And am your ever affec[te]
Mary Stanhope.

From the Same to the Same
Dear Fanny

I had but just sealed my last letter to you when my Mother came up and told me she wanted to speak to me on a very particular subject.

"Ah! I know what you mean; (said I) That old fool Mr Watts has told you all about it, tho' I bid him not. However you shant force me to have him if I don't like it."

"I am not going to force you Child, but only want to know what your resolution is with regard to his Proposals, and to insist upon your making up your mind one way or t'other, that if *you* don't accept him *Sophy* may."

"Indeed (replied I hastily) Sophy need not trouble herself for I shall certainly marry him myself."

"If that is your resolution (said my Mother) why should you be afraid of my forcing your inclinations?"

"Why, because I have not settled whether I shall have him or not."

"You are the strangest Girl in the World Mary. What you say one moment, you unsay the next. Do tell me once for all, whether you intend to marry Mr Watts or not?"

"Law Mama how can I tell you what I dont know myself?"

"Then I desire you will know, and quickly too, for Mr Watts says he wont be kept in suspense."

"That depends upon me."

"No it does not, for if you do not give him your final Answer tomorrow when he drinks Tea with us, he intends to pay his Addresses to Sophy."

"Then I shall tell all the World that he behaved very ill to me."

"What good will that do? Mr Watts has been too long abused by all the World to mind it now."

"I wish I had a Father or a Brother because then they should fight him."

"They would be cunning if they did, for Mr Watts would run away first; and therefore you must and shall resolve either to accept or refuse him before tomorrow evening."

"But why if I don't have him, must he offer to my Sisters?"

"Why! Because he wishes to be allied to the Family and because they are as pretty as you are."

"But will Sophy marry him Mama if he offers to her?"

"Most likely. Why should not she? If however she does not choose it, then Georgiana must, for I am determined not to let such an opportunity escape of settling one of my Daughters so advantageously. So, make the most of your time; I leave you to settle the Matter with yourself." And then she went away. The only thing I can think of my dear Fanny is to ask Sophy and Georgiana whether they would have him were he to make proposals to them, and if they say they would not I am resolved to refuse him too, for I hate him more than you can imagine. As for the Duttons if he marries one of *them* I shall still have the triumph of having refused him first. So, adeiu my dear Freind

—Y^{rs} ever M. S.

Miss Georgiana Stanhope to Miss x x x

Wednesday

My dear Anne

Sophy and I have just been practising a little deceit on our eldest Sister, to which we are not perfectly reconciled, and yet the circumstances were such that if any thing will excuse it, they must. Our neighbour Mr Watts has made proposals to Mary; Proposals which she knew not how to receive, for tho' she has a particular Dislike to him (in which she is not singular) yet she would willingly marry him sooner than risk his offering to Sophy or me which in case of a refusal from herself, he told her he should do, for you must know that the poor Girl considers our marrying before her as one of the greatest misfortunes that can possibly befall her, and to prevent it would willingly ensure herself everlasting Misery by a Marriage with Mr Watts. An hour ago she came to us to sound our inclinations respecting the affair which were to determine hers. A little before she came my Mother had given us an account of it, telling us that she certainly would not let him go farther than our family for a Wife. "And therefore (said she) If Mary wont have him Sophy must, and if Sophy wont Georgiana *shall.*" Poor Georgiana!—We neither of us attempted to alter my Mother's resolution, which I am sorry to say is generally more strictly kept than rationally formed. As soon as she was gone however I broke silence to assure Sophy that if Mary should refuse Mr Watts I should not expect her to sacrifice *her* happiness by becoming his Wife from a motive of

Generosity to me, which I was afraid her Good nature and Sisterly affection might induce her to do.

"Let us flatter ourselves (replied She) that Mary will not refuse him. Yet how can I hope that my Sister may accept a Man who cannot make her happy."

"*He* cannot it is true but his Fortune his Name, his House, his Carriage will and I have no doubt but that Mary will marry him; indeed why should she not? He is not more than two and thirty; a very proper age for a Man to marry at; He is rather plain to be sure, but then what is Beauty in a Man; if he has but a genteel figure and a sensible looking Face it is quite sufficient."

"This is all very true Georgiana but Mr Watts's figure is unfortunately extremely vulgar and his Countenance is very heavy.

"And then as to his temper; it has been reckoned bad, but may not the World be deceived in their Judgement of it. There is an open Frankness in his Disposition which becomes a Man; They say he is stingy; We'll call that Prudence. They say he is suspicious. That proceeds from a warmth of Heart always excusable in Youth, and in short I see no reason why he should not make a very good Husband, or why Mary should not be very happy with him."

Sophy laughed; I continued,

"However whether Mary accepts him or not I am resolved. My determination is made. I never would marry Mr Watts were Beggary the only alternative. So deficient in every respect! Hideous in his person and without one good Quality to make amends for it. His fortune to be sure is good. Yet not so very large! Three thousand a year. What is three thousand a year? It is but six times as much as my Mother's income. It will not tempt me."

"Yet it will be a noble fortune for Mary" said Sophy laughing again.

"For Mary! Yes indeed it will give me pleasure to see *her* in such affluence."

Thus I ran on to the great Entertainment of my Sister till Mary came into the room to appearance in great agitation. She sate down. We made room for her at the fire. She seemed at a loss how to begin and at last said in some confusion

"Pray Sophy have you any mind to be married?"

"To be married! None in the least. But why do you ask me? Are you acquainted with any one who means to make me proposals?"

"I—no, how should I? But may'nt I ask a common question?"

"Not a very common one Mary surely." (said I) She paused and after some moments silence went on—

"How should you like to marry Mr Watts Sophy?"

I winked at Sophy and replied for her. "Who is there but must rejoice to marry a man of three thousand a year?"

"Very true (she replied) That's very true. So you would have him if he would offer, Georgiana. And would *you* Sophy?"

Sophy did not like the idea of telling a lie and deceiving her Sister; she prevented the first and saved half her conscience by equivocation.

"I should certainly act just as Georgiana would do."

"Well then said Mary with triumph in her Eyes, *I* have had an offer from Mr Watts." We were of course very much surprised; "Oh! do not accept him said I, and then perhaps he may have me."

In short my scheme took and Mary is resolved to do *that* to prevent our supposed happiness which she would not have done to ensure it in reality. Yet after all my Heart cannot acquit me and Sophy is even more scrupulous. Quiet our Minds my dear Anne by writing and telling us you approve our conduct. Consider it well over. Mary will have real pleasure in being a married Woman, and able to chaprone us, which she certainly shall do, for I think myself bound to Contribute as much as possible to her happiness in a State I have made her choose. They will probably have a new Carriage, which will be paradise to her, and if we can prevail on Mr W. to set up his Phaeton she will be too happy. These things however would be no consolation to Sophy or me for domestic Misery. Remember all this and do not condemn us.

Friday.

Last night Mr Watts by appointment drank tea with us. As soon as his Carriage stopped at the Door, Mary went to the Window.

"Would you beleive it Sophy (said she) the old Fool wants to have his new Chaise just the colour of the old one, and hung as low too. But it shant—I *will* carry my point. And if he wont let it be as high as the Duttons, and blue spotted with Silver, I wont have him. Yes I will too. Here he comes. I know he'll be rude; I know he'll be illtempered and wont say one civil thing to me! nor behave at all like a Lover." She then sate down and Mr Watts entered.

"Ladies your most obedient." We paid our Compliments and he seated himself.

"Fine Weather Ladies." Then turning to Mary, "Well Miss Stanhope I hope you have *at last* settled the Matter in your own mind; and will be so good as to let me know whether you will *condescend* to marry me or not."

"I think Sir (said Mary) you might have asked in a genteeler way than that. I do not know whether I *shall* have you if you behave so odd."

"Mary!" (said my Mother) "Well Mama if he will be so cross....."

"Hush, hush, Mary, you shall not be rude to Mr Watts."

"Pray Madam do not lay any restraint on Miss Stanhope by obliging her to be civil. If she does not choose to accept my hand, I can offer it else where, for as I am by no means guided by a particular preference to you above your Sisters it is equally the Same to me which I marry of the three." Was there ever such a Wretch! Sophy reddened with Anger, and I felt *so* spiteful!

"Well then (said Mary in a peevish Accent) I *will* have you if I *must.*"

"I should have thought Miss Stanhope that when such Settlements are offered as I have offered to you there can be no great violence done to the inclinations in accepting of them."

Mary mumbled out something, which I who sate close to her could just distinguish to be "What's the use of a great Jointure if Men live forever?" And then audibly "Remember the pin money; two hundred a year."

"A hundred and seventy five Madam."

"Two hundred indeed Sir" said my Mother.

"And Remember I am to have a new Carriage hung as high as the Duttons', and blue spotted with silver; and I shall expect a new Saddle horse, a suit of fine lace, and an infinite number of the most valuable Jewels. Diamonds such as never were seen! And Pearls, Rubies, Emeralds, and Beads out of number. You must set up your Phaeton which must be cream coloured with a wreath of silver flowers round it, You must buy 4 of the finest Bays in the Kingdom and you must drive me in it every day. This is not all; You must entirely new furnish your House after my Taste, You must hire two new Footmen to attend me, two Women to wait on me, must always let me do just as I please and make a very good husband."

Here she stopped, I beleive rather out of breath.

"This is all very reasonable Mr Watts for my Daughter to expect."

"And it is very reasonable Mrs Stanhope that your daughter should be disappointed." He was going on but Mary interrupted him.

"You must build me an elegant Greenhouse and stock it with plants. You must let me spend every Winter in Bath, every Spring in Town, Every Summer in taking some Tour, And every Autumn at a Watering Place, And if we are at home the rest of the year" (Sophy and I laughed) "You must do nothing but give Balls and Masquerades. You must build a room on purpose and a Theatre to act Plays in. The first Play we have shall be *Which is the Man* and I will do Lady Bell Bloomer."

"And pray Miss Stanhope (said Mr Watts) What am I to expect from you in return for all this."

"Expect? why you may expect to have me pleased."

"It would be odd if I did not. Your expectations Madam are too high for me, and I must apply to Miss Sophy who perhaps, may not have raised her's so much."

"You are mistaken Sir in supposing so, (said Sophy) for tho' they may not be exactly in the same Line, yet my expectations are to the full as high as my Sister's; for I expect my Husband to be good tempered and Chearful; to consult my Happiness in all his Actions, and to love me with Constancy and Sincerity."

Mr Watts stared. "These are very odd Ideas truly Young Lady. You had better discard them before you marry, or you will be obliged to do it afterwards."

My Mother in the meantime was lecturing Mary who was sensible that she had gone too far, and when Mr Watts was just turning towards me in order I beleive to address me, she spoke to him in a voice half humble, half sulky.

"You are mistaken Mr Watts if you think I was in earnest when I said I expected so much. However I must have a new Chaise."

"Yes Sir, you must allow that Mary has a right to expect that."

"Mrs Stanhope, I *mean* and have always meant to have a new one on my Marriage. But it shall be the colour of my present one."

"I think Mr Watts you should pay my Girl the compliment of consulting her Taste on such Matters."

Mr Watts would not agree to this, and for some time insisted upon its being a Chocolate colour, while Mary was as eager for having it blue with silver Spots. At length however Sophy proposed that to please Mr W. it should be a dark brown and to please Mary it should be hung rather high and have a silver Border. This was at length agreed to, tho' reluctantly on both sides, as each had intended to carry their point entire. We then proceeded to other Matters, and it was settled that they should be married as soon as the Writings could be completed. Mary was very eager for a Special Licence and Mr Watts talked of Banns. A common Licence was at last agreed on. Mary is to have all the Family Jewels which are very inconsiderable I beleive and Mr W. promised to buy her a Saddle horse; but in return she is not to expect to go to Town or any other public place for these three Years. She is to have neither Greenhouse, Theatre or Phaeton; to be contented with one Maid without an additional Footman. It engrossed the whole Evening to settle these affairs; Mr W. supped with us and did not go till twelve. As soon as he was gone Mary exclaimed "Thank Heaven! he's off at last; how I do hate him!" It was in vain that Mama represented to her the impropriety she was guilty of in disliking him who was to be her Husband, for she persisted in declaring her Aversion to him and hoping she might never see him again. What a Wedding will this be! Adeiu my dear Anne

—Y^r faithfully Sincere
Georgiana Stanhope

From the Same to the Same
Dear Anne   Saturday
Mary eager to have every one know of her approaching Wedding and more particularly desirous of triumphing as she called it over the Duttons, desired us to walk with her this Morning to Stoneham. As we had nothing else to do we readily agreed, and had as pleasant a walk as we could have with Mary whose conversation entirely consisted in abusing the Man she is so soon to marry and in longing for a blue Chaise spotted with Silver. When we reached the Duttons we found the two Girls in the dressing-room with a very handsome Young Man, who was of course introduced to us. He is the son of Sir Henry Brudenell of Leicestershire. Mr Brudenell is the handsomest Man I ever saw in my Life; we are all three very much pleased with him. Mary, who from the moment of our reaching the Dressing-room had been swelling with the knowledge of her own importance and with the Desire of making it known, could not remain long silent on the Subject after we were seated, and soon addressing herself to Kitty said,

"Dont you think it will be necessary to have all the Jewels new set?"

"Necessary for what?"

"For What! Why for my appearance."

"I beg your pardon but I really do not understand you. What Jewels do you speak of, and where is your appearance to be made?"

"At the next Ball to be sure after I am married."

You may imagine their Surprise. They were at first incredulous, but on our joining in the Story they at last beleived it. "And who is it to" was of course the first Question. Mary pretended Bashfulness, and answered in Confusion her Eyes cast down "to Mr Watts." This also required Confirmation from us, for that anyone who had the Beauty and fortune (tho' small yet a provision) of Mary would willingly marry Mr Watts, could by them scarcely be credited. The subject being now fairly introduced and she found herself the object of every one's attention in company, she lost all her confusion and became perfectly unreserved and communicative.

"I wonder you should never have heard of it before for in general things of this Nature are very well known in the Neighbourhood."

"I assure you said Jemima I never had the least suspicion of such an affair. Has it been in agitation long?"

"Oh! Yes, ever since Wednesday."

They all smiled particularly Mr Brudenell.

"You must know Mr Watts is very much in love with me, so that it is quite a match of Affection on his side."

"Not on his only, I suppose" said Kitty.

"Oh! when there is so much Love on one side there is no occasion for it on the other. However I do not much dislike him tho' he is very plain to be sure."

Mr Brudenell stared, the Miss Duttons laughed and Sophy and I were heartily ashamed of our Sister. She went on.

"We are to have a new Postchaise and very likely may set up our Phaeton."

This we knew to be false but the poor Girl was pleased at the idea of persuading the company that such a thing was to be and I would not deprive her of so harmless an Enjoyment. She continued.

"Mr Watts is to present me with the family Jewels which I fancy are very considerable." I could not help whispering Sophy "I fancy not."

"These Jewels are what I suppose must be new set before they can be worn. I shall not wear them till the first Ball I go to after my Marriage. If Mrs Dutton should not go to it, I hope you will let me chaprone you; I shall certainly take Sophy and Georgiana."

"You are very good (said Kitty) and since you are inclined to undertake the Care of young Ladies, I should advise you to prevail on Mrs Edgecumbe to let you chaprone her six Daughters which with your two Sisters and ourselves will make your Entrée very respectable."

Kitty made us all smile except Mary who did not understand her Meaning and coolly said, that she should not like to chaperone so many.

Sophy and I now endeavoured to change the conversation but succeeded only for a few Minutes, for Mary took care to bring back their attention to her and her approaching Wedding.

I was sorry for my Sister's sake to see that Mr Brudenell seemed to take pleasure in listening to her account of it, and even encouraged her by his Questions and Remarks, for it was evident that his only Aim was to laugh at her. I am afraid he found her very ridiculous. He kept his Countenance extremely well, yet it was easy to see that it was with difficulty he kept it. At length however he seemed fatigued and Disgusted with her ridiculous Conversation, as he turned from her to us, and spoke but little to her for about half an hour before we left Stoneham. As soon as we were out of the House we all joined in praising the Person and Manners of Mr Brudenell.

We found Mr Watts at home.

"So, Miss Stanhope (said he) you see I am come a courting in a true Lover like Manner."

"Well you need not have *told* me that. I knew why you came very well."

Sophy and I then left the room, imagining of course that we must be in the way, if a Scene of Courtship were to begin. We were surprised at being followed almost immediately by Mary.

"And is your Courting so soon over?" said Sophy.

"Courting! (replied Mary) we have been quarrelling. Watts is such a Fool! I hope I shall never see him again."

"I am afraid you will, (said I) as he dines here to day. But what has been your dispute?"

"Why only because I told him that I had seen a Man much handsomer than he was this Morning, he flew into a great Passion and called me a Vixen, so I only stayed to tell him I thought him a Blackguard and came away."

"Short and sweet, (said Sophy) but pray Mary how will this be made up?"

"He ought to ask my pardon; but if he did, I would not forgive him."

"His Submission then would not be very useful." When we were dressed we returned to the Parlour where Mama and Mr Watts were in close Conversation. It seems that he had been complaining to her of her Daughter's behaviour, and she had persuaded him to think no more of it. He therefore met Mary with all his accustomed Civility, and except one touch at the Phaeton and another at the Greenhouse, the Evening went off with great Harmony and Cordiality. Watts is going to Town to hasten the preparations for the Wedding. I am your affec^{te} Freind G. S.

To Miss Jane Anna Elizabeth Austen

My Dear Neice

Though you are at this period not many degrees removed from Infancy, Yet trusting that you will in time be older, and that through the care of your excellent Parents, You will one day or another be able to read written hand, I dedicate to You the following Miscellanious Morsels, convinced that if you seriously attend to them, You will derive from them very important Instructions, with regard to your Conduct in Life.—If such my hopes should hereafter be realized, never shall I regret the Days and Nights that have been spent in composing these Treatises for your Benefit. I am my dear Neice

Your very Affectionate
Aunt.
The Author.

June 2^d
1793–

A FRAGMENT—WRITTEN TO INCULCATE THE PRACTISE OF VIRTUE.[*]

We all know that many are unfortunate in their progress through the world, but we do not know all that are so. To seek them out to study their wants, and to leave them unsupplied is the duty, and ought to be the Business of Man. But few have time, fewer still have inclination, and no one has either the one or the other for such employments. Who amidst those that perspire away their Evenings in crouded assemblies can have leisure to bestow a thought on such as sweat under the fatigue of their daily Labour.

---

[*] In Jane Austen's original manuscript, the title is scored through with horizontal lines and the remainder with a combination of horizontal, diagonal and vertical lines. Austen clearly thought better of continuing with this parody of didactic treatises.

A BEAUTIFUL DESCRIPTION OF THE DIFFERENT EFFECTS OF SENSIBILITY ON DIFFERENT MINDS.

I AM BUT JUST returned from Melissa's Bedside, and in my Life tho' it has been a pretty long one, and I have during the course of it been at many Bedsides, I never saw so affecting an object as she exhibits. She lies wrapped in a book muslin bedgown, a chambray gauze shift, and a french net nightcap. Sir William is constantly at her bedside. The only repose he takes is on the Sopha in the Drawing room, where for five minutes every fortnight he remains in an imperfect Slumber, starting up every Moment and exclaiming "Oh! Melissa, Ah! Melissa," then sinking down again, raises his left arm and scratches his head. Poor Mrs Burnaby is beyond measure afflicted. She sighs every now and then, that is about once a week; while the melancholy Charles says every Moment, "Melissa, how are you?" The lovely Sisters are much to be pitied. Julia is ever lamenting the situation of her freind, while lying behind her pillow and supporting her head—Maria more mild in her greif talks of going to Town next week, and Anna is always recurring to the pleasures we once enjoyed when Melissa was well.—I am usually at the fire cooking some little delicacy for the unhappy invalid—Perhaps hashing up the remains of an old Duck, toasting some cheese or making a Curry which are the favourite Dishes of our poor freind.—In these situations we were this morning surprised by receiving a visit from Dr Dowkins; "I am come to see Melissa," said he. "How is She?" "Very weak indeed," said the fainting Melissa—. "Very weak, replied the punning Doctor, aye indeed it is more than a very *week* since you have taken to your bed—How is your appetite?" "Bad, very bad, said Julia."

"That *is* very bad—replied he. Are her spirits good Madam?" "So poorly Sir that we are obliged to strengthen her with cordials every Minute."— "Well then she receives *Spirits* from your being with her. Does she sleep?" "Scarcely ever—." "And Ever Scarcely I suppose when she does. Poor thing! Does she think of dieing?" "She has not strength to think at all." "Nay then she cannot think to have Strength."

THE GENEROUS CURATE—

a moral Tale, setting forth the Advantages of being Generous and a Curate.

IN A PART LITTLE known of the County of Warwick, a very worthy Clergyman lately resided. The income of his living which amounted to about two hundred pound, and the interest of his Wife's fortune which was nothing at all, was entirely sufficient for the Wants and Wishes of a Family who neither wanted or wished for anything beyond what their income afforded them. Mr Williams had been in possession of his living above twenty Years, when this history commences, and his Marriage which had taken place soon after his presentation to it, had made him the father of six very fine Children. The eldest had been placed at the Royal Academy for Seamen at Portsmouth when about thirteen years old, and from thence had been discharged on board of one of the Vessels of a small fleet destined for Newfoundland, where his promising and amiable disposition had procured him many freinds among the Natives, and from whence he regularly sent home a large Newfoundland Dog every Month to his family. The second, who was also a Son had been adopted by a neighbouring Clergyman with the intention of educating him at his own expence, which would have been a very desirable Circumstance had the Gentleman's fortune been equal to his generosity, but as he had nothing to support himself and a very large family but a Curacy of fifty pound a year, Young Williams knew nothing more at the age of 18 than what a twopenny Dame's School in the village could teach him. His Character however was perfectly amiable though his genius might be cramped, and he was addicted to no vice, or ever guilty of any fault beyond what his age and situation rendered perfectly excusable. He had indeed sometimes been detected in flinging Stones at a Duck or putting brickbats into his Benefactor's bed; but these innocent efforts of wit were considered by that good Man rather as the effects of a lively imagination, than of anything bad in his Nature, and if any punishment were decreed for the offence it was in general no greater than that the Culprit should pick up the Stones or take the brickbats away.—

FINIS.

ODE TO PITY

To Miss Austen, the following Ode to Pity is dedicated,
from a thorough knowledge of her pitiful Nature,
by her obed^t hum^{le} Servt
The Author

1

Ever musing I delight to tread
    The Paths of honour and the Myrtle Grove
Whilst the pale Moon her beams doth shed
    On disappointed Love.
While Philomel on airy hawthorn Bush
    Sings sweet and Melancholy, And the Thrush
Converses with the Dove.

2.

Gently brawling down the turnpike road,
    Sweetly noisy falls the Silent Stream—
The Moon emerges from behind a Cloud
    And darts upon the Myrtle Grove her beam.
Ah! then what Lovely Scenes appear,
    The hut, the Cot, the Grot, and Chapel queer,
And eke the Abbey too a mouldering heap,
    Conceal'd by aged pines her head doth rear
And quite invisible doth take a peep.

END OF THE FIRST VOLUME.
June 3^d 1793—

VOLUME THE SECOND

EX DONO MEI PATRIS[*]

---

[*] **Ex dono mei Patris**: Latin for 'a gift from my father'. Probably the notebook was given in 1790, the date of the earliest items in Volume II.

LOVE AND FREINDSHIP
*a novel
in a series of Letters—.*

"Deceived in Freindship and Betrayed in Love."

*To Madame La Comtesse De Feuillide
This Novel is inscribed
by
Her obliged Humble Servant
The Author*

LETTER THE FIRST

From Isabel to Laura

How often, in answer to my repeated intreaties that you would give my Daughter a regular detail of the Misfortunes and Adventures of your Life, have you said "No, my freind never will I comply with your request till I may be no longer in Danger of again experiencing such dreadful ones."

Surely that time is now at hand. You are this Day 55. If a woman may ever be said to be in safety from the determined Perseverance of disagreable Lovers and the cruel Persecutions of obstinate Fathers, surely it must be at such a time of Life.

Isabel.

VOLUME THE SECOND

LETTER 2^D

Laura to Isabel

Altho' I cannot agree with you in supposing that I shall never again be exposed to Misfortunes as unmerited as those I have already experienced, yet to avoid the imputation of Obstinacy or ill-nature, I will gratify the curiosity of your daughter; and may the fortitude with which I have suffered the many Afflictions of my past Life, prove to her a useful Lesson for the support of those which may befall her in her own.

Laura

LETTER 3^D

Laura to Marianne

As the Daughter of my most intimate freind I think you entitled to that knowledge of my unhappy Story, which your Mother has so often solicited me to give you.

My Father was a native of Ireland and an inhabitant of Wales; my Mother was the natural Daughter of a Scotch Peer by an italian Opera-girl—I was born in Spain and received my Education at a Convent in France.

When I had reached my eighteenth Year I was recalled by my Parents to my paternal roof in Wales. Our mansion was situated in one of the most romantic parts of the Vale of Uske. Tho' my Charms are now considerably softened and somewhat impaired by the Misfortunes I have undergone, I was once beautiful. But lovely as I was the Graces of my Person were the least of my Perfections. Of every accomplishment accustomary to my sex, I was Mistress.—When in the Convent, my progress had always exceeded my instructions; my Acquirements had been wonderfull for my Age, and I had shortly surpassed my Masters.

[82]

In my Mind, every Virtue that could adorn it was centered; it was the Rendez-vous of every good Quality and of every noble sentiment.

A sensibility too tremblingly alive to every affliction of my Freinds, my Acquaintance and particularly to every affliction of my own, was my only fault, if a fault it could be called. Alas! how altered now! Tho' indeed my own Misfortunes do not make less impression on me, than they ever did, yet now I never feel for those of an other. My accomplishments too, begin to fade—I can neither sing so well nor Dance so gracefully as I once did—and I have entirely forgot the *Minuet Dela Cour*—

Adeiu.
Laura

LETTER 4TH

Laura to Marianne

Our neighbourhood was small, for it consisted only of your Mother. She may probably have already told you that being left by her Parents in indigent Circumstances she had retired into Wales on eoconomical motives. There it was, our freindship first commenced—. Isabel was then one and twenty—Tho' pleasing both in her Person and Manners (between ourselves) she never possessed the hundredth part of my Beauty or Accomplishments. Isabel had seen the World. She had passed 2 Years at one of the first Boarding-schools in London; had spent a fortnight in Bath and had supped one night in Southampton.

"Beware my Laura (she would often say) Beware of the insipid Vanities and idle Dissipations of the Metropolis of England; Beware of the unmeaning Luxuries of Bath and of the Stinking fish of Southampton."

"Alas! (exclaimed I) how am I to avoid those evils I shall never be exposed to? What probability is there of my ever tasting the Dissipations of London, the Luxuries of Bath, or the stinking Fish of Southampton? I who am doomed to waste my Days of Youth and Beauty in an humble Cottage in the Vale of Uske."

Ah! little did I then think I was ordained so soon to quit that humble Cottage for the Deceitfull Pleasures of the World.

adeiu
Laura—

LETTER 5TH

Laura to Marianne

One Evening in December as my Father, my Mother and myself, were arranged in social converse round our Fireside, we were on a sudden, greatly astonished, by hearing a violent knocking on the outward Door of our rustic Cot.

My Father started—"What noise is that," (said he.) "It sounds like a loud rapping at the Door"—(replied my Mother.) "it does indeed." (cried I.) "I am of your opinion; (said my Father) it certainly does appear to proceed from some uncommon violence exerted against our unoffending Door." "Yes (exclaimed I) I cannot help thinking it must be somebody who knocks for Admittance."

"That is another point (replied he;) We must not pretend to determine on what motive the person may knock—tho' that someone *does* rap at the Door, I am partly convinced."

Here, a 2^d tremendous rap interrupted my Father in his speech and somewhat alarmed my Mother and me.

"Had we not better go and see who it is? (said she) the servants are out." "I think we had." (replied I.) "Certainly, (added my Father) by all means." "Shall we go now?" (said my Mother). "The sooner the better." (answered he.) "Oh! Let no time be lost." (cried I.)

A third more violent Rap than ever again assaulted our ears. "I am certain there is somebody knocking at the Door." (said my Mother.) "I think there must," (replied my Father) "I fancy the Servants are returned; (said I) I think I hear Mary going to the Door." "I'm glad of it" (cried my Father) "for I long to know who it is."

I was right in my Conjecture, for Mary instantly entering the Room, informed us that a young Gentleman and his Servant were at the Door, who had lossed their way, were very cold and begged leave to warm themselves by our fire.

"Wont you admit them?" (said I) "You have no objection, my Dear?" (said my Father.) "None in the World." (replied my Mother.)

Mary, without waiting for any further commands immediately left the room and quietly returned introducing the most beauteous and amiable Youth, I had ever beheld. The servant, She kept to herself.

My natural Sensibility had already been greatly affected by the sufferings of the unfortunate Stranger and no sooner did I first behold him, than I felt that on him the happiness or Misery of my future Life must depend.—

adeiu
Laura

letter 6th

Laura to Marianne

The noble Youth informed us that his name was Lindsay—. for particular reasons however I shall conceal it under that of Talbot. He told us that he was the son of an English Baronet, that his Mother had been many years no more and that he had a Sister of the middle size. "My Father (he continued) is a mean and mercenary wretch—it is only to such particular freinds as this Dear Party that I would thus betray his failings—. Your Virtues my amiable Polydore (addressing himself to my father) yours Dear Claudia and yours my Charming Laura call on me to repose in you my Confidence." We bowed. "My Father, seduced by the false glare of Fortune and the Deluding Pomp of Title, insisted on my giving my hand to Lady Dorothea. No never exclaimed I. Lady Dorothea is lovely and Engaging; I prefer no woman to her; but Know Sir, that I scorn to marry her in compliance with your Wishes. No! Never shall it be said that I obliged my Father."

We all admired the noble Manliness of his reply. He continued.

"Sir Edward was surprised; he had perhaps little expected to meet with so spirited an opposition to his will. 'Where Edward in the name of Wonder (said he) did you pick up this unmeaning Gibberish? You have been studying Novels I suspect.' I scorned to answer: it would have been beneath my Dignity. I mounted my Horse and followed by my faithful William set forwards for my Aunts.

"My Father's house is situated in Bedfordshire, my Aunt's in Middlesex, and tho' I flatter myself with being a tolerable proficient in Geography, I know not how it happened, but I found myself entering this beautifull Vale which I find is in South Wales, when I had expected to have reached my Aunts.

"After having wandered some time on the Banks of the Uske without knowing which way to go, I began to lament my cruel Destiny in the bitterest and most pathetic Manner. It was now perfectly Dark, not a single Star was there to direct my steps, and I know not what might have befallen me had I not at length discerned thro' the solemn Gloom that surrounded me a distant Light, which as I approached it, I discovered to be the chearfull Blaze of your fire. Impelled by the combination of Misfortunes under which I laboured, namely Fear, Cold and Hunger I hesitated not to ask admittance which at length I have gained; and now my Adorable Laura (continued he taking my Hand) when may I hope to receive that reward of all the painfull sufferings I have undergone during the course of my Attachment to you, to which I have ever aspired? Oh! when will you reward me with Yourself?"

"This instant, Dear and Amiable Edward." (replied I.). We were immediately united by my Father, who tho' he had never taken orders had been bred to the Church.

adeiu
Laura.

LETTER 7TH

Laura to Marianne

We remained but a few Days after our Marriage, in the Vale of Uske—. After taking an affecting Farewell of my Father, my Mother and my Isabel, I accompanied Edward to his Aunt's in Middlesex. Philippa received us both with every expression of affectionate Love. My arrival was indeed a most agreable surprize to her as she had not only been totally ignorant of my Marriage with her Nephew, but had never even had the slightest idea of there being such a person in the World.

Augusta, the sister of Edward was on a visit to her when we arrived. I found her exactly what her Brother had described her to be—of the middle size. She received me with equal surprise though not with equal Cordiality, as Philippa. There was a Disagreable Coldness and Forbidding Reserve in her reception of me which was equally Distressing and Unexpected. None of that interesting Sensibility or amiable Simpathy in her Manners and Address to me, when we first met which should have Distinguished our introduction to each other—. Her Language was neither warm, nor affectionate, her expressions of regard were neither animated nor cordial; her arms were not opened to receive me to her Heart, tho' my own were extended to press her to mine.

A short Conversation between Augusta and her Brother, which I accidentally overheard encreased my Dislike to her, and convinced me that her Heart was no more formed for the soft ties of Love than for the endearing intercourse of Freindship.

"But do you think that my Father will ever be reconciled to this imprudent connection?" (said Augusta.)

"Augusta (replied the noble Youth) I thought you had a better opinion of me, than to imagine I would so abjectly degrade myself as to consider my Father's Concurrence in any of my Affairs, either of Consequence or concern to me—. Tell me Augusta tell me with sincerity; did you ever know me consult his inclinations or follow his Advice in the least trifling Particular since the age of fifteen?"

"Edward (replied she) you are surely too diffident in your own praise—. Since you were fifteen only!—My Dear Brother since you were five years old, I entirely acquit you of ever having willingly contributed to the Satisfaction of your Father. But still I am not without apprehensions of your being shortly obliged to degrade yourself in your own eyes by seeking a Support for your Wife in the Generosity of Sir Edward."

"Never, never Augusta will I so demean myself. (said Edward). Support! What support will Laura want which she can receive from him?"

"Only those very insignificant ones of Victuals and Drink." (answered she.)

"Victuals and Drink! (replied my Husband in a most nobly contemptuous Manner) and dost thou then imagine that there is no other support for an exalted Mind (such as is my Laura's) than the mean and indelicate employment of Eating and Drinking?"

"None that I know of, so efficacious." (returned Augusta)

"And did you then never feel the pleasing Pangs of Love, Augusta? (replied my Edward). Does it appear impossible to your vile and corrupted Palate, to exist on Love? Can you not conceive the Luxury of living in every Distress that Poverty can inflict, with the object of your tenderest affection?"

"You are too ridiculous (said Augusta) to argue with; perhaps however you may in time be convinced that...."

Here I was prevented from hearing the remainder of her Speech, by the appearance of a very Handsome young Woman, who was ushured into the Room at the Door of which I had been listening. On hearing her announced by the Name of "Lady Dorothea", I instantly quitted my Post and followed her into the Parlour, for I well remembered that she was the Lady, proposed as a Wife for my Edward by the Cruel and Unrelenting Baronet.

Altho' Lady Dorothea's visit was nominally to Philippa and Augusta, yet I have some reason to imagine that (acquainted with the Marriage and arrival of Edward) to see me was a principal motive to it.

I soon perceived that tho' Lovely and Elegant in her Person and tho' Easy and Polite in her Address, she was of that inferior order of Beings with regard to Delicate Feeling, tender Sentiments, and refined Sensibility, of which Augusta was one.

She staid but half an hour and neither in the Course of her Visit, confided to me any of her Secret thoughts, nor requested me to confide in her, any of Mine. You will easily imagine therefore my Dear Marianne that I could not feel any ardent Affection or very sincere Attachment for Lady Dorothea.

Adeiu
Laura.

letter 8th

Laura to Marianne, in continuation

Lady Dorothea had not left us long before another visitor as unexpected a one as her Ladyship, was announced. It was Sir Edward, who informed by Augusta of her Brother's marriage, came doubtless to reproach him for having dared to unite himself to me without his Knowledge. But Edward foreseeing his design, approached him with heroic fortitude as soon as he entered the Room, and addressed him in the following Manner.

"Sir Edward, I know the motive of your Journey here—You come with the base Design of reproaching me for having entered into an indissoluble engagement with my Laura without your Consent—But Sir, I glory in the Act—. It is my greatest boast that I have incurred the Displeasure of my Father!"

So saying, he took my hand and whilst Sir Edward, Philippa, and Augusta were doubtless reflecting with Admiration on his undaunted Bravery, led me from the Parlour to his Father's Carriage which yet remained at the Door and in which we were instantly conveyed from the pursuit of Sir Edward.

The Postilions had at first received orders only to take the London road; as soon as we had sufficiently reflected However, we ordered them to Drive to M——. the seat of Edward's most particular freind, which was but a few miles distant.

At M——. we arrived in a few hours; and on sending in our names were immediately admitted to Sophia, the Wife of Edward's freind. After having been deprived during the course of 3 weeks of a real freind (for such I term your Mother) imagine my transports at beholding one, most truly worthy of the Name. Sophia was rather above the middle size; most elegantly formed. A soft Languor spread over her lovely features, but increased their Beauty—. It was the Charectaristic of her Mind—. She was all Sensibility and Feeling. We flew into each others arms and after having exchanged vows of mutual Freindship for the rest of our Lives, instantly unfolded to each other the most inward Secrets of our Hearts—. We were interrupted in this Delightfull Employment by the entrance of Augustus, (Edward's freind) who was just returned from a solitary ramble.

Never did I see such an affecting Scene as was the meeting of Edward and Augustus.

"My Life! my Soul!" (exclaimed the former). "My Adorable Angel!" (replied the latter) as they flew into each other's arms.—It was too pathetic for the feelings of Sophia and myself—We fainted Alternately on a Sofa.

Adeiu
Laura

LETTER THE 9TH—

From the same to the same

Towards the close of the Day we received the following Letter from Philippa.

"Sir Edward is greatly incensed by your abrupt departure; he has taken back Augusta with him to Bedfordshire. Much as I wish to enjoy again your charming Society, I cannot determine to Snatch you from that, of such dear and deserving Freinds—When your Visit to them is terminated, I trust you will return to the arms of your"

"Philippa."

We returned a suitable answer to this affectionate Note and after thanking her for her kind invitation assured her that we would certainly avail ourselves of it, whenever we might have no other place to go to. Tho' certainly nothing could to any reasonable Being, have appeared more satisfactory, than so gratefull a reply to her invitation, yet I know not how it was, but she was certainly capricious enough to be displeased with our behaviour and in a few weeks after, either to revenge our Conduct, or releive her own solitude, married a young and illiterate Fortune-hunter. This imprudent Step (tho' we were sensible that it would probably deprive us of that fortune which Philippa had ever taught us to expect) could not on our own accounts, excite from our exalted Minds a single sigh; yet fearfull lest it might prove a source of endless misery to the deluded Bride, our trembling Sensibility was greatly affected when we were first informed of the Event. The affectionate Entreaties of Augustus and Sophia that we would for ever consider their House as our Home, easily prevailed on us to determine never more to leave them—. In the Society of my Edward and this Amiable Pair, I passed the happiest moments of my Life; Our time was most delightfully spent, in mutual Protestations of Freindship, and in vows of unalterable Love, in which we were secure from being interrupted, by intruding and disagreable Visitors, as Augustus and Sophia had on their first Entrance in the Neighbourhood, taken due care to inform the surrounding Families, that as their Happiness centered wholly in themselves, they wished for no other society. But alas! my Dear Marianne such Happiness as I then enjoyed was too perfect to be lasting. A most severe and unexpected Blow at once destroyed every Sensation of Pleasure. Convinced as you must be from what I have already told you concerning Augustus and Sophia, that there never were a happier Couple, I need not I imagine inform you that their union had been contrary to the inclinations of their Cruel and Mercenary Parents; who had vainly endeavoured with obstinate Perseverance to force them into a Marriage with those whom they had ever abhorred; but with an Heroic Fortitude worthy to be related and Admired, they had both, constantly refused to submit to such despotic Power.

After having so nobly disentangled themselves from the Shackles of Parental Authority, by a Clandestine Marriage, they were determined never to forfeit the good opinion they had gained in the World, in so doing, by accepting any proposals of reconciliation that might be offered them by their Fathers—to this farther tryal of their noble independence however they never were exposed.

They had been married but a few months when our visit to them commenced during which time they had been amply supported by a considerable Sum of Money which Augustus had gracefully purloined from his Unworthy father's Escritoire, a few days before his union with Sophia.

By our arrival their Expenses were considerably encreased tho' their means for supplying them were then nearly exhausted. But they, Exalted Creatures!, scorned to reflect a moment on their pecuniary Distresses and would have blushed at the idea of paying their Debts.—Alas! what was their Reward for such disinterested Behaviour! The beautifull Augustus was arrested and we were all undone. Such perfidious Treachery in the merciless perpetrators of the Deed will shock your gentle nature Dearest Marianne as much as it then affected the Delicate Sensibility of Edward, Sophia, your Laura, and of Augustus himself. To compleat such unparalelled Barbarity we were informed that an Execution in the House would shortly take place. Ah! what could we do but what we did! We sighed and fainted on the Sofa.

Adeiu
Laura

LETTER 10TH

Laura in continuation

When we were somewhat recovered from the overpowering Effusions of our Greif, Edward desired that we would consider what was the most prudent step to be taken in our unhappy situation while he repaired to his imprisoned freind to lament over his misfortunes. We promised that we would, and he set forwards on his Journey to Town. During his Absence we faithfully complied with his Desire and after the most mature Deliberation, at length agreed that the best thing we could do was to leave the House; of which we every moment expected the Officers of Justice to take possession. We waited therefore with the greatest impatience, for the return of Edward in order to impart to him the result of our Deliberations—. But no Edward appeared—. In vain did we count the tedious Moments of his Absence—in vain did we weep—in vain even did we sigh—no Edward returned—. This was too cruel, too unexpected a Blow to our Gentle Sensibility—. we could not support it—we could only faint—. At length collecting all the Resolution I was Mistress of, I arose and after packing up some necessary Apparel for Sophia and myself, I dragged her to a Carriage I had ordered and we instantly set out for London. As the Habitation of Augustus was within twelve miles of Town, it was not long e'er we arrived there, and no sooner had we entered Holbourn than letting down one of the Front Glasses I enquired of every decent-looking Person that we passed "If they had seen my Edward"?

But as we drove too rapidly to allow them to answer my repeated Enquiries, I gained little, or indeed, no information concerning him. "Where am I to Drive?" said the Postilion. "To Newgate Gentle Youth (replied I), to see Augustus." "Oh! no, no, (exclaimed Sophia) I cannot go to Newgate; I shall not be able to support the sight of my Augustus in so cruel a confinement—my feelings are sufficiently shocked by the *recital*, of his Distress, but to behold it will overpower my Sensibility." As I perfectly agreed with her in the Justice of her Sentiments the Postilion was instantly directed to return into the Country. You may perhaps have been somewhat surprised my Dearest Marianne, that in the Distress I then endured, destitute of any Support, and unprovided with any Habitation, I should never once have remembered my Father and Mother or my paternal Cottage in the Vale of Uske. To account for this seeming forgetfullness I must inform you of a trifling Circumstance concerning them which I have as yet never mentioned—. The death of my Parents a few weeks after my Departure, is the circumstance I allude to. By their decease I became the lawfull Inheritress of their House and Fortune. But alas! the House had never been their own and their Fortune had only been an Annuity on their own Lives.—Such is the Depravity of the World! To your Mother I should have returned with Pleasure, should have been happy to have introduced to her, my Charming Sophia and should with Chearfullness have passed the remainder of my Life in their dear Society in the Vale of Uske, had not one obstacle to the execution of so agreable a Scheme, intervened; which was the Marriage and Removal of your Mother to a Distant part of Ireland.

Adeiu.
Laura.

LETTER 11TH

Laura in continuation

"I have a Relation in Scotland (said Sophia to me as we left London) who I am certain would not hesitate in receiving me." "Shall I order the Boy to drive there?" said I—but instantly recollecting myself, exclaimed, "Alas I fear it will be too long a Journey for the Horses." Unwilling however to act only from my own inadequate Knowledge of the Strength and Abilities of Horses, I consulted the Postilion, who was entirely of my Opinion concerning the Affair. We therefore determined to change Horses at the next

Town and to travel Post the remainder of the Journey.—. When we arrived at the last Inn we were to stop at, which was but a few miles from the House of Sophia's Relation, unwilling to intrude our Society on him unexpected and unthought of, we wrote a very elegant and well-penned Note to him containing an Account of our Destitute and melancholy Situation, and of our intention to spend some months with him in Scotland. As soon as we had dispatched this Letter, we immediately prepared to follow it in person and were stepping into the Carriage for that Purpose when our Attention was attracted by the Entrance of a coroneted Coach and 4 into the Inn-yard. A Gentleman considerably advanced in years, descended from it—. At his first Appearance my Sensibility was wonderfully affected and e'er I had gazed at him a 2d time, an instinctive Sympathy whispered to my Heart, that he was my Grandfather.

Convinced that I could not be mistaken in my conjecture I instantly sprang from the Carriage I had just entered, and following the Venerable Stranger into the Room he had been shewn to, I threw myself on my knees before him and besought him to acknowledge me as his Grand-Child.—He started, and after having attentively examined my features, raised me from the Ground and throwing his Grand-fatherly arms around my Neck, exclaimed, "Acknowledge thee! Yes dear resemblance of my Laurina and my Laurina's Daughter, sweet image of my Claudia and my Claudia's Mother, I do acknowledge thee as the Daughter of the one and the Grandaughter of the other." While he was thus tenderly embracing me, Sophia astonished at my precipitate Departure, entered the Room in search of me—. No sooner had she caught the eye of the venerable Peer, than he exclaimed with every mark of Astonishment—"Another Grandaughter! Yes, yes, I see you are the Daughter of my Laurina's eldest Girl; Your resemblance to the beauteous Matilda sufficiently proclaims it." "Oh!" replied Sophia, "when I first beheld you the instinct of Nature whispered me that we were in some degree related—But whether Grandfathers, or Grandmothers, I could not pretend to determine." He folded her in his arms, and whilst they were tenderly embracing, the Door of the Apartment opened and a most beautifull Young Man appeared. On perceiving him Lord St Clair started and retreating back a few paces, with uplifted Hands, said, "Another Grand-child! What an unexpected Happiness is this! to discover in the space of 3 minutes, as many of my Descendants! This, I am certain is Philander the son of my Laurina's 3ᵈ Girl the amiable Bertha; there wants now but the presence of Gustavus to compleat the Union of my Laurina's Grand-Children."

"And here he is; (said a Gracefull Youth who that instant entered the room) here is the Gustavus you desire to see. I am the son of Agatha your Laurina's 4th and Youngest Daughter." "I see you are indeed; replied Lord St. Clair—But tell me (continued he looking fearfully towards the Door) tell me, have I any other Grand-Children in the House." "None my Lord." "Then I will provide for you all without farther delay—Here are 4 Banknotes of 50£ each—Take them and remember I have done the Duty of a Grandfather—." He instantly left the Room and immediately afterwards the House.

Adeiu.
Laura.

LETTER THE 12TH

Laura in continuation

You may imagine how greatly we were surprized by the sudden departure of Lord St. Clair—. "Ignoble Grandsire!" exclaimed Sophia. "Unworthy Grand-father!" said I, and instantly fainted in each other's arms. How long we remained in this situation I know not; but when we recovered we found ourselves alone, without either Gustavus, Philander, or the Bank-notes. As we were deploring our unhappy fate, the Door of the Apartment opened and "Macdonald" was announced. He was Sophia's cousin. The haste with which he came to our releif so soon after the receipt of our Note, spoke so greatly in his favour that I hesitated not to pronounce him at first sight, a tender and simpathetic Freind. Alas! he little deserved the name—for though he told us that he was much concerned at our Misfortunes, yet by his own account it appeared that the perusal of them, had neither drawn from him a single sigh, nor induced him to bestow one curse on our vindictive Stars.—. He told Sophia that his Daughter depended on her returning with him to Macdonald-Hall, and that as his Cousin's freind he should be happy to see me there also. To Macdonald-Hall, therefore we went, and were received with great kindness by Janetta the daughter of Macdonald, and the Mistress of the Mansion. Janetta was then only fifteen; naturally well disposed, endowed with a susceptible Heart, and a simpathetic Disposition, she might, had these amiable Qualities been properly encouraged, have been an ornament to human Nature; but unfortunately her Father possessed not a soul sufficiently exalted to admire so promising a Disposition, and had endeavoured by every means in his power to prevent its encreasing with her Years. He had actually so far extinguished the natural noble Sensibility of her Heart, as to prevail on her to accept an offer from a young Man of his Recommendation. They were to be married in a few Months, and Graham, was in the House when we arrived. *We* soon saw through his Character—. He was just such a Man as one might have expected to be the choice of Macdonald. They said he was Sensible, well-informed, and Agreable; we did not pretend to Judge of such trifles, but as we were convinced he had no soul, that he had never read the Sorrows of Werter, and that his Hair bore not the least resemblance to auburn, we were certain that Janetta could feel no affection for him, or at least that she ought to feel none. The very circumstance of his being her father's choice too, was so much in his disfavour, that had he been deserving her, in every other respect yet *that* of itself ought to have been a sufficient reason in the Eyes of Janetta for rejecting him. These considerations we were determined to represent to her in their proper light and doubted not of meeting with the desired Success from one naturally so well disposed, whose errors in the Affair had only arisen from a want of proper confidence in her own opinion, and a suitable contempt of her father's. We found her indeed all that our warmest wishes could have hoped for; we had no difficulty to convince her that it was impossible she could love Graham, or that it was her Duty to disobey her Father; the only thing at which she rather seemed to hesitate was our assertion that she must be attached to some other Person. For some time, she persevered in declaring that she knew no other young Man for whom she had the smallest Affection; but upon explaining the impossibility of such a thing she said that she beleived she *did like* Captain M'Kenzie better than any one she knew besides. This confession satisfied us and after having enumerated the good Qualites of M'Kenzie and assured her that she was violently in love with him, we desired to know whether he had ever in anywise declared his Affection to her.

"So far from having ever declared it, I have no reason to imagine that he has ever felt any for me." said Janetta. "That he certainly adores you (replied Sophia) there can be no doubt—. The Attachment must be reciprocal—. Did he never gaze on you with Admiration—tenderly press your hand—drop an involantary tear—and leave the room abruptly?" "Never (replied She) that I remember—he has always left the room indeed when his visit has been ended, but has never gone away particularly abruptly or without making a bow." "Indeed my Love (said I) you must be mistaken—: for it is absolutely impossible that he should ever have left you but with, Confusion, Despair, and Precipitation—. Consider but for a moment Janetta, and you must be convinced how absurd it is to suppose that he could ever make a Bow, or behave like any other Person." Having settled this Point to our satisfaction, the next we took into consideration was, to determine in what manner we should inform M'Kenzie of the favourable Opinion Janetta entertained of him.—. We at length agreed to acquaint him with it by an anonymous Letter which Sophia drew up in the following Manner.

"Oh! happy Lover of the beautifull Janetta, oh! enviable Possessor of *her* Heart whose hand is destined to another, why do you thus delay a confession of your Attachment to the amiable Object of it? Oh! consider that a few weeks will at once put an end to every flattering Hope that you may now entertain, by uniting the unfortunate Victim of her father's Cruelty to the execrable and detested Graham.

"Alas! why do you thus so cruelly connive at the projected Misery of her and of yourself by delaying to communicate that scheme which has doubtless long possessed your imagination? A secret Union will at once secure the felicity of both."

The amiable M'Kenzie, whose modesty as he afterwards assured us had been the only reason of his having so long concealed the violence of his affection for Janetta, on receiving this Billet flew on the wings of Love to Macdonald-Hall, and so powerfully pleaded his Attachment to her who inspired it, that after a few more private interviews, Sophia and I experienced the Satisfaction of seeing them depart for Gretna-Green, which they chose for the celebration of their Nuptials, in preference to any other place although it was at a considerable distance from Macdonald-Hall.

Adeiu—
Laura—

LETTER THE 13TH

Laura in Continuation

They had been gone nearly a couple of Hours, before either Macdonald or Graham had entertained any suspicion of the affair—. And they might not even then have suspected it, but for the following little Accident. Sophia happening one Day to open a private Drawer in Macdonald's Library with one of her own keys, discovered that it was the Place where he kept his Papers of consequence and amongst them some bank notes of considerable amount. This discovery she imparted to me; and having agreed together that it would be a proper treatment of so vile a Wretch as Macdonald to deprive him of Money, perhaps dishonestly gained, it was determined that the next time we should either of us happen to go that way, we would take one or more of the Bank notes from the drawer. This well-meant Plan we had often successfully put in Execution; but alas! on the very day of Janetta's Escape, as Sophia was majestically removing the 5th Bank-note from the Drawer to her own purse, she was suddenly most impertinently interrupted in her employment by the entrance of Macdonald himself, in a most abrupt and precipitate Manner. Sophia (who though naturally all winning sweetness could when occasions demanded it call forth the Dignity of her Sex) instantly put on a most forbiding look, and darting an angry frown on the undaunted Culprit, demanded in a haughty tone of voice "Wherefore her retirement was thus insolently broken in on?" The unblushing Macdonald without even endeavouring to exculpate himself from the crime he was charged with, meanly endeavoured to reproach Sophia with ignobly defrauding him of his Money . . . The dignity of Sophia was wounded; "Wretch (exclaimed she, hastily replacing the Banknote in the Drawer) how darest thou to accuse me of an Act, of which the bare idea makes me blush?" The base wretch was still unconvinced and continued to upbraid the justly-offended Sophia in such opprobious Language, that at length he so greatly provoked the gentle sweetness of her Nature, as to induce her to revenge herself on him by informing him of Janetta's Elopement, and of the active Part we had both taken in the Affair. At this period of their Quarrel I entered the Library and was as you may imagine equally offended as Sophia at the ill-grounded Accusations of the malevolent and contemptible Macdonald. "Base Miscreant! (cried I) how canst thou thus undauntedly endeavour to sully the spotless reputation of such bright Excellence? Why dost thou not suspect *my* innocence as soon?"

"Be satisfied Madam" (replied he) "I *do* suspect it, and therefore must desire that you will both leave this House in less than half an hour."

"We shall go willingly; (answered Sophia) our hearts have long detested thee, and nothing but our freindship for thy Daughter could have induced us to remain so long beneath thy roof."

"Your Freindship for my Daughter has indeed been most powerfully exerted by throwing her into the arms of an unprincipled Fortune-hunter." (replied he)

"Yes, (exclaimed I) amidst every misfortune, it will afford us some consolation to reflect that by this one act of Freindship to Janetta, we have amply discharged every obligation that we have received from her father."

"It must indeed be a most gratefull reflection, to your exalted minds." (said he.)

As soon as we had packed up our wardrobe and valuables, we left Macdonald Hall, and after having walked about a mile and a half we sate down by the side of a clear limpid stream to refresh our exhausted limbs. The place was suited to meditation—. A Grove of full-grown Elms sheltered us from the East—. A Bed of full-grown Nettles from the West—. Before us ran the murmuring brook and behind us ran the turn-pike road. We were in a mood for contemplation and in a Disposition to enjoy so beautifull a spot. A mutual Silence which had for some time reigned between us, was at length broke by my exclaiming—"What a lovely Scene! Alas why are not Edward and Augustus here to enjoy its Beauties with us?"

"Ah! my beloved Laura (cried Sophia) for pity's sake forbear recalling to my remembrance the unhappy situation of my imprisoned Husband. Alas, what would I not give to learn the fate of my Augustus!—to know if he is still in Newgate, or if he is yet hung.—But never shall I be able so far to conquer my tender sensibility as to enquire after him. Oh! do not I beseech you ever let me again hear you repeat his beloved Name—. It affects me too deeply—. I cannot bear to hear him mentioned, it wounds my feelings."

"Excuse me my Sophia for having thus unwillingly offended you—" replied I—and then changing the conversation, desired her to admire the Noble Grandeur of the Elms which Sheltered us from the Eastern Zephyr. "Alas! my Laura (returned she) avoid so melancholy a subject, I intreat you—Do not again wound my Sensibility by Observations on those elms—. They remind me of

Augustus—. He was like them, tall, magestic—he possessed that noble grandeur which you admire in them."

I was silent, fearfull lest I might any more unwillingly distress her by fixing on any other subject of conversation which might again remind her of Augustus.

"Why do you not speak my Laura? (said she after a short pause) I cannot support this silence—you must not leave me to my own reflections; they ever recur to Augustus."

"What a beautifull Sky! (said I) How charmingly is the azure varied by those delicate streaks of white!"

"Oh! my Laura (replied she hastily withdrawing her Eyes from a momentary glance at the sky) do not thus distress me by calling my Attention to an object which so cruelly reminds me of my Augustus's blue Sattin Waistcoat striped with white! In pity to your unhappy freind avoid a subject so distressing." What could I do? The feelings of Sophia were at that time so exquisite, and the tenderness she felt for Augustus so poignant that I had not power to start any other topic, justly fearing that it might in some unforseen manner again awaken all her sensibility by directing her thoughts to her Husband.—Yet to be silent would be cruel; She had intreated me to talk.

From this Dilemma I was most fortunately releived by an accident truly apropos; it was the lucky overturning of a Gentleman's Phaeton, on the road which ran murmuring behind us. It was a most fortunate Accident as it diverted the Attention of Sophia from the melancholy reflections which she had been before indulging. We instantly quitted our seats and ran to the rescue of those who but a few moments before had been in so elevated a situation as a fashionably high Phaeton, but who were now laid low and sprawling in the Dust—. "What an ample subject for reflection on the uncertain Enjoyments of this World, would not that Phaeton and the Life of Cardinal Wolsey afford a thinking Mind"! said I to Sophia as we were hastening to the field of Action.

She had not time to answer me, for every thought was now engaged by the horrid Spectacle before us. Two Gentlemen most elegantly attired but weltering in their blood was what first struck our Eyes—we approached—they were Edward and Augustus—Yes dearest Marianne they were our Husbands. Sophia shreiked and fainted on the Ground—I screamed and instantly ran mad—. We remained thus mutually deprived of our Senses, some minutes, and on regaining them were deprived of them again—. For an Hour and a Quarter did we continue in this unfortunate Situation—Sophia fainting every moment and I running Mad as often—. At length a Groan from the hapless Edward (who alone retained any share of Life) restored us to ourselves—. Had we indeed before imagined that either of them lived, we should have been more sparing of our Greif—but as we had supposed when we first beheld them that they were no more, we knew that nothing could remain to be done but what we were about—. No sooner therefore did we hear my Edward's groan than postponing our Lamentations for the present, we hastily ran to the Dear Youth and kneeling on each side of him implored him not to die—. "Laura (said He fixing his now languid Eyes on me) I fear I have been overturned."

I was overjoyed to find him yet sensible—.

"Oh! tell me Edward (said I) tell me I beseech you before you die, what has befallen you since that unhappy Day in which Augustus was arrested and we were separated—"

"I will" (said he) and instantly fetching a Deep sigh, Expired—. Sophia immediately sunk again into a swoon—. *My* Greif was more audible. My Voice faltered, My Eyes assumed a vacant Stare, My face became as pale as Death, and my Senses were considerably impaired—.

"Talk not to me of Phaetons (said I, raving in a frantic, incoherent manner)—Give me a violin—. I'll play to him and sooth him in his melancholy Hours—Beware ye gentle Nymphs of Cupid's Thunderbolts, avoid the piercing Shafts of Jupiter—Look at that Grove of Firs—I see a Leg of Mutton—They told me Edward was not Dead; but they deceived me—they took him for a Cucumber—" Thus I continued wildly exclaiming on my Edward's Death—. For two Hours did I rave thus madly and should not then have left off, as I was not in the least fatigued, had not Sophia who was just recovered from her swoon, intreated me to consider that Night was now approaching and that the Damps began to fall. "And whither shall we go (said I) to shelter us from either"? "To that white Cottage." (replied she pointing to a neat Building which rose up amidst the Grove of Elms and which I had not before observed—) I agreed and we instantly walked to it—we knocked at the door—it was opened by an old Woman; on being requested to afford us a Night's Lodging, she informed us that her House was but small, that she had only two Bedrooms, but that However we should be wellcome to one of them. We were satisfied and followed the good Woman into the House where we were greatly cheered by the Sight of a comfortable fire—. She was a Widow and had only one Daughter, who was then just Seventeen—One of the best of ages; but alas! she was very plain and her name was Bridget.... Nothing therefore could be expected from her... she could not be supposed to possess either exalted Ideas, Delicate Feelings or refined Sensibilities—She was nothing more than a mere good-tempered, civil and obliging Young Woman; as such we could scarcely dislike her—she was only an Object of Contempt—.

Adeiu
Laura—

LETTER THE 14TH

Laura in continuation

Arm yourself my amiable Young Freind with all the philosophy you are Mistress of; Summon up all the fortitude you possess, for Alas! in the perusal of the following Pages your sensibility will be most severely tried. Ah! what were the Misfortunes I had before experienced and which I have already related to you, to the one I am now going to inform you of! The Death of my Father my Mother, and my Husband though almost more than my gentle Nature could support, were trifles in comparison to the misfortune I am now proceeding to relate. The morning after our arrival at the Cottage, Sophia complained of a violent pain in her delicate limbs, accompanied with a disagreable Head-ake. She attributed it to a cold caught by her continual faintings in the open Air as the Dew was falling the Evening before. This I feared was but too probably the case; since how could it be otherwise accounted for that I should have escaped the same indisposition, but by supposing that the bodily Exertions I had undergone in my repeated fits of frenzy had so effectually circulated and warmed my Blood as to make me proof against the chilling Damps of Night, whereas, Sophia lying totally inactive on the Ground must have been exposed to all their Severity. I was most seriously alarmed by her illness which trifling as it may appear to you, a certain instinctive Sensibility whispered me, would in the End be fatal to her.

Alas! my fears were but too fully justified; she grew gradually worse—and I daily became more alarmed for her.—At length she was obliged to confine herself solely to the Bed allotted us by our worthy Landlady—. Her disorder turned to a galloping Consumption and in a few Days carried her off. Amidst all my Lamentations for her (and violent you may suppose they were) I yet received some consolation in the reflection of my having paid every Attention to her, that could be offered, in her illness. I had wept over her every Day—had bathed her sweet face with my tears and had pressed her fair Hands continually in mine—. "My beloved Laura (said she to me a few Hours before she died) take warning from my unhappy End and avoid the imprudent conduct which has occasioned it . . . Beware of fainting-fits . . . Though at the time they may be refreshing and Agreable yet beleive me they will in the end, if too often repeated and at improper seasons, prove destructive to your Constitution . . . My fate will teach you this . . . I die a Martyr to my greif for the loss of Augustus . . . One fatal swoon has cost me my Life . . . Beware of swoons Dear Laura. . . . A frenzy fit is not one quarter so pernicious; it is an exercise to the Body and if not too violent, is I dare say conducive to Health in its consequences—Run mad as often as you chuse; but do not faint—".

These were the last words she ever addressed to me ... It was her dieing Advice to her afflicted Laura, who has ever most faithfully adhered to it.

After having attended my lamented freind to her Early Grave, I immediately (tho' late at night) left the detested Village in which she died, and near which had expired my Husband and Augustus. I had not walked many yards from it before I was overtaken by a Stage-Coach, in which I instantly took a place, determined to proceed in it to Edinburgh, where I hoped to find some kind some pitying Freind who would receive and comfort me in my Afflictions.

It was so dark when I entered the Coach that I could not distinguish the Number of my Fellow-travellers; I could only perceive that they were Many. Regardless however of any thing concerning them, I gave myself up to my own sad Reflections. A general Silence prevailed—A Silence, which was by nothing interrupted but by the loud and repeated Snores of one of the Party.

"What an illiterate villain must that Man be! (thought I to myself) What a total Want of delicate refinement must he have, who can thus shock our senses by such a brutal Noise! He must I am certain be capable of every bad Action! There is no crime too black for such a Character!" Thus reasoned I within myself, and doubtless such were the reflections of my fellow travellers.

At length, returning Day enabled me to behold the unprincipled Scoundrel who had so violently disturbed my feelings. It was Sir Edward the father of my Deceased Husband. By his side, sate Augusta, and on the same seat with me were your Mother and Lady Dorothea. Imagine my Surprize at finding myself thus seated amongst my old Acquaintance. Great as was my astonishment, it was yet increased, when on looking out of Windows, I beheld the Husband of Philippa, with Philippa by his side, on the Coach-box, and when on looking behind I beheld, Philander and Gustavus in the Basket. "Oh! Heavens, (exclaimed I) is it possible that I should so unexpectedly be surrounded by my nearest Relations and Connections"? These words rouzed the rest of the Party, and every eye was directed to the corner in which I sat. "Oh! my Isabel (continued I throwing myself, across Lady Dorothea into her arms) receive once more to your Bosom the unfortunate Laura. Alas! when we last parted in the Vale of Usk, I was happy in being united to the best of Edwards; I had then a Father and a Mother, and had never known misfortunes—But now deprived of every freind but you—"

"What! (interrupted Augusta) is my Brother dead then? Tell us I intreat you what is become of him?"

"Yes, cold and insensible Nymph, (replied I) that luckless Swain your Brother, is no more, and you may now glory in being the Heiress of Sir Edward's fortune."

Although I had always despised her from the Day I had overheard her conversation with my Edward, yet in civility I complied with hers and Sir Edward's intreaties that I would inform them of the whole melancholy Affair. They were greatly shocked—Even the obdurate Heart of Sir Edward and the insensible one of Augusta, were touched with Sorrow, by the unhappy tale. At the request of your Mother I related to them every other misfortune which had befallen me since we parted. Of the imprisonment of Augustus and the Absence of Edward—of our arrival in Scotland—of our unexpected Meeting with our Grand-father and our cousins—of our visit to Macdonald-Hall—of the singular Service we there performed towards Janetta—of her Fathers ingratitude for it.... of his inhuman Behaviour, unaccountable suspicions, and barbarous treatment of us, in obliging us to leave the House.... of our Lamentations on the loss of Edward and Augustus and finally of the melancholy Death of my beloved Companion.

Pity and Surprise were strongly depicted in your Mother's Countenance, during the whole of my narration, but I am sorry to say, that to the eternal reproach of her Sensibility, the latter infinitely predominated. Nay, faultless as my Conduct had certainly been during the whole Course of my late Misfortunes and Adventures, she pretended to find fault with my Behaviour in many of the situations in which I had been placed. As I was sensible myself, that I had always behaved in a manner which reflected Honour on my Feelings and Refinement, I paid little attention to what she said, and desired her to satisfy my Curiosity by informing me how she came there, instead of wounding my spotless reputation with unjustifiable Reproaches. As soon as she had complied with my wishes in this particular and had given me an accurate detail of every thing that had befallen her since our separation (the particulars of which if you are not already acquainted with, your Mother will give you) I applied to Augusta for the same information respecting herself, Sir Edward and Lady Dorothea.

She told me that having a considerable taste for the Beauties of Nature, her curiosity to behold the delightful scenes it exhibited in that part of the World had been so much raised by Gilpin's Tour to the Highlands, that she had prevailed on her Father to undertake a Tour to Scotland and had persuaded Lady Dorothea to accompany them. That they had arrived at Edinburgh a few Days before and from thence had made daily Excursions into the Country around in the Stage Coach they were then in, from one of which Excursions they were at that time returning. My next enquiries were concerning Philippa and her Husband, the latter of whom I learned having spent all her fortune, had recourse for subsistance to the talent in which, he had always most excelled, namely, Driving, and that having sold every thing which belonged to them except their Coach, had converted it into a Stage and in order to be removed from any of his former Acquaintance, had driven it to Edinburgh from whence he went to Sterling every other Day; That Philippa still retaining her affection for her ungratefull Husband, had followed him to Scotland and generally accompanied him in his little Excursions to Sterling. "It has only been to throw a little money into their Pockets (continued Augusta) that my Father has always travelled in their Coach to veiw the beauties of the Country since our arrival in Scotland—for it would certainly have been much more agreable to us, to visit the Highlands in a Postchaise than merely to travel from Edinburgh to Sterling and from Sterling to Edinburgh every other Day in a crouded and uncomfortable Stage." I perfectly agreed with her in her sentiments on the Affair, and secretly blamed Sir Edward for thus sacrificing his Daughter's Pleasure for the sake of a ridiculous old Woman whose folly in marrying so young a Man ought to be punished.

His Behaviour however was entirely of a peice with his general Character; for what could be expected from a Man who possessed not the smallest atom of Sensibility, who scarcely knew the meaning of Simpathy, and who actually snored—.

Adeiu
Laura.

LETTER THE 15TH

Laura in continuation.

When we arrived at the town where we were to Breakfast, I was determined to speak with Philander and Gustavus, and to that purpose as soon as I left the Carriage, I went to the Basket and tenderly enquired after their Health, expressing my fears of the uneasiness of their Situation. At first they seemed rather confused at my Appearance dreading no doubt that I might call them to account for the money which our Grandfather had left me and which they had unjustly deprived me of, but finding that I mentioned nothing of the Matter, they desired me to step into the Basket as we might there converse with greater ease. Accordingly I entered and whilst the rest of the party were devouring Green tea and buttered toast, we feasted ourselves in a more refined and Sentimental Manner by a confidential Conversation. I informed them of every thing which had befallen me during the course of my Life, and at my request they related to me every incident of theirs.

"We are the sons as you already know, of the two youngest Daughters which Lord St. Clair had by Laurina an italian Opera-girl. Our mothers could neither of them exactly ascertain who were our Fathers; though it is generally beleived that Philander, is the son of one Philip Jones a Bricklayer and that my Father was Gregory Staves a Staymaker of Edinburgh. This is however of little consequence, for as our Mothers were certainly never married to either of them, it reflects no Dishonour on our Blood, which is of a most ancient and unpolluted kind. Bertha (the Mother of Philander) and Agatha (my own Mother) always lived together. They were neither of them very rich; their united fortunes had originally amounted to nine thousand Pounds, but as they had always lived upon the principal of it, when we were fifteen it was diminished to nine Hundred. This nine Hundred, they always kept in a Drawer in one of the Tables which stood in our common sitting Parlour, for the Convenience of having it always at Hand. Whether it was from this circumstance, of its being easily taken, or from a wish of being independent, or from an excess of Sensibility (for which we were always remarkable) I cannot now determine, but certain it is that when we had reached our 15th Year, we took the Nine Hundred Pounds and ran away. Having obtained this prize we were determined to manage it with eoconomy and not to spend it either with folly or Extravagance. To this purpose we therefore divided it into nine parcels, one of which we devoted to Victuals, the 2^d to Drink, the 3^d to Housekeeping, the 4th to Carriages, the 5th to Horses, the 6th to Servants, the 7th to Amusements the 8th to Cloathes and the 9th to Silver Buckles. Having thus arranged our Expences for two Months (for we expected to make the nine Hundred Pounds last as long) we hastened to London and had the good luck to spend it in 7 weeks and a Day which was 6 Days sooner than we had intended. As soon as we had thus happily disencumbered ourselves from the weight of so much Money, we began to think of returning to our Mothers, but accidentally hearing that they were both starved to Death, we gave over the design and determined to engage ourselves to some strolling Company of Players, as we had always a turn for the Stage. Accordingly we offered our Services to one and were accepted; our Company was indeed rather small, as it consisted only of the Manager his Wife and ourselves, but there were fewer to pay and the only inconvenience attending it was the Scarcity of Plays which for want of People to fill the Characters, we could perform.—. We did not mind trifles however—. One of our most admired Performances was *Macbeth*, in which we were truly great. The Manager always played *Banquo* himself, his Wife my *Lady Macbeth*, I did the *Three Witches* and Philander acted *all the rest*. To say the truth this tragedy was not only the Best, but the only Play we ever performed; and after having acted it all over England, and Wales, we came to Scotland to exhibit it over the remainder of Great Britain. We happened to be quartered in that very Town, where you came and met your Grandfather—. We were in the Inn-yard when his Carriage entered and perceiving by the Arms to whom it belonged, and knowing that Lord St. Clair was our Grand-father, we agreed to endeavour to get something from him by discovering the Relationship—. You know how well it succeeded—. Having obtained the two Hundred Pounds, we instantly left the Town, leaving our Manager and his Wife to act *Macbeth* by themselves, and took the road to Sterling, where we spent our little fortunes with great *eclat*. We are now returning to Edinburgh in order to get some preferment in the Acting way; and such my Dear Cousin is our History."

I thanked the amiable Youth for his entertaining Narration, and after expressing my Wishes for their Welfare and Happiness, left them in their little Habitation and returned to my other Freinds who impatiently expected me.

My Adventures are now drawing to a close my dearest Marianne; at least for the present.

When we arrived at Edinburgh Sir Edward told me that as the Widow of his Son, he desired I would accept from his Hands of four Hundred a year. I graciously promised that I would, but could not help observing that the unsimpathetic Baronet offered it more on account of my being the Widow of Edward than in being the refined and Amiable Laura.

I took up my Residence in a romantic Village in the Highlands of Scotland, where I have ever since continued, and where I can uninterrupted by unmeaning Visits, indulge in a melancholy Solitude, my unceasing Lamentations for the Death of my Father, my Mother, my Husband and my Freind.

Augusta has been for several Years united to Graham the Man of all others most suited to her; she became acquainted with him during her stay in Scotland.

Sir Edward in hopes of gaining an Heir to his Title and Estate, at the same time married Lady Dorothea—. His wishes have been answered.

Philander and Gustavus, after having raised their reputation by their Performances in the Theatrical Line at Edinburgh, removed to Covent Garden, where they still Exhibit under the assumed names of *Lewis* and *Quick.*

Philippa has long paid the Debt of Nature, Her Husband however still continues to drive the Stage-Coach from Edinburgh to Sterling:—

Adeiu my Dearest Marianne—.
Laura—

FINIS
June 13th 1790

LESLEY CASTLE
an unfinished Novel in Letters.

To Henry Thomas Austen Esqre—.

Sir
 I am now availing myself of the Liberty you have frequently honoured me with of dedicating one of my Novels to you. That it is unfinished, I greive; yet fear that from me, it will always remain so; that as far as it is carried, it Should be so trifling and so unworthy of you, is

another concern to your obliged humble Servant
The Author

Messrs Demand and Co—please to pay Jane Austen Spinster the sum of one hundred guineas on account of your Hum^{bl} Servant.

H T Austen.

£ 105.0.0

LETTER THE FIRST IS FROM

Miss Margaret Lesley to Miss Charlotte Lutterell.
Lesley-Castle Jan^{ry} 3^{d}—1792.

My Brother has just left us. "Matilda (said he at parting) you and Margaret will I am certain take all the care of my dear little one, that she might have received from an indulgent, an affectionate an amiable Mother." Tears rolled down his Cheeks as he spoke these words—the remembrance of her, who had so wantonly disgraced the Maternal character and so openly violated the conjugal Duties, prevented his adding anything farther; he embraced his sweet Child and after saluting Matilda and Me hastily broke from us—and seating himself in his Chaise, pursued the road to Aberdeen. Never was there a better young Man! Ah! how little did he deserve the misfortunes he has experienced in the Marriage State. So good a Husband to so bad a Wife!, for you know my dear Charlotte that the Worthless Louisa left him, her Child and reputation a few weeks ago in company with Danvers and dishonour.[a] Never was there a sweeter face, a finer form, or a less amiable Heart than Louisa owned! Her child already possesses the personal Charms of her unhappy Mother! May she inherit from her Father all his mental ones! Lesley is at present but five and twenty, and has already given himself up to melancholy and Despair; what a difference between him and his Father!, Sir George is 57 and still remains the Beau, the flighty stripling, the gay Lad, and sprightly Youngster, that his Son was really about five years back, and that *he* has affected to appear ever since my remembrance. While our father is fluttering about the Streets of London, gay, dissipated, and Thoughtless at the age of 57, Matilda and I continue secluded from Mankind in our old and Mouldering Castle, which is situated two miles from Perth on a bold projecting Rock, and commands an extensive veiw of the Town and its delightful Environs. But tho' retired from almost all the World, (for we visit no one but the M'Leods, The M'Kenzies, the M'Phersons, the M'Cartneys, the M'donalds, The M'kinnons, the M'lellans, the M'kays, the Macbeths and the Macduffs) we are neither dull nor unhappy; on the contrary there never were two more lively, more agreable or more witty Girls, than we are; not an hour in the Day hangs heavy on our hands. We read, we work, we walk, and when fatigued with these Employments releive

---

[a] Rakehelly Dishonor Esqre [JA's note]

our spirits, either by a lively song, a graceful Dance, or by some smart bon-mot, and witty repartée. We are handsome my dear Charlotte, very handsome and the greatest of our Perfections is, that we are entirely insensible of them ourselves. But why do I thus dwell on myself? Let me rather repeat the praise of our dear little Neice the innocent Louisa, who is at present sweetly smiling in a gentle Nap, as she reposes on the Sofa. The dear Creature is just turned of two years old; as handsome as tho' 2 and 20, as sensible as tho' 2 and 30, and as prudent as tho' 2 and 40. To convince you of this, I must inform you that she has a very fine complexion and very pretty features, that she already knows the two first Letters in the Alphabet, and that she never tears her frocks—. If I have not now convinced you of her Beauty, Sense and Prudence, I have nothing more to urge in support of my assertion, and you will therefore have no way of deciding the Affair but by coming to Lesley-castle, and by a personal acquaintance with Louisa, determine for yourself. Ah! my dear Freind, how happy should I be to see you within these venerable Walls! It is now four years since my removal from School has separated me from you; that two such tender Hearts, so closely linked together by the ties of simpathy and Freindship, should be so widely removed from each other, is vastly moving. I live in Perthshire, You in Sussex. We might meet in London, were my Father disposed to carry me there, and were your Mother to be there at the same time. We might meet at Bath, at Tunbridge, or any where else indeed, could we but be at the same place together. We have only to hope that such a period may arrive. My Father does not return to us till Autumn; my Brother will leave Scotland in a few Days; he is impatient to travel. Mistaken Youth! He vainly flatters himself that change of Air will heal the Wounds of a broken Heart! You will join with me I am certain my dear Charlotte, in prayers for the recovery of the unhappy Lesley's peace of Mind, which must ever be essential to that of your sincere freind

M. Lesley.

VOLUME THE SECOND

LETTER THE SECOND

From Miss C. Lutterell to Miss M. Lesley in answer
Glenford Feb^{ry} 12

I have a thousand excuses to beg for having so long delayed thanking you my dear Peggy for your agreable Letter, which beleive me I should not have deferred doing, had not every moment of my time during the last five weeks been so fully employed in the necessary arrangements for my sisters Wedding, as to allow me no time to devote either to you or myself. And now what provokes me more than any thing else is that the Match is broke off, and all my Labour thrown away. Imagine how great the Dissapointment must be to me, when you consider that after having laboured both by Night and by Day, in order to get the Wedding dinner ready by the time appointed, after having roasted Beef, Broiled Mutton, and Stewed Soup enough to last the new-married Couple through the Honey-moon, I had the mortification of finding that I had been Roasting, Broiling and Stewing both the Meat and Myself to no purpose. Indeed my dear Freind, I never remember suffering any vexation equal to what I experienced on last Monday when my Sister came running to me in the Store-room with her face as White as a Whipt syllabub, and told me that Hervey had been thrown from his Horse, had fractured his Scull and was pronounced by his Surgeon to be in the most emminent Danger.

"Good God! (said I) you dont say so? why what in the name of Heaven will become of all the Victuals! We shall never be able to eat it while it is good. However, we'll call in the Surgeon to help us—. I shall be able to manage the Sir-loin myself; my Mother will eat the Soup, and You and the Doctor must finish the rest." Here I was interrupted, by seeing my poor Sister fall down to appearance Lifeless upon one of the Chests, where we keep our Table linen. I immediately called my Mother and the Maids, and at last we brought her to herself again; as soon as ever she was sensible, she expressed a determination of going instantly to Henry, and was so wildly bent on this Scheme, that we had the greatest Difficulty in the World to prevent her putting it in execution; at last however more by Force than Entreaty we prevailed on her to go into her room; we laid her upon the Bed, and she continued for some Hours in the most dreadful Convulsions. My Mother and I continued in the room with her, and when any intervals of tolerable Composure in Eloisa would allow us, we joined in heartfelt lamentations on the dreadful Waste in our provisions which this Event must occasion, and in concerting some plan for getting rid of them. We agreed that the best thing we could do was to begin eating them immediately, and accordingly we ordered up the cold Ham and Fowls, and instantly began our Devouring Plan on them with great Alacrity. We would have persuaded Eloisa to have taken a Wing of a Chicken, but she would not be persuaded. She was however much quieter than she had been; the Convulsions she had before suffered having given way to an almost perfect Insensibility. We endeavoured to rouse her by every means in our power, but to no purpose. I talked to her of Henry. "Dear Eloisa (said I) there's no occasion for your crying so much about such a trifle. (for I was willing to make light of it in order to comfort her) I beg you would not mind it—. You see it does not vex me in the least; though perhaps *I* may suffer most from it after all; for I shall not only be obliged to eat up all the Victuals I have dressed already, but must if Hervey should recover (which however is not very likely) dress as much for you again; or should he die (as I suppose he will) I shall still have to prepare a Dinner for you whenever you marry any one else. So you see that tho' perhaps for the present it may afflict you to think of Henry's sufferings, Yet I dare say he'll die soon, and then his pain will be over and you will be easy, whereas my Trouble will last much longer for work as hard as I may, I am certain that the pantry cannot be cleared in less than a fortnight." Thus I did all in my power to console her, but without any effect, and at last as I saw that she did not seem to listen to me, I said no more, but leaving her with my Mother I took down the remains of The Ham and Chicken, and sent William to ask how Hervey did. He was not expected to live many Hours; he died the same day. We took all possible Care to break the Melancholy Event to Eloisa in the tenderest manner; yet in spite of every precaution, her Sufferings on hearing it were too violent for her reason, and she continued for many hours in a high Delirium. She is still extremely ill, and her Physicians are greatly afraid of her going into a Decline. We are therefore preparing for Bristol, where we mean to be in the course of the next Week. And now my dear Margaret let me talk a little of your affairs; and in the first place I must inform you that it is confidently reported, your Father is going to be married; I am very unwilling to beleive so unpleasing a report, and at the same time cannot wholly discredit it. I have written to my freind Susan Fitzgerald, for information concerning it, which as she is at present in Town, she will be very able to give me. I know not who is the Lady. I think your Brother is extremely right in the resolution he has taken of travelling, as it will perhaps contribute to obliterate from his remembrance, those disagreable Events, which have lately so much afflicted him—I am happy to find that tho' secluded from all the World, neither You nor Matilda are dull or unhappy—that you may never know what it is to be either is the Wish of your Sincerely Affectionate

C. L.

P.S. I have this instant received an answer from my freind Susan, which I enclose to you, and on which you will make your own reflections.

The enclosed Letter
My dear Charlotte

You could not have applied for information concerning the report of Sir George Lesleys Marriage, to any one better able to give it you than I am. Sir George is certainly married; I was myself present at the Ceremony, which you will not be surprised at when I subscribe myself your

Affectionate Susan Lesley

LETTER THE THIRD

From Miss Margaret Lesley to Miss C. Lutterell

Lesley Castle February the 16th

I *have* made my own reflections on the letter you enclosed to me, my Dear Charlotte and I will now tell you what those reflections were. I reflected that if by this second Marriage Sir George should have a second family, our fortunes must be considerably diminished—that if his Wife should be of an extravagant turn, she would encourage him to persevere in that Gay and Dissipated way of Life to which little encouragement would be necessary, and which has I fear already proved but too detrimental to his health and fortune—that she would now become Mistress of those Jewels which once adorned our Mother, and which Sir George had always promised us—that if they did not come into Perthshire I should not be able to gratify my curiosity of beholding my Mother-in-law, and that if they did, Matilda would no longer sit at the head of her Father's table—. These my dear Charlotte were the melancholy reflections which crouded into my imagination after perusing Susan's letter to you, and which instantly occurred to Matilda when she had perused it likewise. The same ideas, the same fears, immediately occupied her Mind, and I know not which reflection distressed her most, whether the probable Diminution of our Fortunes, or her own Consequence. We both wish very much to know whether Lady Lesley is handsome and what is your opinion of her; as you honour her with the appellation of your freind, we flatter ourselves that she must be amiable. My Brother is already in Paris. He intends to quit it in a few Days, and to begin his route to Italy. He writes in a most chearfull Manner, says that the air of France has greatly recovered both his Health and Spirits; that he has now entirely ceased to think of Louisa with any degree either of Pity or Affection, that he even feels himself obliged to her for her Elopement, as he thinks it very good fun to be single again. By this, you may perceive that he has entirely regained that chearful Gaiety, and sprightly Wit, for which he was once so remarkable. When he first became acquainted with Louisa which was little more than three years ago, he was one of the most lively, the most agreable young Men of the age—. I beleive you never yet heard the particulars of his first acquaintance with her. It commenced at our cousin Colonel Drummond's; at whose house in Cumberland he spent the Christmas, in which he attained the age of two and twenty. Louisa Burton was the Daughter of a distant Relation of Mrs. Drummond, who dieing a few Months before in extreme poverty, left his only Child then about eighteen to the protection of any of his Relations who would protect her. Mrs. Drummond was the only one who found herself so disposed—Louisa was therefore removed from a miserable Cottage in Yorkshire to an elegant Mansion in Cumberland, and from every pecuniary Distress that Poverty could inflict, to every elegant Enjoyment that Money could purchase—. Louisa was naturally ill-tempered and Cunning; but she had been taught to disguise her real Disposition, under the appearance of insinuating Sweetness, by a father who but too well knew, that to be married, would be the only chance she would have of not being starved, and who flattered himself that with such an extroidinary share of personal beauty, joined to a gentleness of Manners, and an engaging address, she might stand a good chance of pleasing some young Man who might afford to marry a Girl without a Shilling. Louisa perfectly entered into her father's schemes and was determined to forward them with all her care and attention. By dint of Perseverance and Application, she had at length so thoroughly disguised her natural disposition under the mask of Innocence and Softness, as to impose upon every one who had not by a long and constant intimacy with her discovered her real Character. Such was Louisa when the hapless Lesley first beheld her at Drummond-house. His heart which (to use your favourite comparison) was as delicate as sweet and as tender as a Whipt-syllabub, could not resist her attractions. In a very few Days, he was falling in love, shortly after actually fell, and before he had known her a Month, he had married her. My Father was at first highly displeased at so hasty and imprudent a connection; but when he found that they did not mind it, he soon became perfectly reconciled to the match. The Estate near Aberdeen which my brother possesses by the bounty of his great Uncle independant of Sir George, was entirely sufficient to support him and my Sister in Elegance and Ease. For the first twelvemonth, no one could be happier than Lesley, and no one more amiable to appearance than Louisa, and so plausibly did she act and so cautiously behave that tho' Matilda and I often spent several weeks together with them, yet we neither of us had any suspicion of her real Disposition. After the birth of Louisa however, which one would have thought would have strengthened her regard for Lesley, the mask she had so long supported was by degrees thrown aside, and as probably she then thought herself secure in the affection of her Husband (which did indeed appear if possible augmented by the birth of his Child) she seemed to take no pains to prevent that affection from ever diminishing. Our visits therefore to Dunbeath, were now less frequent and by far less agreable than they used to be. Our absence was however never either mentioned or lamented by Louisa who in the society of young Danvers with whom she became acquainted at Aberdeen (he was at one of the Universities there,) felt infinitely happier than in that of Matilda and your freind, tho' there certainly never were pleasanter Girls than we are. You know the sad end of all Lesleys connubial happiness; I will not repeat it—. Adeiu my dear Charlotte; although I have not yet mentioned any thing of the matter, I hope you will do me the justice to beleive that I *think* and *feel*, a great deal for your Sisters affliction. I do not doubt but that the healthy air of the Bristol-downs will intirely remove it, by erasing from her Mind the remembrance of Henry. I am my dear Charlotte y^{rs} ever

ML—

LETTER THE FOURTH

From Miss C. Lutterell to Miss M. Lesley

Bristol February 27th

My dear Peggy

I have but just received your letter, which being directed to Sussex while I was at Bristol was obliged to be forwarded to me here, and from some unaccountable Delay, has but this instant reached me—. I return you many thanks for the account it contains of Lesley's acquaintance, Love and Marriage with Louisa, which has not the less entertained me for having often been repeated to me before.

I have the satisfaction of informing you that we have every reason to imagine our pantry is by this time nearly cleared, as we left particular orders with the Servants to eat as hard as they possibly could, and to call in a couple of Chairwomen to assist them. We brought a cold Pigeon-pye, a cold turkey, a cold tongue, and half a dozen Jellies with us, which we were lucky enough with the help of our Landlady, her husband, and their three children, to get rid of, in less than two days after our arrival. Poor Eloisa is still so very indifferent both in Health and Spirits, that I very much fear, the air of the Bristol-downs, healthy as it is, has not been able to drive poor Henry from her remembrance—.

You ask me whether your new Mother in law is handsome and amiable—I will now give you an exact description of her bodily and Mental charms. She is short, and extremely well-made; is naturally pale, but rouges a good deal; has fine eyes, and fine teeth, as she will take care to let you know as soon as she sees you, and is altogether very pretty. She is remarkably good-tempered when she has her own way, and very lively when she is not out of humour. She is naturally extravagant and not very affected; she never reads any thing but the letters she receives from me, and never writes anything but her answers to them. She plays, sings and Dances, but has no taste for either, and excells in none, tho' she says she is passionately fond of all. Perhaps you may flatter me so far as to be surprised that one of whom I speak with so little affection should be my particular freind; but to tell you the truth, our freindship arose rather from Caprice on her side, than Esteem on mine. We spent two or three days together with a Lady in Berkshire with whom we both happened to be connected—. During our visit, the Weather being remarkably bad, and our party particularly stupid, she was so good as to conceive a violent partiality for me, which very soon settled in a downright Freindship, and ended in an established correspondence. She is probably by this time as tired of me, as I am of her; but as she is too polite and I am too civil to say so, our letters are still as frequent and affectionate as ever, and our Attachment as firm and Sincere as when it first commenced.—As she has a great taste for the pleasures of London, and of Brighthelmstone, he will I dare say find some difficulty in prevailing on herself ever to satisfy the curiosity I dare say she feels of beholding you, at the expence of quitting those favourite haunts of Dissipation, for the melancholy tho' venerable gloom of the castle you inhabit. Perhaps however if she finds her health impaired by too much amusement, she may acquire fortitude sufficient to undertake a Journey to Scotland in the hope of its proving at least beneficial to her health, if not conducive to her happiness. Your fears I am sorry to say, concerning your father's extravagance, your own fortunes, your Mothers Jewels and your Sister's consequence, I should suppose are but too well founded. My freind herself has four thousand pounds, and will probably spend nearly as much every year in Dress and Public places, if she can get it—she will certainly not endeavour to reclaim Sir George from the manner of living to which he has been so long accustomed, and there is therefore some reason to fear that you will be very well off, if you get any fortune at all. The Jewels I should imagine too will undoubtedly be hers, and there is too much reason to think that she will preside at her Husbands table in preference to his Daughter. But as so melancholy a subject must necessarily extremely distress you, I will no longer dwell on it—.

Eloisa's indisposition has brought us to Bristol at so unfashionable a season of the year, that we have actually seen but one genteel family since we came. Mr and Mrs Marlowe are very agreable people; the ill health of their little boy occasioned their arrival here; you may imagine that being the only family with whom we can converse, we are of course on a footing of intimacy with them; we see them indeed almost every day, and dined with them yesterday. We spent a very pleasant Day, and had a very good Dinner, tho' to be sure the Veal was terribly underdone, and the Curry had no seasoning. I could not help wishing all dinner-time that I had been at the dressing it—. A brother of Mrs Marlowe, Mr Cleveland is with them at present; he is a good-looking young Man and seems to have a good deal to say for himself. I tell Eloisa that she should set her cap at him, but she does not at all seem to relish the proposal. I should like to see the girl married and Cleveland has a very good estate. Perhaps you may wonder that I do not consider *myself* as well as my Sister in my matrimonial Projects; but to tell you the truth I never wish to act a more principal part at a Wedding than the superintending and directing the Dinner, and therefore while I can get any of my acquaintance to marry for me, I shall never think of doing it myself, as I very much suspect that I should not have so much time for dressing my own Wedding-dinner, as for dressing that of my freinds. Y^{rs} sincerely

CL.

LETTER THE FIFTH

Miss Margaret Lesley to Miss Charlotte Luttrell

Lesley-Castle March 18th

On the same day that I received your last kind letter, Matilda received one from Sir George which was dated from Edinburgh, and informed us that he should do himself the pleasure of introducing Lady Lesley to us on the following Evening. This as you may suppose considerably surprised us, particularly as your account of her Ladyship had given us reason to imagine there was little chance of her visiting Scotland at a time that London must be so gay. As it was our business however to be delighted at such a mark of condescension as a visit from Sir George and Lady Lesley, we prepared to return them an answer expressive of the happiness we enjoyed in expectation of such a Blessing, when luckily recollecting that as they were to reach the Castle the next Evening, it would be impossible for my father to receive it before he left Edinburgh, We contented ourselves with leaving them to suppose that we were as happy as we ought to be. At nine in the Evening on the following day, they came, accompanied by one of Lady Lesleys brothers. Her Ladyship perfectly answers the description you sent me of her, except that I do not think her so pretty as you seem to consider her. She has not a bad face, but there is something so extremely unmajestic in her little diminutive figure, as to render her in comparison with the elegant height of Matilda and Myself, an insignificant Dwarf. Her curiosity to see us (which must have been great to bring her more than four hundred miles) being now perfectly gratified, she already begins to mention their return to town, and has desired us to accompany her—. We cannot refuse her request since it is seconded by the commands of our Father, and thirded by the entreaties of Mr Fitzgerald who is certainly one of the most pleasing young Men, I ever beheld. It is not yet determined when we are to go, but when we do we shall certainly take our little Louisa with us. Adeiu my dear Charlotte; Matilda unites in best wishes to You and Eloisa, with yours ever

ML

LETTER THE SIXTH

Lady Lesley to Miss Charlotte Luttrell
Lesley-Castle March 20th
We arrived here my sweet Freind about a fortnight ago, and I already heartily repent that I ever left our charming House in

Portman-Square for such a dismal old Weather-beaten Castle as this. You can form no idea sufficiently hideous, of its dungeon-like form. It is actually perched upon a Rock to appearance so totally inaccessible, that I expected to have been pulled up by a rope; and sincerely repented having gratified my curiosity to behold my Daughters at the expence of being obliged to enter their prison in so dangerous and ridiculous a Manner. But as soon as I once found myself safely arrived in the inside of this tremendous building, I comforted myself with the hope of having my spirits revived, by the sight of two beautifull Girls, such as the Miss Lesleys had been represented to me, at Edinburgh. But here again, I met with nothing but Disapointment and Surprise. Matilda and Margaret Lesley are two great, tall, out of the way, overgrown, Girls, just of a proper size to inhabit a Castle almost as Large in comparison as themselves. I wish my dear Charlotte that you could but behold these Scotch Giants; I am sure they would frighten you out of your wits. They will do very well as foils to myself, so I have invited them to accompany me to London where I hope to be in the course of a fortnight. Besides these two fair Damsels, I found a little humoured Brat here who I beleive is some relation to them; they told me who she was, and gave me a long rigmerole Story of her father and a Miss *Somebody* which I have entirely forgot. I hate Scandal and detest Children.—. I have been plagued ever since I came here with tiresome visits from a parcel of Scotch wretches, with terrible hard-names; they were so civil, gave me so many invitations, and talked of coming again so soon, that I could not help affronting them. I suppose I shall not see them any more, and yet as a family party we are so stupid, that I do not know what to do with myself. These girls have no Music, but Scotch Airs, no Drawings but Scotch Mountains, and no Books but Scotch Poems—And I hate everything Scotch. In general I can spend half the Day at my toilett with a great deal of pleasure, but why should I dress here, since there is not a creature in the House whom I have any wish to please.—. I have just had a conversation with my Brother in which he has greatly offended me, and which as I have nothing more entertaining to send you I will give you the particulars of. You must know that I have for these 4 or 5 Days past strongly suspected William of entertaining a partiality for my eldest Daughter. I own indeed that had *I* been inclined to fall in love with any woman, I should not have made choice of Matilda Lesley for the object of my passion; for there is nothing I hate so much as a tall Woman: but however there is no accounting for some men's taste and as William is himself nearly six feet high, it is not wonderful that he should be partial to that height. Now as I have very great affection for my Brother and should be extremely sorry to see him unhappy, which I suppose he means to be if he cannot marry Matilda, as moreover I know that his Circumstances will not allow him to marry any one without a fortune, and that Matilda's is entirely dependent on her Father, who will neither have his own inclination nor my permission to give her anything at present, I thought it would be doing a good-natured action by my Brother to let him know as much, in order that he might choose for himself, whether to conquer his passion, or Love and Despair. Accordingly finding myself this Morning alone with him in one of the horrid old rooms of this Castle, I opened the cause to him in the following Manner.

"Well my dear William what do you think of these girls? for my part, I do not find them so plain as I expected: but perhaps you may think me partial to the Daughters of my Husband and perhaps you are right—They are indeed so very like Sir George that it is natural to think....."

"My Dear Susan (cried he in a tone of the greatest amazement) You do not really think they bear the least resemblance to their Father! He is so very plain!—but I beg your pardon—I had entirely forgotten to whom I was speaking—"

"Oh! pray don't mind me; (replied I) every one knows Sir George is horribly ugly, and I assure you I always thought him a fright."

"You surprise me extremely (answered William) by what you say both with respect to Sir George and his Daughters. You cannot think Your Husband so deficient in personal Charms as you speak of, nor can you surely see any resemblance between him and the Miss Lesleys who are in my opinion perfectly unlike him and perfectly Handsome."

"If that is your opinion with regard to the girls it certainly is no proof of their Father's beauty, for if they are perfectly unlike him and very handsome at the same time, it is natural to suppose that he is very plain."

"By no means, (said he) for what may be pretty in a Woman, may be very unpleasing in a Man."

"But, you yourself (replied I) but a few Minutes ago allowed him to be very plain."

"Men are no Judges of Beauty in their own Sex." (said he)

"Neither Men nor Women can think Sir George tolerable."

"Well, well, (said he) we will not dispute about *his* Beauty, but your opinion of his *Daughters* is surely very singular, for if I understood you right, you said you did not find them so plain as you expected to do."!

"Why, do *you* find them plainer then?" (said I)

"I can scarcely beleive you to be serious (returned he) when you speak of their persons in so extroidinary a Manner. Do not you not think the Miss Lesleys are two very handsome Young Women?"

"Lord! No! (cried I) I think them terribly plain!"

"Plain! (replied He) My dear Susan, you cannot really think so! Why what single Feature in the face of either of them, can you possibly find fault with?"

"Oh! trust me for that; (replied I). Come I will begin with the eldest—with Matilda. Shall I, William?" (I looked as cunning as I could when I said it, in order to shame him.)

"They are so much alike (said he) that I should suppose the faults of one, would be the faults of both."

"Well, then, in the first place, they are both so horribly tall!"

"They are *taller* than you are indeed." (said he with a saucy smile.)

"Nay, (said I) I know nothing of that."

"Well, but (he continued) tho' they may be above the common size, their figures are perfectly elegant; and as to their faces, their Eyes are beautifull—."

"I never can think such tremendous, knock-me-down figures in the least degree elegant, and as for their eyes, they are so tall that I never could strain my neck enough to look at them."

"Nay, (replied he) I know not whether you may not be in the right in not attempting it, for perhaps they might dazzle you with their Lustre."

"Oh! Certainly. (said I, with the greatest Complacency, for I assure you my dearest Charlotte I was not in the least offended tho' by what followed, one would suppose that William was conscious of having given me just cause to be so, for coming up to me and taking my hand, he said) "You must not look so grave Susan; you will make me fear I have offended you!"

"Offended me! Dear Brother, how came such a thought in your head! (returned I) No really! I assure you that I am not in the least surprised at your being so warm an advocate for the Beauty of these Girls—"

"Well, but (interrupted William) remember that we have not yet concluded our dispute concerning them. What fault do you find with their complexion?"

"They are so horridly pale."

"They have always a little colour, and after any exercise it is considerably heightened."

"Yes, but if there should ever happen to be any rain in this part of the world, they will never be able to raise more than their common stock—except indeed they amuse themselves with running up and Down these horrid old Galleries and Antichambers—"

"Well, (replied my Brother in a tone of vexation, and glancing an impertinent look at me) if they *have* but little colour, at least, it is all their own."

This was too much my dear Charlotte, for I am certain that he had the impudence by that look, of pretending to suspect the reality of mine. But you I am sure will vindicate my character whenever you may hear it so cruelly aspersed, for you can witness how often I have protested against wearing Rouge, and how much I always told you I disliked it. And I assure you that my opinions are still the same.—. Well, not bearing to be so suspected by my Brother,

I left the room immediately, and have been ever since in my own Dressing-room writing to you. What a long Letter have I made of it. But you must not expect to receive such from me when I get to Town; for it is only at Lesley castle, that one has time to write even to a Charlotte Luttrell.—. I was so much vexed by William's Glance, that I could not summon Patience enough, to stay and give him that Advice respecting his Attachment to Matilda which had first induced me from pure Love to him to begin the conversation; and I am now so thoroughly convinced by it, of his violent passion for her, that I am certain he would never hear reason on the Subject, and I shall therefore give myself no more trouble either about him or his favourite. Adeiu my dear Girl—

Y^{rs} affectionately Susan L.

LETTER THE SEVENTH

From Miss C. Luttrell to Miss M. Lesley

Bristol the 27th of March

I have received Letters from You and your Mother-in-law within this week which have greatly entertained me, as I find by them that you are both downright jealous of each others Beauty. It is very odd that two pretty Women tho' actually Mother and Daughter cannot be in the same House without falling out about their faces. Do be convinced that you are both perfectly handsome and say no more of the Matter. I suppose this Letter must be directed to Portman Square where probably (great as is your affection for Lesley Castle) you will not be sorry to find yourself. In spite of all that People may say about Green fields and the Country I was always of opinion that London and its Amusements must be very agreable for a while, and should be very happy could my Mother's income allow her to jockey us into its Public-places, during Winter. I always longed particularly to go to Vaux-hall, to see whether the cold Beef there is cut so thin as it is reported, for I have a sly suspicion that few people understand the act of cutting a slice of cold Beef so well as I do: nay it would be hard of I did not know something of the Matter, for it was a part of my Education that I took by far the most pains with. Mama always found me *her* best Scholar, tho' when Papa was alive Eloisa was *his*. Never to be sure were there two more different Dispositions in the World. We both loved Reading. *She* preferred Histories, and *I* Receipts. She loved drawing Pictures, and I drawing Pullets. No one could sing a better Song than She, and no one make a better Pye than I.—And so it has always continued since we have been no longer Children. The only difference is that all disputes on the superior excellence of our Employments *then* so frequent are now no more. We have for many years entered into an agreement always to admire each other's works; I never fail listening to *her* Music, and she is as constant in eating *my* pies. Such at least was the case till Henry Hervey made his appearance in Sussex. Before the arrival of his Aunt in our neighbourhood where she established herself you know about a twelvemonth ago, his visits to her had been at stated times, and of equal and settled Duration; but on her removal to the Hall which is within a walk from our House, they became both more frequent and longer. This as you may suppose could not be pleasing to Mrs Diana who is a professed Enemy to everything which is not directed by Decorum and Formality, or which bears the least resemblance to Ease and Good-breeding. Nay so great was her aversion to her Nephews behaviour that I have often heard her give such hints of it before his face that had not Henry at such times been engaged in conversation with Eloisa, they must have caught his Attention and have very much distressed him. The alteration in my Sister's behaviour which I have before hinted at, now took place. The Agreement we had entered into of admiring each others productions she no longer seemed to regard, and tho' I constantly applauded even every Country-dance, She play'd, yet not even a pidgeon-pye of my making could obtain from her a single word of Approbation. This was certainly enough to put any one in a Passion; however, I was as cool as a Cream-cheese and having formed my plan and concerted a scheme of Revenge, I was determined to let her have her own way and not even to make her a single reproach. My Scheme was to treat her as she treated me, and tho' she might even draw my own Picture or play Malbrook (which is the only tune I ever really liked) not to say so much as "Thank you Eloisa"; tho' I had for many years constantly hollowed whenever she played, *Bravo, Bravissimo, Encora, Da Capro, allegretto, con espressioné,* and *Poco presto* with many other such outlandish words, all of them as Eloisa told me expressive of my Admiration; and so indeed I suppose they are, as I see some of them in every Page of every Music-book, being the Sentiments I imagine of the Composer.

I executed my Plan with great Punctuality, I can not say success, for Alas! my silence while she played seemed not in the least to displease her; on the contrary she actually said to me one day "Well Charlotte, I am very glad to find that you have at last left off that ridiculous custom of applauding my Execution on the Harpsichord till you made *my* head ake, and yourself hoarse. I feel very much obliged to you for keeping your Admiration to yourself." I never shall forget the very witty answer I made to this speech.

"Eloisa (said I) I beg you would be quite at your Ease with respect to all such fears in future, for be assured that I shall always keep my Admiration to myself and my own pursuits and never extend it to yours." This was the only very severe thing I ever said in my Life; not but that I have often felt myself extremely satirical but it was the only time I ever made my feelings public.

I suppose there never were two young people who had a greater affection for each other than Henry and Eloisa; no, the Love of your Brother for Miss Burton could not be so strong tho' it might be more violent. You may imagine therefore how provoked my Sister must have been to have him play her such a trick. Poor Girl! She still laments his Death, with undiminished Constancy, notwithstanding he has been dead more than six weeks; but some people mind such things more than others. The ill state of Health into which his Loss has thrown her makes her so weak, and so unable to support the least exertion, that she has been in tears all this morning merely from having taken leave of Mrs Marlowe who with her Husband, Brother and Child are to leave Bristol this Morning. I am sorry to have them go because they are the only family with whom we have here any acquaintance, but I never thought of crying; to be sure Eloisa and Mrs Marlowe have always been more together than with me, and have therefore contracted a kind of affection for each other, which does not make Tears so inexcusable in them as they would be in me. The Marlowes are going to Town, Cleveland accompanies them; as neither Eloisa nor I could catch him I hope You or Matilda may have better Luck. I know not when we shall leave Bristol, Eloisa's Spirits are so low that she is very averse to moving, and yet is certainly by no means mended by her residence here. A week or two will I hope determine our Measures—in the mean time beleive me

etc—etc—Charlotte Luttrell

LETTER THE EIGHTH

Miss Luttrell to Mrs Marlowe.

Bristol April 4th

I feel myself greatly obliged to you my dear Emma for such a mark of your affection as I flatter myself was conveyed in the proposal you made me of our Corresponding; I assure you that it will be a great releif to me to write to you and as long as my Health and Spirits will allow me, you will find me a very constant Correspondent; I will not say an entertaining one, for you know my situation sufficiently not to be ignorant that in me Mirth would be improper and I know my own Heart too well not to be sensible that it would be unnatural. You must not expect News for we see no one with whom we are in the least acquainted, or in whose proceedings we have any Interest. You must not expect Scandal for by the same rule we are equally debarred either from hearing or inventing it.—You must expect from me nothing but the melancholy effusions of a broken Heart which is ever reverting to the Happiness it once enjoyed and which ill supports its present Wretchedness. The Possibility of being able to write, to speak, to you of my losst Henry will be a Luxury to me, and your Goodness will not I know refuse to read what it will so much releive my Heart to write. I once thought that to have what is in general called a Freind (I mean one of my own Sex to whom I might speak with less reserve than to any other person) independant of my Sister would never be an object of my wishes, but how much was I mistaken! Charlotte is too much engrossed by two confidential Correspondents of that sort, to supply the place of one to me, and I hope you will not think me girlishly romantic, when I say that to have some kind and compassionate Freind who might listen to my Sorrows without endeavouring to console me was what I had for some time wished for, when our acquaintance with you, the intimacy which followed it and the particular affectionate Attention you paid me almost from the first, caused me to entertain the flattering Idea of those attentions being improved on a closer acquaintance into a Freindship which, if you were what my wishes formed you would be the greatest Happiness I could be capable of enjoying. To find that such Hopes are realized is a satisfaction indeed, a satisfaction which is now almost the only one I can ever experience.—I feel myself so languid that I am sure were you with me you would oblige me to leave off writing, and I can not give you a greater proof of my Affection for you than by acting, as I know you would wish me to do, whether Absent or Present. I am my dear Emmas sincere freind

E. L.

LETTER THE NINTH

Mrs Marlowe to Miss Lutterell

Grosvenor Street, April 10th

Need I say my dear Eloisa how wellcome your Letter was to me? I cannot give a greater proof of the pleasure I received from it, or of the Desire I feel that our Correspondence may be regular and frequent than by setting you so good an example as I now do in answering it before the end of the week—. But do not imagine that I claim any merit in being so punctual; on the contrary I assure you, that it is a far greater Gratification to me to write to you, than to spend the Evening either at a Concert or a Ball. Mr Marlowe is so desirous of my appearing at some of the Public places every evening that I do not like to refuse him, but at the same time so much wish to remain at Home, that independant of the Pleasure I experience in devoting any portion of my Time to my Dear Eloisa, yet the Liberty I claim from having a Letter to write of spending an Evening at home with my little Boy, You know me well enough to be sensible, will of itself be a sufficient Inducement (if one is necessary) to my maintaining with Pleasure a Correspondence with you. As to the Subjects of your Letters to me, whether Grave or Merry, if they concern you they must be equally interesting to me; Not but that I think the Melancholy Indulgence of your own Sorrows by repeating them and dwelling on them to me, will only encourage and increase them, and that it will be more prudent in you to avoid so sad a subject; but yet knowing as I do what a soothing and Melancholy Pleasure it must afford you, I cannot prevail on myself to deny you so great an Indulgence, and will only insist on your not expecting me to encourage you in it, by my own Letters; on the contrary I intend to fill them with such lively Wit and entertaining Humour as shall even provoke a Smile in the sweet but Sorrowfull Countenance of my Eloisa.

In the first place you are to learn that I have met your Sisters three freinds Lady Lesley and her Daughters, twice in Public since I have been here. I know you will be impatient to hear my opinion of the Beauty of three Ladies of whom You have heard so much. Now, as you are too ill and too unhappy to be vain, I think I may venture to inform you that I like none of their faces so well as I do your own. Yet they are all handsome—Lady Lesley indeed I have seen before; her Daughters I beleive would in general be said to have a finer face than her Ladyship, and Yet what with the charms of a Blooming Complexion, a little Affectation and a great deal of Small-talk, (in each of which She is superior to the Young Ladies) she will I dare say gain herself as many Admirers as the more regular features of Matilda, and Margaret. I am sure you will agree with me in saying that they can none of them be of a proper size for real Beauty, when you know that two of them are taller and the other shorter than ourselves. In spite of this Defect (or rather by reason of it) there is something very noble and majestic in the figures of the Miss Lesleys, and something agreably Lively in the Appearance of their pretty little Mother-in-law. But tho' one may be majestic and the other Lively, yet the faces of neither possess that Bewitching Sweetness of my Eloisas, which her present Languor is so far from diminushing. What would my Husband and Brother say of us, if they knew all the fine things I have been saying to you in this Letter. It is very hard that a pretty Woman is never to be told she is so by any one of her own Sex, without that person's being suspected to be either her determined Enemy, or her professed Toad-eater.* How much more amiable are women in that particular! one Man may say forty civil things to another without our supposing that he is ever paid for it, and provided he does his Duty by our Sex, we care not how Polite he is to his own.

Mrs Luttrell will be so good as to accept my Compliments, Charlotte, my Love, and Eloisa the best wishes for the recovery of her Health and Spirits that can be offered by her Affectionate Freind E. Marlowe.

I am afraid this Letter will be but a poor Specimen of my Powers in the Witty Way; and your opinion of them will not be greatly increased when I assure you that I have been as entertaining as I possibly could—.

---

* **Toad-eater:** a sycophant. The term comes from mountebanks' assistants pretending to swallow toads, so that the mountebanks could impress their audience by pretending to expel the poisons supposedly ingested.

LETTER THE TENTH

From Miss Margaret Lesley to Miss Charlotte Luttrell

Portman Square April 13th

My dear Charlotte

We left Lesley-Castle on the 28th of Last Month, and arrived safely in London after a Journey of seven Days; I had the pleasure of finding your Letter here waiting my Arrival, for which you have my grateful Thanks. Ah! my dear Freind I every day more regret the serene and tranquil Pleasures of the Castle we have left, in exchange for the uncertain and unequal Amusements of this vaunted City. Not that I will pretend to assert that these uncertain and unequal Amusements are in the least Degree unpleasing to me; on the contrary I enjoy them extremely and should enjoy them even more, were I not certain that every appearance I make in Public but rivetts the Chains of those unhappy Beings whose Passion it is impossible not to pity, tho' it is out of my power to return. In short my Dear Charlotte it is my sensibility for the sufferings of so many amiable Young Men, my Dislike of the extreme Admiration I meet with, and my Aversion to being so celebrated both in Public, in Private, in Papers, and in Printshops, that are the reasons why I cannot more fully enjoy, the Amusements so various and pleasing of London. How often have I wished that I possessed as little personal Beauty as you do; that my figure were as inelegant; my face as unlovely; and my Appearance as unpleasing as yours! But Ah! what little chance is there of so desirable an Event; I have had the Small-pox, and must therefore submit to my unhappy fate.

I am now going to intrust you my dear Charlotte with a secret which has long disturbed the tranquility of my days, and which is of a kind to require the most inviolable Secrecy from you. Last Monday se'night Matilda and I accompanied Lady Lesley to a Rout at the Honourable Mrs Kickabout's; we were escorted by Mr Fitzgerald who is a very amiable Young Man in the main, tho' perhaps a little Singular in his Taste—He is in love with Matilda—. We had scarcely paid our Compliments to the Lady of the House and curtseyed to half a Score different people when my Attention was attracted by the appearance of a Young Man the most lovely of his Sex, who at that Moment entered the Room with another Gentleman and Lady. From the first moment I beheld him, I was certain that on him depended the future Happiness of my Life. Imagine my surprise when he was introduced to me by the name of Cleveland—I instantly recognized him as the Brother of Mrs Marlowe, and the acquaintance of my Charlotte at Bristol. Mr and Mrs M. were the Gentleman and Lady who accompanied him. (You do not think Mrs Marlowe handsome?) The elegant address of Mr Cleveland, his polished Manners and Delightful Bow, at once confirmed my attachment. He did not speak; but I can imagine every thing he would have said, had he opened his Mouth. I can picture to myself the cultivated Understanding, the Noble Sentiments, and elegant Language which would have shone so conspicuous in the conversation of Mr Cleveland. The approach of Sir James Gower (one of my too numerous Admirers) prevented the Discovery of any such Powers, by putting an end to a Conversation we had never commenced, and by attracting my attention to himself. But Oh! how inferior are the accomplishments of Sir James to those of his so greatly envied Rival! Sir James is one of the most frequent of our Visitors, and is almost always of our Parties. We have since often met Mr and Mrs Marlowe but no Cleveland—he is always engaged some where else. Mrs Marlowe fatigues me to Death every time I see her by her tiresome Conversations about You and Eloisa. She is so Stupid! I live in the hope of seeing her irresistable Brother to night, as we are going to Lady Flambeau's, who is I know intimate with the Marlowes. Our party will be Lady Lesley, Matilda, Fitzgerald, Sir James Gower, and myself. We see little of Sir George, who is almost always at the Gaming-table. Ah! my poor Fortune where art thou by this time? We see more of Lady L. who always makes her appearance (highly rouged) at Dinner-time. Alas! what Delightful Jewels will she be decked in this evening at Lady Flambeau's! Yet I wonder how she can herself delight in wearing them; surely she must be sensible of the ridiculous impropriety of loading her little diminutive figure with such superfluous ornaments; is it possible that she can not know how greatly superior an elegant simplicity is to the most studied apparel? Would she but present them to Matilda and me, how greatly should we be obliged to her. How becoming would Diamonds be on our fine majestic figures! And how surprising it is that such an Idea should never have occurred to *her*. I am sure if I have reflected in this Manner once, I have fifty times. Whenever I see Lady Lesley dressed in them such reflections immediately come across me. My own Mother's Jewels too! But I will say no more on so melancholy a Subject—Let me entertain you with something more pleasing—Matilda had a letter this Morning from Lesley, by which we have the pleasure of finding that he is at Naples has turned Roman-catholic, obtained one of the Pope's Bulls for annulling his 1st Marriage and has since actually married a Neapolitan Lady of great Rank and Fortune. He tells us moreover that much the same sort of affair has befallen his first Wife the worthless Louisa who is likewise at Naples has turned Roman-catholic, and is soon to be married to a Neapolitan Nobleman of great and Distinguished Merit. He says, that they are at present very good Freinds, have quite forgiven all past errors and intend in future to be very good Neighbours. He invites Matilda and me to pay him a visit in Italy and to bring him his little Louisa whom both her Mother, Step-Mother, and himself are equally desirous of beholding. As to our accepting his invitation, it is at present very uncertain; Lady Lesley advises us to go without loss of time; Fitzgerald offers to escort us there, but Matilda has some doubts of the Propriety of such a Scheme—She owns it would be very agreable. I am certain she likes the Fellow. My Father desires us not to be in a hurry, as perhaps if we wait a few months both he and Lady Lesley will do themselves the pleasure of attending us. Lady Lesley says no, that nothing will ever tempt her to forego the Amusements of Brighthelmstone for a Journey to Italy merely to see our Brother. "No (says the disagreable Woman) I have once in my Life been fool enough to travel I dont know how many hundred Miles to see two of the Family, and I found it did not answer, so Deuce take me, if ever I am so foolish again." So says her Ladyship, but Sir George still perseveres in saying that perhaps in a Month or two, they may accompany us.

Adeiu my Dear Charlotte—
Y^r faithful Margaret Lesley

THE HISTORY OF ENGLAND

*from the reign of
Henry the 4th
to the death of
Charles the 1st.*

By a partial, prejudiced, and ignorant Historian

*To Miss Austen eldest daughter of the Revd George Austen, this Work is inscribed with all due respect by
The Author*

N. B. There will be very few Dates in this History.

HENRY THE 4TH

Henry the 4th ascended the throne of England much to his own satisfaction in the year 1399, after having prevailed on his cousin and predecessor Richard the 2ᵈ, to resign it to him, and to retire for the rest of his Life to Pomfret Castle,[1] where he happened to be murdered. It is to be supposed that Henry was Married, since he had certainly four sons, but it is not in my power to inform the Reader who was his Wife.[2] Be this as it may, he did not live for ever, but falling ill, his son the Prince of Wales came and took away the crown; whereupon the King made a long speech, for which I must refer the Reader to Shakespear's Plays, and the Prince made a still longer. Things being thus settled between them the King died, and was succeeded by his Son Henry who had previously beat Sir William Gascoigne.[3]

HENRY THE 5TH

This Prince after he succeeded to the throne grew quite reformed and Amiable, forsaking all his dissipated Companions, and never thrashing Sir William again. During his reign, Lord Cobham[4] was burnt alive, but I forget what for. His Majesty then turned his thoughts to France, where he went and fought the famous Battle of Agincourt.[5] He afterwards married the King's daughter Catherine, a very agreable Woman by Shakespear's account. Inspite of all this however he died, and was succeeded by his son Henry.

HENRY THE 6TH

I CANNOT SAY much for this Monarch's Sense—Nor would I if I could, for he was a Lancastrian. I suppose you know all about the Wars between him and the Duke of York who was of the right side; if you do not, you had better read some other History, for I shall not be very diffuse in this, meaning by it only to vent my Spleen *against*, and shew my Hatred *to* all those people whose parties or principles do not suit with mine, and not to give information. This King married Margaret of Anjou, a Woman whose distresses and Misfortunes were so great as almost to make me who hate her, pity her.[6] It was in this reign that Joan of Arc lived and made such a *row* among the English. They should not have burnt her—but they did. There were several Battles between the Yorkists and Lancastrians, in which the former (as they ought) usually conquered. At length they were entirely over come; The King was murdered—The Queen was sent home—and Edward the 4th Ascended the Throne.

VOLUME THE SECOND

EDWARD THE 4TH.

This Monarch was famous only for his Beauty and his Courage, of which the Picture we have here given of him, and his undaunted Behaviour in marrying one Woman while he was engaged to another, are sufficient proofs. His Wife was Elizabeth Woodville, a Widow who, poor Woman!, was afterwards confined in a Convent by that Monster of Iniquity and Avarice Henry the 7th. One of Edward's Mistresses was Jane Shore,[7] who has had a play written about her, but it is a tragedy and therefore not worth reading. Having performed all these noble actions, his Majesty died, and was succeeded by his son.

EDWARD THE 5TH

This unfortunate Prince lived so little a while that no body had time to draw his picture. He was murdered by his Uncle's Contrivance, whose name was Richard the 3ᵈ.

RICHARD THE 3ᴰ

The Character of this Prince has been in general very severely treated by Historians, but as he was a *York*, I am rather inclined to suppose him a very respectable Man. It has indeed been confidently asserted that he killed his two Nephews and his Wife, but it has also been declared the he did *not* kill his two Nephews, which I am inclined to beleive true; and if this is the case, it may also be affirmed that he did not kill his Wife, for if Perkin Warbeck was really the Duke of York, why might not Lambert Simnel be the Widow of Richard.[8] Whether innocent or guilty, he did not reign long in peace, for Henry Tudor E. of Richmond as great a Villain as ever lived, made a great fuss about getting the Crown and having killed the King at the battle of Bosworth, he succeeded to it.

HENRY THE 7TH

THIS MONARCH soon after his accession married the Princess Elizabeth of York; by which alliance he plainly proved that he thought his own right inferior to hers, tho' he pretended to the contrary.[9] By this Marriage he had two sons and two daughters, the elder of which Daughters was married to the King of Scotland and had the happiness of being grandmother to one of the first Characters in the World. But of *her*, I shall have occasion to speak more at large in future. The Youngest, Mary, married first the King of France and secondly the D. of Suffolk, by whom she had one daughter, afterwards the Mother of Lady Jane Grey, who tho' inferior to her lovely Cousin the Queen of Scots, was yet an amiable young Woman and famous for reading Greek while other people were hunting. It was in the reign of Henry the 7th that Perkin Warbeck and Lambert Simnel before mentioned made their appearance, the former of whom was set in the Stocks, took shelter in Beaulieu Abbey, and was beheaded with the Earl of Warwick, and the latter was taken into the King's Kitchen. His Majesty died and was succeeded by his son Henry whose only merit was his not being *quite* so bad as his daughter Elizabeth.

HENRY THE 8TH—

IT WOULD BE AN affront to my Readers were I to suppose that they were not as well acquainted with the particulars of this King's reign as I am myself. It will therefore be saving *them* the task of reading again what they have read before, and *myself* the trouble of writing what I do not perfectly recollect, by giving only a slight sketch of the principal Events which marked his reign. Among these may be ranked Cardinal Wolsey's[10] telling the father Abbott of Leicester Abbey that "he was come to lay his bones among them," the reformation in Religion, and the King's riding through the Streets of London with Anna Bullen. It is however but Justice, and my Duty to declare that this amiable Woman was entirely innocent of the Crimes with which she was accused, of which her Beauty, her Elegance, and her Sprightliness were sufficient proofs, not to mention her solemn protestations of Innocence, the weakness of the Charges against her, and the King's Character; all of which add some confirmation, tho' perhaps slight ones when in comparison with those before alledged in her favour.[11] Tho' I do not profess giving many dates, yet as I think it proper to give some and shall of course Make choice of those which it is most necessary for the Reader to know, I think it right to inform him that her letter to the

King was dated on the 6th of May. The Crimes and Cruelties of this Prince, were too numerous to be mentioned, (as this history I trust has fully shewn;) and nothing can be said in his vindication, but that his abolishing Religious Houses and leaving them to the ruinous depredations of time has been of infinite use to the landscape of England in general, which probably was a principal motive for his doing it, since otherwise why should a Man who was of no Religion himself be at so much trouble to abolish one which had for Ages been established in the Kingdom. His Majesty's 5th Wife was the Duke of Norfolk's Neice who, tho' universally acquitted of the crimes for which she was beheaded, has been by many people supposed to have led an abandoned Life before her Marriage—Of this however I have many doubts, since she was a relation of that noble Duke of Norfolk who was so warm in the Queen of Scotland's cause, and who at last fell a victim to it.[12] The King's last wife contrived to survive him, but with difficulty effected it. He was succeeded by his only son Edward.

EDWARD THE 6TH

As this prince was only nine years old at the time of his Father's death, he was considered by many people as too young to govern, and the late King happening to be of the same opinion, his mother's Brother the Duke of Somerset was chosen Protector of the realm during his minority.[13] This Man was on the whole of a very amiable Character, and is somewhat of a favourite with me, tho' I would by no means pretend to affirm that he was equal to those first of Men

Robert Earl of Essex, Delamere, or Gilpin. He was beheaded, of which he might with reason have been proud, had he known that such was the death of Mary Queen of Scotland; but as it was impossible that he should be conscious of what had never happened, it does not appear that he felt particularly delighted with the manner of it. After his decease the Duke of Northumberland had the care of the King and the Kingdom, and performed his trust of both so well that the King died and the Kingdom was left to his daughter in law the Lady Jane Grey, who has been already mentioned as reading Greek. Whether she really understood that language or whether such a Study proceeded only from an excess of vanity for which I beleive she was always rather remarkable, is uncertain. Whatever might be the cause, she preserved the same appearance of Knowledge, and contempt of what was generally esteemed pleasure, during the whole of her Life, for she declared herself displeased with being appointed Queen, and while conducting to the Scaffold, she wrote a Sentence in Latin and another in Greek on seeing the dead Body of her Husband accidentally passing that way.

MARY

THIS WOMAN HAD the good luck of being advanced to the throne of England, inspite of the Superior pretensions, Merit, and *Beauty* of her Cousins Mary Queen of Scotland and Jane Grey. Nor can I pity the Kingdom for the misfortunes they experienced during her Reign, since they fully deserved them, for having allowed her to succeed her Brother—which was a double peice of folly, since they might have foreseen that as she died without Children, she would be succeeded by that disgrace to humanity, that pest of society, Elizabeth. Many were the people who fell Martyrs to the protestant Religion during her reign; I suppose not fewer than a dozen. She married Philip King of Spain who in her Sister's reign was famous for building Armadas. She died without issue, and then the dreadful moment came in which the destroyer of all comfort, the deceitful Betrayer of trust reposed in her, and the Murderess of her Cousin succeeded to the Throne.—

ELIZABETH—

IT WAS THE PECULIAR Misfortune of this Woman to have bad Ministers—Since wicked as she herself was, she could not have committed such extensive Mischeif, had not these vile and abandoned Men connived at, and encouraged her in her Crimes. I know that it has by many people been asserted and beleived that Lord Burleigh, Sir Francis Walsingham, and the rest of those who filled the cheif Offices of State were deserving, experienced, and able Ministers. But Oh! how blinded such Writers and such Readers must be to true Merit, to Merit despised, neglected and defamed, if they can persist in such opinions when they reflect that these Men, these boasted Men were such Scandals to their Country and their Sex as to allow and assist their Queen in confining for the space of nineteen years, a *Woman* who if the claims of Relationship and Merit were of no avail, yet as a Queen and as one who condescended to place confidence in her, had every reason to expect Assistance and protection; and at length in allowing Elizabeth to bring this amiable Woman to an untimely, unmerited, and scandalous Death. Can any one if he reflects but for a moment on this blot, this everlasting blot upon their Understanding and their Character, allow any praise to Lord Burleigh or Sir Francis Walsingham?[14] Oh! what must this bewitching Princess whose only freind was then the Duke of Norfolk, and whose only ones are now Mr Whitaker, Mrs Lefroy, Mrs Knight and myself, who was abandoned by her Son, confined by her Cousin, Abused, reproached and vilified by all, what must not her most noble Mind have suffered when informed that Elizabeth had given orders for her Death![15] Yet she bore it with a most unshaken fortitude; firm in her Mind; Constant in her Religion; and prepared herself to meet the cruel fate to which she was doomed, with a magnanimity that could alone proceed from conscious Innocence. And Yet could you Reader have beleived it possible that some hardened and zealous Protestants have even abused her for that Steadfastness in the Catholic Religion which reflected on her so much credit? But this is a striking proof of *their* narrow Souls and prejudiced Judgements who accuse her. She was executed in the Great Hall at Fotheringay Castle! (sacred Place!) on Wednesday the 8th of February—1586—to the everlasting Reproach of Elizabeth, her Ministers, and of England in general. It may not be unnecessary before I entirely conclude my account of this ill-fated Queen, to observe that she had been accused of several crimes during the time of her reigning in Scotland, of which I now most seriously do assure my Reader that she was entirely innocent; having never been guilty of anything more than Imprudencies into which she was betrayed by the openness of her Heart, her Youth, and her Education. Having I trust by this assurance entirely done away every Suspicion and every doubt which might have arisen in the Reader's mind, from what other Historians have written of her, I shall proceed to mention the remaining Events, that marked Elizabeth's reign. It was about this time that Sir Francis Drake the first English Navigator who sailed round the World, lived, to be the ornament of his Country and his profession. Yet great as he was, and justly celebrated as a Sailor, I cannot help foreseeing that he will be equalled in this or the next Century by one who tho' now but young, already promises to answer all the ardent and sanguine expectations of his Relations and Freinds, amongst whom I may class the amiable Lady to whom this work is dedicated, and my no less amiable Self.[16]

Though of a different profession, and shining in a different Sphere of Life, yet equally conspicuous in the Character of an *Earl*, as Drake was in that of a *Sailor*, was Robert Devereux Lord Essex.[17] This unfortunate young Man was not unlike in Character to that equally unfortunate one *Frederic Delamere*. The simile may be carried still farther, and Elizabeth the torment of Essex may be compared to the Emmeline of Delamere. It would be endless to recount the misfortunes of this noble and gallant Earl. It is sufficient to say that he was beheaded on the 25th of Feb^{ry}, after having been Lord Leuitenant of Ireland, after having clapped his hand on his Sword, and after performing many other services to his Country. Elizabeth did not long survive his loss, and died *so* miserable that were it not an injury to the memory of Mary I should pity her.

JAMES THE 1ST

THOUGH THIS King had some faults, among which and as the most principal, was his allowing his Mother's death, yet considered on the whole I cannot help liking him. He married Anne of Denmark, and had several Children; fortunately for him his eldest son Prince Henry died before his father or he might have experienced the evils which befell his unfortunate Brother.

As I am myself partial to the roman catholic religion, it is with infinite regret that I am obliged to blame the Behaviour of any Member of it; yet Truth being I think very excusable in an Historian, I am necessitated to say that in this reign the roman Catholics of England did not behave like Gentlemen to the protestants. Their Behaviour indeed to the Royal Family and both Houses of Parliament might justly be considered by them as very uncivil, and even Sir Henry Percy tho' certainly the best bred Man of the party, had none of that general politeness which is so universally pleasing, as his Attentions were entirely Confined to Lord Mounteagle.[18]

Sir Walter Raleigh flourished in this and the preceding reign, and is by many people held in great veneration and respect—But as he was an enemy of the noble Essex, I have nothing to say in praise of him, and must refer all those who may wish to be acquainted with the particulars of his Life, to Mr Sheridan's play of the Critic, where they will find many interesting Anecdotes as well of him as of his freind Sir Christopher Hatton.[19]—His Majesty was of that amiable disposition which inclines to Freindships, and in such points was possessed of a keener penetration in Discovering Merit than many other people.[20] I once heard an excellent Sharade on a Carpet, of which the subject I am now on reminds me, and as I think it may afford my Readers some Amusement to *find it out*, I shall here take the liberty of presenting it to them.

Sharade
My first is what my second was to King James the 1st, and you tread on my whole.

The principal favourites of his Majesty were Car, who was afterwards created Earl of Somerset and whose name perhaps may have some share in the above-mentioned Sharade, and George Villiers afterwards Duke of Buckingham. On his Majesty's death he was succeeded by his son Charles.

CHARLES THE 1ST

THIS AMIABLE Monarch seems born to have suffered Misfortunes equal to those of his lovely Grandmother; Misfortunes which he could not deserve since he was her descendant. Never certainly were there before so many detestable Characters at one time in England as in this period of its History; Never were amiable Men so Scarce. The number of them throughout the whole Kingdom amounting only to *five*, besides the inhabitants of Oxford who were always loyal to their King and faithful to his interests. The names of this noble five who never forgot the duty of the Subject, or swerved from their attachment to his Majesty, were as follows—The King himself, ever stedfast in his own support—Archbishop Laud, Earl of Strafford, Viscount Faulkland and Duke of Ormond, who were scarcely less strenuous or zealous in the cause.[21] While the *Villains* of the time would make too long a list to be written or read; I shall therefore content myself with mentioning the leaders of the Gang. Cromwell, Fairfax, Hampden, and Pym may be considered as the original Causers of all the disturbances, Distresses, and Civil Wars in which England for many years was embroiled. In this reign as well as in that of Elizabeth, I am obliged in spite of my Attachment to the Scotch, to consider them as equally guilty with the generality of the English, since they dared to think differently from their Sovereign, to forget the Adoration which as *Stuarts* it was their Duty to pay them, to rebel against, dethrone and imprison the unfortunate Mary; to oppose, to deceive, and to sell the no less unfortunate Charles. The Events of this Monarch's reign are too numerous for my pen, and indeed the recital of any Events (except what I make myself) is uninteresting to me; my principal reason for undertaking the History of England being to prove the innocence of the Queen of Scotland, which I flatter myself with having effectually done, and to abuse Elizabeth, tho' I am rather fearful of having fallen short in the latter part of my Scheme.—. As therefore it is not my intention to give any particular account of the distresses into which this King was involved through the misconduct and Cruelty of his Parliament, I shall satisfy myself with vindicating him from the Reproach of Arbitrary and tyrannical Government with which he has often been Charged. This, I feel, is not difficult to be done, for with one argument I am certain of satisfying every sensible and well disposed person whose opinions have been properly guided by a good Education—and this Argument is that he was a **Stuart**.

FINIS
Saturday Nov. 26th 1791

NOTES TO 'THE HISTORY OF ENGLAND'

EXPLANATORY NOTES TO
'THE HISTORY OF ENGLAND'

For an introduction to the 'History', see General Notes.

1. Pomfret Castle is Pontefract in Yorkshire, used by Shakespeare as the scene of the murder of Richard II.
2. In Shakespeare's *Henry IV*, Henry's two wives do not appear.
3. The anecdote of Sir William Gascoigne, in which as Lord Chief Justice he supposedly sent Prince Hal to prison for striking him appears in Shakespeare's *Henry IV, Part 2* and in Goldsmith's *History*. Henry V's renunciation of his 'dissipated Companions' occurs in both Shakespeare and Goldsmith.
4. Lord Cobham, formerly Sir John Oldcastle, was probably Shakespeare's model for Falstaff. He was executed for heresy in 1417.
5. The English victory at Agincourt (1415) takes up much of Shakespeare's *Henry V*. Henry married Catherine of Valois, daughter of the French king.
6. Margaret of Anjou married Henry VI in 1445. In his trilogy *Henry VI*, Shakespeare depicts her as scheming, taking advantage of a feeble king. After Henry VI was murdered, Margaret was banished, both events occurring in Shakespeare's plays.
7. Jane Shore was the mistress of Edward IV, accused of witchcraft after his death.
8. Perkin Warbeck and Lambert Simnel were imposters in the reign of Henry VII (Henry Tudor) who seized the throne after the defeat and death of Richard III at the Battle of Bosworth Field (1485). Perkin Warbeck claimed to be Richard, Duke of York, son of Edward IV; Lambert Simnel claimed to be Edward, Earl of Warwick, nephew of Edward IV.
9. Elizabeth of York was the daughter of Edward IV. By marrying Henry VII she united the houses of York and Lancaster.

10. The death of Cardinal Wolsey, once Henry VIII's favourite advisor, is described at length in *Henry VIII*, partially written by Shakespeare. During the Reformation, with the establishing of the Church of England, the Catholic monasteries were dissolved and many of their buildings fell into ruins.
11. Anne Boleyn (Anna Bullen), second wife of Henry VIII, was charged with adultery, and executed in 1536. Shakespeare and Goldsmith believed her innocent and treated her sympathetically, especially as the mother of their admired Elizabeth I.
12. Catherine Howard, niece of the Duke of Norfolk, was Henry VIII's fifth wife; she was executed in 1542. Henry's last wife was Catherine Parr; she survived him.
13. Edward Seymour, Duke of Somerset, was the brother of Henry VIII's third wife, Jane Seymour, and uncle of Edward VI. He became Lord Protector when his nine-year-old nephew was crowned king in 1547. Somerset was beheaded when his rival, the Duke of Northumberland, triumphed. Northumberland arranged the marriage of his son to the famously learned and Protestant Lady Jane Grey, great-granddaughter of Henry VII, whom Northumberland intended to make queen, so excluding Henry VIII's daughters, Mary and Elizabeth. Lady Jane Grey was beheaded in 1554 after the Catholic Mary became queen. The number of Protestants Goldsmith describes Mary as burning was much reduced by Jane Austen.
14. William Cecil, Lord Burghley and Sir Francis Walsingham were Elizabeth I's councillors, seen as enemies of Mary Queen of Scots.
15. Mary Queen of Scots was imprisoned and executed by Elizabeth in Fotheringhay Castle in Northamptonshire in 1587 (Jane Austen wrote 1586 because she was referring to the the old calendar which began the year on 25 March; Mary was beheaded in February.). Beyond Jane Austen, her contemporary supporters are listed as John Whitaker, author of *Mary Queen of Scots Vindicated* (1787), Anne Lefroy, Jane Austen's close freind (see the poem on her death in *Later Manuscripts*), and Catherine, wife of Thomas Knight who adopted Jane's brother Edward as his heir.
16. The young man compared with the heroic circumnavigator of the world, Sir Francis Drake, was probably Jane's brother Francis, then a midshipman (see dedication to 'Jack and Alice').

NOTES TO 'THE HISTORY OF ENGLAND'

17. Robert Devereux, Earl of Essex, was Elizabeth I's favourite courtier towards the end of her life. He was executed in 1601 following a failed rebellion against the Queen.
18. According to Goldsmith, the Gunpowder Plot of 1605, a Catholic conspiracy to blow up James I and the House of Commons (unmentioned by Jane Austen), was discovered when Sir Henry Percy wrote anonymously to Lord Mounteagle warning him to avoid Parliament on the designated day.
19. The famous explorers Sir Walter Raleigh and Sir Christopher Hatton were courtiers in Elizabeth's reign. Raleigh was executed by James I in 1618.
20. James I, son of Mary Queen of Scots, married Anne of Denmark. He was known for his attraction to handsome young men including Sir Robert Carr and George Villiers, later Duke of Buckingham. Possibly the 'keener penetration' is a double entendre and the charade a naughty coupling of 'Carr' and 'pet'.
21. William Laud, Archbishop of Canterbury, Sir Thomas Wentworth, Earl of Strafford, Lucius Cary, Viscount Falkland, and James Butler, first Duke of Ormond, were Royalist supporters of Charles I in the seventeenth-century Civil Wars between King and Parliament. Oliver Cromwell, Thomas Fairfax, John Hampden and John Pym were Parliamentarian soldiers and statesmen. Jane Austen was especially hostile to Cromwell, Lord Protector of England from 1653 to his death in 1658; she held him responsible for the execution of Charles I in 1649.

A COLLECTION OF LETTERS—

To Miss Cooper—

Cousin
Conscious of the Charming Character which in every Country, and every Clime in Christendom is Cried, Concerning you, With Caution and Care I Commend to your Charitable Criticism this Clever Collection of Curious Comments, which have been Carefully Culled, Collected and Classed by your Comical Cousin

The Author.

LETTER THE FIRST

From a Mother to her freind.

My Children begin now to claim all my attention in a different Manner from that in which they have been used to receive it, as they are now arrived at that age when it is necessary for them in some measure to become conversant with the World. My Augusta is 17 and her Sister scarcely a twelvemonth younger. I flatter myself that their education has been such as will not disgrace their appearance in the World, and that they will not disgrace their Education I have every reason to beleive. Indeed they are sweet Girls—. Sensible yet unaffected—Accomplished yet Easy—. Lively yet Gentle—. As their progress in every thing they have learnt has been always the same, I am willing to forget the difference of age, and to introduce them together into Public. This very Evening is fixed on as their first entrée into Life, as we are to drink tea with Mrs Cope and her Daughter. I am glad that we are to meet no one for my Girls sake, as it would be awkward for them to enter too wide a Circle on the very first day. But we shall proceed by degrees—. Tomorrow Mr Stanly's family will drink tea with us, and perhaps the Miss Phillips's will meet them. On Tuesday we shall pay Morning-Visits—On Wednesday we are to dine at Westbrook. On Thursday we have Company at home. On Friday we are to be at a private Concert at Sir John Wynne's—and on Saturday we expect Miss Dawson to call in the Morning—which will complete my Daughters Introduction into Life. How they will bear so much dissipation I cannot imagine; of their Spirits I have no fear, I only dread their health.

―――

This mighty affair is now happily over, and my Girls *are out*.—As the moment approached for our departure, you can have no idea how the sweet Creatures trembled with fear and Expectation. Before the Carriage drove to the door, I called them into my dressing-room, and as soon as they were seated thus addressed them. "My dear Girls the moment is now arrived when I am to reap the rewards of all my Anxieties and Labours towards you during your Education. You are this Evening to enter a World in which you will meet with many wonderfull Things; Yet let me warn you against suffering yourselves to be meanly swayed by the Follies and Vices of others, for believe me my beloved Children that if you do——I shall be very sorry for it." They both assured me that they would ever remember my Advice with Gratitude, and follow it with Attention; That they were prepared to find a World full of things to amaze and to shock them: but that they trusted their behaviour would never give me reason to repent the Watchful Care with which I had presided over their infancy and formed their Minds—"With such expectations and such intentions (cried I) I can have nothing to fear from you—and can chearfully conduct you to Mrs Cope's without a fear of your being seduced by her Example, or contaminated by her Follies. Come, then my Children (added I) the Carriage is driving to the door, and I will not a moment delay the happiness you are so impatient to enjoy." When we arrived at Warleigh, poor Augusta could scarcely breathe, while Margaret was all Life and Rapture. "The long-expected Moment is now arrived (said she) and we shall soon be in the World."—In a few Moments we were in Mrs Cope's parlour—, where with her daughter she sate ready to receive us. I observed with delight the impression my Children made on them—. They were indeed two sweet, elegant-looking Girls, and tho' somewhat abashed from the peculiarity of their Situation, Yet there was an ease in their Manners and Address which could not fail of pleasing—. Imagine my dear Madam how delighted I must have been in beholding as I did, how attentively they observed every object they saw, how disgusted with some Things, how enchanted with others, how astonished at all! On the whole however they returned in raptures with the World, its Inhabitants, and Manners.

Y^{rs} Ever—A—F—.

LETTER THE SECOND

From a Young Lady crossed in Love to her freind—

Why should this last disappointment hang so heavily on my Spirits? Why should I feel it more, why should it wound me deeper than those I have experienced before? Can it be that I have a greater affection for Willoughby than I had for his amiable predecessors—? Or is it that our feelings become more acute from being often wounded? I must suppose my dear Belle that this is the Case, since I am not conscious of being more sincerely attached to Willoughby than I was to Neville, Fitzowen, or either of the Crawfords, for all of whom I once felt the most lasting affection that ever warmed a Woman's heart. Tell me then dear Belle why I still sigh when I think of the faithless Edward, or why I weep when I behold his Bride?, for too surely this is the case—. My Freinds are all alarmed for me; They fear my declining health; they lament my want of Spirits; they dread the effects of both. In hopes of releiving my Melancholy, by directing my thoughts to other objects, they have invited several of their freinds to spend the Christmas with us. Lady Bridget Dashwood and her Sister-in-Law Miss Jane are expected on Friday; and Colonel Seaton's family will be with us next week. This is all most kindly meant by my Uncle and Cousins; but what can the presence of a dozen indifferent people do to me; but weary and distress me—. I will not finish my Letter till some of our Visitors are arrived.

———

Friday Evening—
Lady Bridget came this Morning, and with her, her sweet Sister* Miss Jane—. Although I have been acquainted with this charming Woman above fifteen Years, Yet I never before observed how lovely she is. She is now about 35, and in spite of sickness, Sorrow and Time is more blooming than I ever saw a Girl of 17. I was delighted with her, the moment she entered the house, and she appeared equally pleased with me, attaching herself to me during the remainder of the day. There is something so sweet, so mild in her Countenance, that she seems more than Mortal. Her Conversation is as bewitching as her appearance—; I could not help telling her how much she engaged my Admiration—. "Oh! Miss Jane (said I)— and stopped from an inability at the moment of expressing myself as I could wish—"Oh! Miss Jane—(I repeated)—I could not think of words to suit my feelings—. She seemed waiting for my Speech—. I was confused—distressed—My thoughts were bewildered—and I could only add—"How do you do?" She saw and felt for my Embarrassment and with admirable presence of mind releived me from it by saying—"My dear Sophia be not uneasy at having exposed Yourself—I will turn the Conversation without appearing to notice it." Oh! how I loved her for her kindness! "Do you ride as much as you used to do?" said she—. "I am advised to ride by my Physician, We have delightful Rides round us, I have a Charming horse, am uncommonly fond of the Amusement," replied I quite recovered from my Confusion, "and in short I ride a great deal." "You are in the right my Love," said

---

* **Sister**: sister-in-law.

She, Then repeating the following Line which was an extempore and equally adapted to recommend both Riding and Candour—

"Ride where you may, Be Candid where You can," She added, "*I rode once, but it is many years ago*"—She spoke this in so Low and tremulous a Voice, that I was silent— Struck with her Manner of Speaking I could make no reply. "I have not ridden, continued she fixing her Eyes on my face, since I was married."

I was never so surprised—"Married, Ma'am!" I repeated. "You may well wear that look of astonishment, said she, since what I have said must appear improbable to you—Yet nothing is more true than that I once was married."

"Then why are you called Miss Jane?"

"I married, my Sophia without the consent or knowledge of my father the late Admiral Annesley. It was therefore necessary to keep the Secret from him and from every one, till some fortunate opportunity might offer of revealing it—. Such an opportunity alas! was but too soon given in the death of my dear Capt Dashwood— Pardon these tears, continued Miss Jane wiping her Eyes, I owe them to my Husband's Memory. He fell my Sophia, while fighting for his Country in America* after a most happy Union of seven Years—. My Children, two sweet Boys and a Girl, who had constantly resided with my Father and me, passing with him and with every one as the Children of a Brother (tho' I had ever been an only Child) had as yet been the Comforts of my Life. But no sooner had I lossed my Henry, than these sweet Creatures fell sick and died—. Conceive dear Sophia what my feelings must have been when as an Aunt I attended my Children to their early Grave—. My Father did not survive them many weeks—He died, poor Good old Man, happily ignorant to his last hour of my Marriage."

"But did not you own it, and assume his name at your husband's death?"

"No; I could not bring myself to do it; more especially when in my Children I lost all inducement for doing it. Lady Bridget, and

---

* Fighting with the British army during the **American War of Independence**, 1775–83.

Yourself are the only persons who are in the knowledge of my having ever been either Wife or Mother. As I could not prevail on myself to take the name of Dashwood (a name which after my Henry's death I could never hear without emotion) and as I was conscious of having no right to that of Annesley, I dropt all thoughts of either, and have made it a point of bearing only my Christian one since my Father's death." She paused—"Oh! my dear Miss Jane (said I) how infinitely am I obliged to you for so entertaining a Story! You cannot think how it has diverted me! But have you quite done?"

"I have only to add my dear Sophia, that my Henry's elder Brother dieing about the same time, Lady Bridget became a Widow like myself, and as we had always loved each other in idea from the high Character in which we had ever been spoken of, though we had never met, we determined to live together. We wrote to one another on the same subject by the same post, so exactly did our feelings and our Actions coincide! We both eagerly embraced the proposals we gave and received of becoming one family, and have from that time lived together in the greatest affection."

"And is this all?" said I, "I hope you have not done."

"Indeed I have; and did you ever hear a Story more pathetic?"

"I never did—and it is for that reason it pleases me so much, for when one is unhappy nothing is so delightful to one's Sensations as to hear of equal Misery."

"Ah! but my Sophia why *are you* unhappy?"

"Have you not heard Madam of Willoughby's Marriage?" "But my Love why lament *his* perfidy, when you bore so well that of many young Men before?" "Ah! Madam, I was used to it then, but when Willoughby broke his Engagements I had not been dissapointed for half a year." "Poor Girl!" said Miss Jane.

LETTER THE THIRD

From A young Lady in distress'd Circumstances to her freind.
A few days ago I was at a private Ball given by Mr Ashburnham. As my Mother never goes out she entrusted me to the care of Lady

Greville who did me the honour of calling for me in her way and of allowing me to sit forwards, which is a favour about which I am very indifferent especially as I know it is considered as confering a great obligation on me. "So Miss Maria (said her Ladyship as she saw me advancing to the door of the Carriage) you seem very smart to night—My poor Girls will appear quite to disadvantage by you—I only hope your Mother may not have distressed herself to set you off. Have you got a new Gown on?"

"Yes Ma'am." replied I, with as much indifference as I could assume.

"Aye, and a fine one too I think—(feeling it, as by her permission I seated myself by her) I dare say it is all very smart— But I must own, for you know I always speak my mind, that I think it was quite a needless peice of expence—Why could not you have worn your old striped one? It is not my way to find fault with people because they are poor, for I always think that they are more to be despised and pitied than blamed for it, especially if they cannot help it, but at the same time I must say that in my opinion your old striped Gown would have been quite fine enough for its wearer—for to tell you the truth (I always speak my mind) I am very much afraid that one half of the people in the room will not know whether you have a Gown on or not—But I suppose you intend to make your fortune tonight—: Well, the sooner the better; and I wish you success."

"Indeed Ma'am I have no such intention—"

"Who ever heard a Young Lady own that she was a Fortune-hunter?" Miss Greville laughed, but I am sure Ellen felt for me.

"Was your Mother gone to bed before you left her?" said her Ladyship—

"Dear Ma'am," said Ellen "it is but nine o'clock."

"True Ellen, but Candles cost money, and Mrs Williams is too wise to be extravagant."

"She was just sitting down to supper Ma'am—"

"And what had she got for Supper?" "I did not observe." "Bread and Cheese I suppose." "I should never wish for a better supper." said Ellen. "You have never any reason" replied her Mother, "as a better is always provided for you." Miss Greville laughed excessively, as she constantly does at her Mother's wit.

Such is the humiliating Situation in which I am forced to appear while riding in her Ladyship's Coach—I dare not be impertinent, as my Mother is always admonishing me to be humble and patient if I wish to make my way in the world. She insists on my accepting every invitation of Lady Greville, or you may be certain that I would never enter either her House, or her Coach, with the disagreable certainty I always have of being abused for my Poverty while I am in them.—When we arrived at Ashburnham, it was nearly ten o'clock, which was an hour and a half later than we were desired to be there; but Lady Greville is too fashionable (or fancies herself to be so) to be punctual. The Dancing however was not begun as they waited for Miss Greville. I had not been long in the room before I was engaged to dance by Mr Bernard, but just as we were going to stand up, he recollected that his Servant had got his white Gloves; and immediately ran out to fetch them. In the mean time the Dancing began and Lady Greville in passing to another room went exactly before me—She saw me and instantly stopping, said to me though there were several people close to us;

"Hey day, Miss Maria! What cannot you get a partner? Poor Young Lady! I am afraid your new Gown was put on for nothing. But do not despair; perhaps you may get a hop before the Evening is over." So saying, she passed on without hearing my repeated assurance of being engaged, and leaving me very much provoked at being so exposed before every one—Mr Bernard however soon returned and by coming to me the moment he entered the room, and leading me to the Dancers my Character I hope was cleared from the imputation Lady Greville had thrown on it, in the eyes of all the old Ladies who had heard her speech. I soon forgot all my vexations in the pleasure of dancing and of having the most agreable partner in the room. As he is moreover heir to a very large Estate I could see that Lady Greville did not look very well pleased when she found who had been his Choice—She was determined to mortify me, and accordingly when we were sitting down between the dances, she came to me with *more* than her usual insulting importance attended by Miss Mason and said loud enough to be heard by half the people in the room, "Pray Miss Maria in what way of business was your Grandfather? for Miss Mason and I cannot agree whether he was a Grocer or a Bookbinder." I saw that she wanted to mortify me, and was resolved if I possibly could to prevent her seeing that her scheme succeeded. "Neither Madam; he was a Wine Merchant." "Aye, I knew he was in some such low way—He broke did not he?" "I beleive not Ma'am." "Did not he abscond?" "I never heard that he did." "At least he died insolvent?" "I was never told so before." "Why, was not your Father as poor as a Rat?" "I fancy not," "Was not he in the Kings Bench once?" "I never saw him there." She gave me *such* a look, and turned away in a great passion; while I was half delighted with myself for my impertinence, and half afraid of being thought too saucy. As Lady Greville was extremely angry with me, she took no further notice of me all the Evening, and indeed had I been in favour I should have been equally neglected, as she was got into a party of great folks and she never speaks to me when she can to anyone else. Miss Greville was with her Mother's party at Supper, but Ellen preferred staying with the Bernards and me. We had a very pleasant Dance and as Lady G— slept all the way home, I had a very comfortable ride.

The next day while we were at dinner Lady Greville's Coach stopped at the door, for that is the time of day she generally contrives it should. She sent in a message by the Servant to say that "she should not get out but that Miss Maria must come to the Coach-door, as she wanted to speak to her, and that she must make haste and come immediately—" "What an impertinent Message Mama!" said I—"Go Maria—" replied She—Accordingly I went and was obliged to stand there at her Ladyships pleasure though the Wind was extremely high and very cold.

"Why I think Miss Maria you are not quite so smart as you were last night—But I did not come to examine your dress, but to tell you that you may dine with us the day after tomorrow— Not tomorrow, remember, do not come tomorrow, for we expect Lord and Lady Clermont and Sir Thomas Stanley's family—There will be no occasion for your being very fine for I shant send the

Carriage—If it rains you may take an umbrella—" I could hardly help laughing at hearing her give me leave to keep myself dry—"And pray remember to be in time, for I shant wait—I hate my Victuals over-done—But you need not come *before* the time—How does your Mother do—? She is at dinner is not she?" "Yes Ma'am we were in the middle of dinner when your Ladyship came." "I am afraid you find it very cold Maria." said Ellen. "Yes, it is an horrible East wind—said her Mother—I assure you I can hardly bear the window down—But you are used to be blown about by the wind Miss Maria and that is what has made your Complexion so ruddy and coarse. You young Ladies who cannot often ride in a Carriage never mind what weather you trudge in, or how the wind shews your legs. I would not have *my* Girls stand out of doors as you do in such a day as this. But some sort of people have no feelings either of cold or Delicacy—Well, remember that we shall expect you on Thursday at 5 o'clock—You must tell your Maid to come for you at night—There will be no Moon—and You will have an horrid walk home—My Comps to your Mother—I am afraid your dinner will be cold—Drive on—" And away she went, leaving me in a great passion with her as she always does.

Maria Williams

LETTER THE FOURTH

From a young Lady rather impertinent to her freind.

We dined yesterday with Mr Evelyn where we were introduced to a very agreable looking Girl his Cousin. I was extremely pleased with her appearance, for added to the charms of an engaging face, her manner and voice had something peculiarly interesting in them. So much so, that they inspired me with a great curiosity to know the history of her Life, who were her Parents, where she came from, and what had befallen her, for it was then only known that she was a relation of Mr Evelyn, and that her name was Grenville. In the evening a favourable opportunity offered to me of attempting at least to know what I wished to know, for every one played at Cards but Mrs Evelyn, My Mother, Dr Drayton, Miss Grenville and myself, and as the two former were engaged in a whispering Conversation, and the Doctor fell asleep, we were of necessity obliged to entertain each other. This was what I wished and being determined not to remain in ignorance for want of asking, I began the Conversation in the following Manner.

"Have you been long in Essex Ma'am?"

"I arrived on Tuesday."

"You came from Derbyshire?"

"No Ma'am—! appearing surprised at my question, from Suffolk." You will think this a good dash of mine my dear Mary, but you know that I am not wanting for Impudence when I have any end in veiw. "Are you pleased with the Country Miss Grenville? Do you find it equal to the one you have left?"

"Much Superior Ma'am in point of Beauty." She sighed. I longed to know for why.

"But the face of any Country however beautiful said I, can be but a poor consolation for the loss of one's dearest Freinds." She shook her head, as if she felt the truth of what I said. My Curiosity was so much raised, that I was resolved at any rate to satisfy it.

"You regret having left Suffolk then Miss Grenville?" "Indeed I do." "You were born there I suppose?" "Yes Ma'am I was and passed many happy years there—"

"That is a great comfort—" said I—"I hope Ma'am that you never spent any *un*happy one's there?"

"Perfect Felicity is not the property of Mortals, and no one has a right to expect uninterrupted Happiness.—*Some* Misfortunes I have certainly met with—"

"*What* Misfortunes dear Ma'am? replied I, burning with impatience to know every thing. "*None* Ma'am I hope that have been the effect of any wilfull fault in me." "I dare say not Ma'am, and have no doubt but that any sufferings you may have experienced could arise only from the cruelties of Relations or the Errors of Freinds." She sighed—"You seem unhappy my dear Miss Grenville—Is it in my power to soften your Misfortunes?" "*Your* power Ma'am replied she extremely surprised; it is in *no ones* power to make me happy." She pronounced these words in so mournfull and Solemn an accent, that for some time I had not courage to reply—I was actually silenced. I recovered myself however in a few moments and looking at her with all the affection I could, "My dear Miss Grenville said I you appear extremely young—and may probably stand in need of some one's advice whose regard for you, joined to superior Age, perhaps superior Judgement might authorise her to give it—. I am that person, and I now challenge you to accept the offer I make you of my Confidence and Freindship, in return to which I shall only ask for yours—"

"You are extremely obliging Ma'am—said She—and I am highly flattered by your attention to me—. But I am in no difficulty, no doubt, no uncertainty of situation in which any Advice can be wanted. Whenever I am however continued she brightening into a complaisant Smile, I shall know where to apply."

I bowed, but felt a good deal mortified by such a repulse; Still however I had not given up my point. I found that by the appearance of Sentiment and Freindship nothing was to be gained and determined therefore to renew my Attacks by Questions and Suppositions.

"Do you intend staying long in this part of England Miss Grenville?"

"Yes Ma'am, some time I beleive."

"But how will Mr and Mrs Grenville bear your Absence?"

"They are neither of them alive Ma'am."

This was an answer I did not expect—I was quite silenced, and never felt so awkward in my Life—.

LETTER THE FIFTH

From a Young Lady very much in love to her Freind.

My Uncle gets more Stingy, my Aunt more particular, and I more in love every day. What shall we all be at this rate by the end of the year! I had this morning the happiness of receiving the following Letter from my dear Musgrove.

Sackville St. Jan^{ry} 7th

It is a month to day since I first beheld my lovely Henrietta, and the sacred anniversary must and shall be kept in a manner becoming the day—by writing to her. Never shall I forget the moment when her Beauties first broke on my sight—No time as you well know can erase it from my Memory. It was at Lady Scudamores. Happy Lady Scudamore to live within a mile of the divine Henrietta! When the lovely Creature first entered the room, Oh! what were my sensations? The sight of you was like the sight of a wonderful fine Thing. I started—I gazed at her with Admiration—She appeared every moment more Charming, and the unfortunate Musgrove became a Captive to your Charms before I had time to look about me. Yes Madam, I had the happiness of adoring you, an happiness for which I cannot be too grateful. "What said he to himself is Musgrove allowed to die for Henrietta,? Enviable Mortal,! and may he pine for her who is the object of universal Admiration, who is adored by a Colonel, and toasted by a Baronet!—Adorable Henrietta how beautiful you are! I declare you are quite divine! You are more than Mortal. You are an Angel. You are Venus herself. In short Madam you are the prettiest Girl I ever saw in my Life—and her Beauty is encreased in her Musgrove's Eyes, by permitting him to love her and allowing me to hope. And Ah! Angelic Miss Henrietta Heaven is my Witness how ardently I do hope for the death of your villanous Uncle and his Abandoned Wife, Since my fair one, will not consent to be mine till their decease has placed her in affluence above what my fortune can procure—. Though it is an improvable Estate—. Cruel Henrietta to persist in such a resolution! I am at present with my Sister where I mean to continue till my own house which tho' an excellent one is at present somewhat out of repair, is ready to receive me. Amiable princess of my Heart farewell—Of that Heart which trembles while it signs itself your most ardent Admirer

and devoted humble Servt
T. Musgrove

A COLLECTION OF LETTERS

There is a pattern for a Love-letter Matilda! Did you ever read such a masterpeice of Writing? Such Sense, Such Sentiment, Such purity of Thought, Such flow of Language and such unfeigned Love in one Sheet? No, never I can answer for it, since a Musgrove is not to be met with by every Girl. Oh! how I long to be with him! I intend to send him the following in answer to his Letter tomorrow.

My dearest Musgrove—. Words cannot express how happy your Letter made me; I thought I should have cried for Joy, for I love you better than any body in the World. I think you the most amiable, and the handsomest Man in England, and so to be sure you are. I never read so sweet a Letter in my Life. Do write me another just like it, and tell me you are in love with me in every other line. I quite die to see you. How shall we manage to see one another—? for we are so much in love that we cannot live asunder. Oh! my dear Musgrove you cannot think how impatiently I wait for the death of my Uncle and Aunt—If they will not die soon, I beleive I shall run mad, for I get more in love with you every day of my Life. How happy your Sister is to enjoy the pleasure of your Company in her house, and how happy every body in London must be because you are there. I hope you will be so kind as to write to me again soon, for I never read such sweet Letters as yours. I am my dearest Musgrove most truly and faithfully Yours for ever and ever

Henrietta Halton—

I hope he will like my answer; it is as good a one as I can write though nothing to his; Indeed I had always heard what a dab he was at a Love-letter. I saw him you know for the first time at Lady Scudamore's—And when I saw her Ladyship afterwards she asked me how I liked her Cousin Musgrove?

"Why upon my word said I, I think he is a very handsome young Man."

"I am glad you think so replied she, for he is distractedly in love with you."

"Law! Lady Scudamore said I, how can you talk so ridiculously?"

"Nay, 'tis very true answered She, I assure you, for he was in love with you from the first moment he beheld you."

"I wish it may be true said I, for that is the only kind of love I would give a farthing for—There is some Sense in being in love at first sight."

"Well, I give you Joy of your conquest, replied Lady Scudamore, "and I beleive it to have been a very complete one; I am sure it is not a contemptible one, for my Cousin is a charming young fellow, has seen a great deal of the World, and writes the best Love-letters I ever read."

This made me very happy, and I was excessively pleased with my conquest. However I thought it was proper to give myself a few Airs—. So I said to her—

"This is all very pretty Lady Scudamore, but you know that we young Ladies who are Heiresses must not throw ourselves away upon Men who have no fortune at all."

"My dear Miss Halton said She, I am as much convinced of that as you can be, and I do assure you that I should be the last person to encourage your marrying any one who had not some pretensions to expect a fortune with you. Mr Musgrove is so far from being poor that he has an estate of Several hundreds an year which is capable of great Improvement, and an excellent House, though at present it is not quite in repair."

"If that is the case replied I, I have nothing more to say against him, and if as you say he is an informed young Man and can write good Love-letters, I am sure I have no reason to find fault with him for admiring me, tho' perhaps I may not marry him for all that Lady Scudamore."

"You are certainly under no obligation to marry him answered her Ladyship, except that which love himself will dictate to you, for if I am not greatly mistaken You are at this very moment unknown to yourself, cherishing a most tender affection for him."

"Law, Lady Scudamore replied I blushing how can you think of such a thing?"

"Because every look, every word betrays it, answered She; "Come my dear Henrietta, consider me as a freind, and be sincere with me—Do not you prefer Mr Musgrove to any man of your acquaintance?"

"Pray do not ask me such questions Lady Scudamore, said I turning away my head, for it is not fit for me to answer them."

"Nay my Love replied she, now you confirm my suspicions. But why Henrietta should you be ashamed to own a well-placed Love, or why refuse to confide in me?"

"I am not ashamed to own it; said I taking Courage. I do not refuse to confide in you or blush to say that I do love your cousin Mr Musgrove, that I am sincerely attached to him, for it is no disgrace to love a handsome Man. If he were plain indeed I might have had reason to be ashamed of a passion which must have been mean since the Object would have been unworthy. But with such a figure and face, and such beautiful hair as your Cousin has, why should I blush to own that such Superior Merit has made an impression on me."

"My Sweet Girl (said Lady Scudamore embracing me with great Affection) what a delicate way of thinking you have in these Matters, and what a quick discernment for one of your years! Oh! how I honour you for such Noble Sentiments!"

"Do you Ma'am,? said I; You are vastly obliging. But pray Lady Scudamore did your Cousin himself tell you of his Affection for me? I shall like him the better if he did, for what is a Lover without a Confidante?"

"Oh! my Love replied She, you were born for each other. Every word you say more deeply convinces me that your Minds are actuated by the invisible power of simpathy, for your opinions and Sentiments so exactly coincide. Nay, the colour of your Hair is not very different. Yes my dear Girl, the poor despairing Musgrove did reveal to me the story of his Love—. Nor was I surprised at it—I know not how it was, but I had a kind of presentiment that he *would* be in love with you."

"Well, but how did he break it to you?"

"It was not till after Supper. We were sitting round the fire together talking on indifferent Subjects, though to say the truth the Conversation was cheifly on my side for he was thoughtful and silent, when on a Sudden he interrupted me in the midst of something I was saying, by exclaiming in a most Theatrical tone—

Yes I'm in love I feel it now

And Henrietta Halton has undone me—"

"Oh! What a sweet Way replied I, of declaring his Passion! To make such a couple of charming Lines about me! What a pity it is that they are not in rhime!"

"I am very glad you like it answered She; To be sure there was a great deal of Taste in it. And are you in love with her, Cousin?, said I, I am very sorry for it, for unexceptionable as you are in every respect, with a pretty Estate capable of Great improvements, and an excellent House tho' somewhat out of repair, Yet who can hope to aspire with Success to the adorable Henrietta who has had an offer from a Colonel and been toasted by a Baronet—" "*That* I have—" cried I. Lady Scudamore continued. "Ah dear Cousin replied he, I am so well convinced of the little Chance I can have of winning her who is adored by thousands, that I need no assurances of yours to make me more thoroughly so. Yet surely neither you or the fair Henrietta herself will deny me the exquisite Gratification of dieing for her, of falling a victim to her Charms. And when I am dead"—continued he—

"Oh Lady Scudamore, said I wiping my eyes, that such a sweet Creature should talk of dieing!"

"It is an affecting Circumstance indeed," replied Lady Scudamore. "When I am dead said he, Let me be carried and lain at her feet, and perhaps she may not disdain to drop a pitying tear on my poor remains."

"Dear Lady Scudamore interrupted I, say no more on this affecting Subject. I cannot bear it."

"Oh! how I admire the sweet Sensibility of your Soul, and as I would not for Worlds wound it too deeply, I will be silent."

"Pray go on." said I. She did so.

"And then added he, Ah! Cousin imagine what my transports will be when I feel the dear precious drops trickle o'er my face! Who would not die to taste such extacy! And when I am interred, may the divine Henrietta bless some happier Youth with her affection,

May he be as tenderly attached to her as the hapless Musgrove and while *he* crumbles to dust, May they live an example of Felicity in the Conjugal state!"

Did you ever hear any thing so pathetic? What a charming Wish, to be lain at my feet when he was dead! Oh! What an exalted mind he must have to be capable of Such a wish! Lady Scudamore went on.

"Ah! my dear Cousin replied I to him, Such noble behaviour as this, must melt the heart of any Woman however obdurate it may naturally be; and could the divine Henrietta but hear your generous wishes for her happiness, all gentle as is her Mind, I have not a doubt but that she would pity your affection and endeavour to return it." "Oh! Cousin answered he, do not endeavour to raise my hopes by such flattering Assurances. No, I cannot hope to please this angel of a Woman, and the only thing which remains for me to do, is to die." "True Love is ever desponding replied I, but *I* my dear Tom will give you even greater hopes of conquering this fair one's heart, than I have yet given you, by assuring you that I watched her with the strictest attention during the whole day, and could plainly discover that she cherishes in her bosom though unknown to herself, a most tender affection for you."

"Dear Lady Scudamore cried I, This is more than I ever knew!"

"Did not I say that it was unknown to yourself? I did not, continued I to him, encourage you by saying this at first, that Surprise might render the pleasure Still Greater." "No Cousin replied he in a languid voice, nothing will convince me that *I* can have touched the heart of Henrietta Halton, and if you are deceived yourself, do not attempt deceiving me." "Inshort my Love it was the work of some hours for me to persuade the poor despairing Youth that you had really a preference for him; but when at last he could no longer deny the force of my arguments, or discredit what I told him, his transports, his Raptures, his Extacies are beyond my power to describe."

"Oh! the dear Creature, cried I, how passionately he loves me! But dear Lady Scudamore did you tell him that I was totally dependant on my Uncle and Aunt?"

"Yes, I told him every thing."

"And what did he say."

"He exclaimed with virulence against Uncles and Aunts; Accused the Laws of England for allowing them to possess their Estates when wanted by their Nephews or Neices, and wished *he* were in the House of Commons, that he might reform the Legislature, and rectify all its abuses."

"Oh! the sweet Man! What a spirit he has!" said I.

"He could not flatter himself he added, that the adorable Henrietta would condescend for his Sake to resign those Luxuries and that Splendor to which She had been used, and accept only in exchange the Comforts and Elegancies which his limited Income could afford her, even supposing that his house were in Readiness to receive her. I told him that it could not be expected that she would; it would be doing her an injustice to suppose her capable of giving up the power she now possesses and so nobly uses of doing such extensive Good to the poorer part of her fellow Creatures, merely for the gratification of you and herself."

"To be sure said I, I *am* very Charitable every now and then. And what did Mr Musgrove say to this?"

"He replied that he was under a melancholy Necessity of owning the truth of what I said, and that therefore if he should be the happy Creature destined to be the Husband of the Beautiful Henrietta he must bring himself to wait, however impatiently, for the fortunate day, when she might be freed from the power of worthless Relations and able to bestow herself on him."

What a noble Creature he is! Oh! Matilda what a fortunate one *I am*, who am to be his Wife! My Aunt is calling me to come and make the pies. So adieu my dear freind.

and beleive me yours etc.—H. Halton.

FINIS

THE FEMALE PHILOSOPHER—
a Letter.

To Miss Fanny Catherine Austen

My dear Neice

As I am prevented by the great distance between Rowling and Steventon from superintending Your Education Myself, the care of which will probably on that account devolve on your Father and Mother, I think it is my particular Duty to prevent your feeling as much as possible the want of my personal instructions, by addressing to You on paper my Opinions and Admonitions on the conduct of Young Women, which you will find expressed in the following pages.—I am my dear Neice

Your affectionate Aunt
The Author.

My dear Louisa

Your freind Mr Millar called upon us yesterday in his way to Bath, whither he is going for his health; two of his daughters were with him, but the oldest and the three Boys are with their Mother in Sussex. Though you have often told me that Miss Millar was remarkably handsome, You never mentioned anything of her Sisters' beauty; yet they are certainly extremely pretty. I'll give you their description.—Julia is eighteen; with a countenance in which Modesty, Sense and Dignity are happily blended, she has a form which at once presents you with Grace, Elegance and Symmetry. Charlotte who is just Sixteen is shorter than her Sister, and though her figure cannot boast the easy dignity of Julia's, yet it has a pleasing plumpness which is in a different way as estimable.

She is fair and her face is expressive sometimes of softness the most bewitching, and at others of Vivacity the most striking. She appears to have infinite Wit and a good humour unalterable; her conversation during the half hour they set with us, was replete with humourous Sallies, Bonmots and reparteés, while the sensible, the amiable Julia uttered Sentiments of Morality worthy of a heart like her own.

Mr Millar appeared to answer the character I had always received of him. My Father met him with that look of Love, that social Shake, and Cordial Kiss which marked his gladness at beholding an old and valued freind from whom thro' various circumstances he had been separated nearly twenty Years. Mr Millar observed (and very justly too) that many events had befallen each during that interval of time, which gave occasion to the lovely Julia for making most sensible reflections on the many changes in their situation which so long a period had occasioned, on the advantages of some, and the disadvantages of others. From this subject she made a short digression to the instability of human pleasures and the uncertainty of their duration, which led her to observe that all earthly Joys must be imperfect. She was proceeding to illustrate this doctrine by examples from the Lives of great Men when the Carriage came to the Door and the amiable Moralist with her Father and Sister was obliged to depart, but not without a promise of spending five or six months with us on their return. We of course mentioned You, and I assure you that ample Justice was done to your Merits by all. "Louisa Clarke (said I) is in general a very pleasant Girl, yet sometimes her good humour is clouded by Peevishness, Envy and Spite. She neither wants Understanding nor is without some pretensions to Beauty, but these are so very trifling, that the value she sets on her personal charms, and the adoration she expects them to be offered are at once a striking example of her vanity, her pride, and her folly." So said I, and to my opinion every one added weight by the concurrence of their own.

Your affec^{te} Arabella Smythe

THE FIRST ACT OF A COMEDY—

CHARACTERS
Popgun
Charles
Postilion
Chorus of ploughboys
and
Strephon

Maria
Pistoletta
Hostess
Cook
and
Chloe

Scene—an Inn—

Enter Hostess, Charles, Maria, and Cook.

Host[ss] *to Maria*) If the gentry in the Lion should want beds, shew them number 9.—
Maria) Yes Mistress. *exit Maria*—
Host[ss] *to Cook*) If their Honours in the Moon ask for the bill of fare, give it to them.
Cook)—I wull, I wull. *exit Cook.*
Host[ss] *to Charles*) If their Ladyships in the Sun ring their Bell—answer it.

Charles) Yes Ma'am.— *Exeunt Severally—*

Scene changes to the Moon, and discovers Popgun and Pistoletta.

Pistol^{tta}) Pray papa how far is it to London?
Popgun) My Girl, my Darling, my favourite of all my Children, who art the picture of thy poor Mother who died two months ago, with whom I am going to Town to marry to Strephon, and to whom I mean to bequeath my whole Estate, it wants seven Miles.

Scene changes to the Sun—
Enter Chloe and a chorus of ploughboys.

Chloe) Where am I? At Hounslow.—Where go I? To London—What to do? To be married—. Unto whom? Unto Strephon. Who is he? A Youth. Then I will sing a Song.

Song
I go to Town
And when I come down,
I shall be married to Stree-phon
And that to me will be fun.

Chorus) Be fun, be fun, be fun,
And that to me will be fun,

Enter Cook

Cook) Here is the bill of fare.
Chloe *reads*) 2 Ducks, a leg of beef, a stinking partridge, and a tart.—I will have the leg of beef and the partridge.
exit Cook.

And now I will sing another Song.

Song—
I am going to have my dinner,
After which I shan't be thinner,

I wish I had here Strephon
For he would carve the partridge if it should be a tough one

Chorus) Tough one, tough one, tough one,
>   For he would carve the partridge if it should be a
>   tough one.

Exit Chloe and Chorus—.
Scene changes to the inside of the Lion.
Enter Strephon and Postilion

Streph.) You drove me from Staines to this place, from whence I mean to go to Town to marry Chloe. How much is your due?

Post.) Eighteen pence.

Streph.) Alas, my freind, I have but a bad guinea with which I mean to support myself in Town. But I will pawn to you an undirected Letter that I received from Chloe.

Post.) Sir, I accept your offer.

END OF THE FIRST ACT.—

A LETTER FROM A YOUNG LADY, WHOSE FEELINGS BEING TOO STRONG FOR HER JUDGEMENT LED HER INTO THE COMMISSION OF ERRORS WHICH HER HEART DISAPPROVED.—

Many have been the cares and vicissitudes of my past life, my beloved Ellinor, and the only consolation I feel for their bitterness is that on a close examination of my conduct, I am convinced that I have strictly deserved them. I murdered my father at a very early period of my Life, I have since murdered my Mother, and I am now going to murder my Sister. I have changed my religion so often that at present I have not an idea of any left. I have been a perjured witness in every public tryal for these last twelve Years, and I have forged my own Will. In short there is scarcely a crime that I have not committed—But I am now going to reform. Colonel Martin of the Horseguards has paid his Addresses to me, and we are to be married in a few days. As there is something Singular in our Courtship, I will give you an account of it. Col. Martin is the second Son of the late Sir John Martin who died immensely rich, but bequeathing only one hundred thousand pound apeice to his three younger Children, left the bulk of his fortune, about eight Million to the present Sir Thomas. Upon his Small pittance the Colonel lived tolerably contented for nearly four months when he took it into his head to determine on getting the whole of his eldest Brother's Estate. A new will was forged and the Colonel produced it in Court—but nobody would swear to it's being the right Will except himself, and he had sworn so much that Nobody believed him. At that moment I happened to be passing by the door of the Court, and was beckoned in by the Judge who told the Colonel that I was a Lady ready to witness anything for the cause of Justice, and advised him to apply to me. In short the Affair was soon adjusted. The Colonel and I swore to its' being the right will, and Sir Thomas has been obliged to resign all his illgotten Wealth. The Colonel in gratitude waited on me the next day with an offer of his hand—. I am now going to murder my Sister.

$\qquad\qquad\qquad\qquad\qquad\qquad$ Y^{rs} Ever,
$\qquad\qquad\qquad\qquad\qquad\qquad\qquad$ Anna Parker.

A TOUR THROUGH WALES—
in a Letter from a young Lady—

My dear Clara

    I have been so long on the ramble that I have not till now had it in my power to thank you for your Letter—. We left our dear home on last Monday Month; and proceeded on our tour through Wales, which is a principality contiguous to England and gives the title to the Prince of Wales. We travelled on horseback by preference. My Mother rode upon our little poney and Fanny and I walked by her side or rather ran, for my Mother is so fond of riding fast that She galloped all the way. You may be sure that we were in a fine perspiration when we came to our place of resting. Fanny has taken a great Many Drawings of the Country, which are very beautiful, tho' perhaps not such exact resemblances as might be wished, from their being taken as she ran along. It would astonish you to see all the Shoes we wore out in our Tour. We determined to take a good Stock with us and therefore each took a pair of our own besides those we set off in. However we were obliged to have them both capped and heelpeiced at Carmarthen, and at last when they were quite gone, Mama was so kind as to lend us a pair of blue Sattin Slippers, of which we each took one and hopped home from Hereford delightfully—

I am your ever affectionate
Elizabeth Johnson.

A TALE.

A GENTLEMAN whose family name I shall conceal, bought a small Cottage in Pembrokeshire about two Years ago. This daring Action was suggested to him by his elder Brother who promised to furnish two rooms and a Closet for him, provided he would take a small house near the borders of an extensive Forest and about three Miles from the Sea. Wilhelminus gladly accepted the Offer and Continued for some time searching after such a retreat when he was one morning agreably releived from his Suspence by reading this advertisement in a Newspaper.

To be Lett
A Neat Cottage on the borders of an extensive forest and about three Miles from the Sea. It is ready furnished except two rooms and a Closet.

The delighted Wilhelminus posted away immediately to his brother, and shewed him the advertisement. Robertus congratulated him and sent him in his Carriage to take possession of the Cottage. After travelling for three days and Six Nights without Stopping, they arrived at the Forest and following a track which led by it's side down a steep Hill over which ten Rivulets meandered, they reached the Cottage in half an hour. Wilhelminus alighted, and after knocking for some time without receiving any answer or hearing anyone stir within, he opened the door which was fastened only by a wooden latch and entered a small room, which he immediately perceived to be one of the two that were unfurnished— From thence he proceeded into a Closet equally bare. A pair of Stairs that went out of it led him into a room above, no less destitute, and these apartments he found composed the whole of the House. He was by no means displeased with this discovery, as he had the comfort of reflecting that he should not be obliged to lay out any thing on furniture himself—. He returned immediately to his Brother, who took him the next day to every Shop in Town, and bought whatever was requisite to furnish the two rooms and the Closet. In a few days everything was completed, and Wilhelminus returned to take possession of his Cottage. Robertus accompanied him, with his Lady the amiable Cecilia and her two lovely Sisters Arabella and Marina to whom Wilhelminus was tenderly attached, and a large number of Attendants.—An ordinary Genius might probably have been embarrassed in endeavouring to accommodate so large a party, but Wilhelminus with admirable presence of Mind, gave orders for the immediate erection of two noble Tents in an open Spot in the Forest adjoining to the house. Their Construction was both simple and elegant—A Couple of old blankets, each supported by four Sticks, gave a striking proof of that Taste for Architecture and that happy ease in overcoming difficulties which were some of Wilhelminus's most striking Virtues.

FINIS

END OF THE SECOND VOLUME.

VOLUME THE THIRD

JANE AUSTEN—MAY 6TH 1792.

EVELYN

To Miss Mary Lloyd,
The following Novel is by permission
Dedicated,
by her Obed[t] humble Serv[t]
The Author

IN A RETIRED part of the County of Sussex there is a village (for what I know to the Contrary) called Evelyn, perhaps one of the most beautiful Spots in the south of England. A Gentleman passing through it on horseback about twenty years ago, was so entirely of my opinion in this respect, that he put up at the little Alehouse in it and enquired with great earnestness whether there were any house to be lett in the Parish. The Landlady, who as well as every one else in Evelyn was remarkably amiable, shook her head at this question, but seemed unwilling to give him any answer. He could not bear this uncertainty—yet knew not how to obtain the information he desired. To repeat a question which had already appear'd to make the good woman uneasy was impossible —. He turned from her in visible agitation. "What a situation am I in!" said he to himself as he walked to the window and threw up the sash. He found himself revived by the Air, which he felt to a much greater degree when he had opened the window than he had done before. Yet it was but for a moment—. The agonizing pain of Doubt and Suspence again weighed down his Spirits. The good woman who had watched in eager silence every turn of his Countenance with that benevolence which characterizes the inhabitants of Evelyn, intreated him to tell her the cause of his uneasiness. "Is there anything Sir in my power to do that may releive Your Greifs—Tell me in what Manner I can sooth them, and beleive me that the freindly balm of Comfort and Assistance shall not be wanting; for indeed Sir I have a simpathetic Soul."

"Amiable Woman (said Mr Gower, affected almost to tears by this generous offer) This Greatness of mind in one to whom I am almost a Stranger, serves but to make me the more warmly wish for a house in this sweet village—. What would I not give to be your Neighbour, to be blessed with your Acquaintance, and with the farther knowledge of your virtues! Oh! with what pleasure would I form myself by such an example! Tell me then, best of Women, is there no possibility?—I cannot speak—you know my meaning—"

"Alas! Sir, replied Mrs Willis, there is *none*. Every house in this village, from the sweetness of the Situation, and the purity of the Air, in which neither Misery, Illhealth, or Vice are ever wafted, is inhabited. And yet, (after a short pause) there is a Family, who tho' warmly attached to the spot, yet from a peculiar Generosity of Disposition would perhaps be willing to oblige you with their house." He eagerly caught at this idea, and having gained a direction to the place, he set off immediately on his walk to it. As he approached the House, he was delighted with its situation. It was in the exact center of a small circular paddock, which was enclosed by a regular paling, and bordered with a plantation of Lombardy poplars, and Spruce firs alternately placed in three rows. A gravel walk ran through this beautiful Shrubbery, and as the remainder of the paddock was unincumbered with any other Timber, the surface of it perfectly even and smooth, and grazed by four white Cows which were disposed at equal distances from each other, the whole appearance of the place as Mr Gower entered the Paddock was uncommonly striking. A beautifully-rounded, gravel road without any turn or interruption led immediately to the house. Mr Gower rang—the Door was soon opened. "Are Mr and Mrs Webb at home?" "My Good Sir they are—" replied the Servant; And leading the way, conducted Mr Gower up stairs into a very elegant Dressing room, where a Lady rising from her seat, welcomed him with all the Generosity which Mrs Willis had attributed to the Family.

"Welcome best of Men—Welcome to this House, and to every thing it contains. William, tell your Master of the happiness I enjoy—invite him to partake of it—. Bring up some Chocolate immediately; Spread a Cloth in the dining Parlour, and carry in the venison pasty—. In the mean time let the Gentleman have some sandwiches, and bring in a Basket of Fruit—Send up some Ices and a bason of Soup, and do not forget some Jellies and Cakes." Then turning to Mr Gower, and taking out her purse, "Accept this my good Sir,—. Beleive me you are welcome to everything that is in my power to bestow.—I wish my purse were weightier, but Mr Webb must make up my deficiencies—. I know he has cash in the house to the amount of an hundred pounds, which he shall bring you immediately." Mr Gower felt overpowered by her generosity as he put the purse in his pocket, and from the excess of his Gratitude, could scarcely express himself intelligibly when he accepted her offer of the hundred pounds. Mr Webb soon entered the room, and repeated every protestation of Freindship and Cordiality which his Lady had already made—. The Chocolate, The Sandwiches, the Jellies, the Cakes, the Ice, and the Soup soon made their appearance, and Mr Gower having tasted something of all, and pocketted the rest, was conducted into the dining parlour, where he eat a most excellent Dinner and partook of the most exquisite Wines, while Mr and Mrs Webb stood by him still pressing him to eat and drink a little more. "And now my good Sir, said Mr Webb, when Mr Gower's repast was concluded, what else can we do to contribute to your happiness and express the Affection we bear you. Tell us what you wish more to receive, and depend upon our gratitude for the communication of your wishes." "Give me then your house and Grounds; I ask for nothing else." "It is yours, exclaimed both at once; from this moment it is yours." This Agreement concluded on and the present accepted by Mr Gower, Mr Webb rang to have the Carriage ordered, telling William at the same time to call the Young Ladies.

"Best of Men, said Mrs Webb, we will not long intrude upon your Time."

"Make no Apologies dear Madam, replied Mr Gower, You are welcome to stay this half hour if you like it."

They both burst forth into raptures of Admiration at his politeness, which they agreed served only to make their Conduct appear more inexcusable in trespassing on his time.

The Young Ladies soon entered the room. The eldest of them was about seventeen, the other, several years younger. Mr Gower had no sooner fixed his Eyes on Miss Webb than he felt that something more was necessary to his happiness than the house he had just received—Mrs Webb introduced him to her daughter. "Our dear freind Mr Gower my Love— He has been so good as to accept of this house, small as it is, and to promise to keep it for ever." "Give me leave to assure you Sir, said Miss Webb, that I am highly sensible of your kindness in this respect, which from the shortness of my Father's and Mother's acquaintance with You, is more than usually flattering." Mr Gower bowed—"You are too obliging Ma'am—I assure you that I like the house extremely— and if they would complete their generosity by giving me their elder daughter in marriage with a handsome portion, I should have nothing more to wish for." This compliment brought a blush into the cheeks of the lovely Miss Webb, who seemed however to refer herself to her father and Mother. *They* looked delighted at each other—At length Mrs Webb breaking silence, said—"We bend under a weight of obligations to you which we can never repay. Take our girl, take our Maria, and on her must the difficult task fall, of endeavouring to make some return to so much Beneficence." Mr Webb added, "Her fortune is but ten thousand pounds, which is almost too small a sum to be offered." This objection however being instantly removed by the generosity of Mr Gower, who declared himself satisfied with the sum mentioned, Mr and Mrs Webb, with their youngest daughter took their leave, and on the next day, the nuptials of their eldest with Mr Gower were celebrated.—This amiable Man now found himself perfectly happy; united to a very lovely and deserving young woman, with an handsome fortune, an elegant house, settled in the village of Evelyn, and by that means enabled to cultivate his acquaintance with Mrs Willis, could he have a wish ungratified?—For some months he found that he could *not*, till one day as he was walking in the Shrubbery with Maria leaning on his arm, they observed a rose full-blown lying on the gravel; it had fallen from a rose tree which with three others had been planted by Mr Webb to give a pleasing variety to the walk. These four Rose trees served also to mark the quarters of the Shrubbery, by which means the Traveller might always know how far in his progress round the Paddock he was got—. Maria stooped to pick up the beautiful flower, and with all her Family Generosity presented it to her Husband. "My dear Frederic, said she, pray take this charming rose." "Rose! exclaimed Mr Gower—. Oh! Maria, of what does not that remind me! Alas my poor Sister, how have I neglected you!" The truth was that Mr Gower was the only son of a very large Family, of which Miss Rose Gower was the thirteenth daughter. This Young Lady whose merits deserved a better fate than she met with, was the darling of her relations—From the clearness of her skin and the Brilliancy of her Eyes, she was fully entitled to all their partial affection. Another circumstance contributed to the general Love they bore her, and that was one of the finest heads of hair in the world. A few Months before her Brother's marriage, her heart had been engaged by the attentions and charms of a young Man whose high rank and expectations seemed to foretell objections from his Family to a match which would be highly desirable to theirs. Proposals were made on the young Man's part, and proper objections on his Father's—He was desired to return from Carlisle where he was with his beloved Rose, to the family seat in Sussex. He was obliged to comply, and the angry father then finding from his Conversation how determined he was to marry no other woman, sent him for a fortnight to the Isle of Wight under the care of the Family Chaplain, with the hope of overcoming his Constancy by Time and Absence in a foreign Country. They accordingly prepared to bid a long adeiu to England—The young Nobleman was not allowed to see his Rosa. They set sail—A storm arose which baffled the arts of the Seamen. The Vessel was wrecked on the coast of Calshot and every Soul on board perished. This sad Event soon reached Carlisle, and the beautiful Rose was affected by it, beyond the power of Expression. It was to soften her affliction by obtaining a picture of her unfortunate Lover that her brother undertook a Journey into Sussex, where he hoped that his petition would not be rejected, by the severe yet afflicted Father. When he reached Evelyn he was not many miles from——Castle, but the pleasing events which befell him in that place had for a while made him totally forget the object of his Journey and his unhappy Sister. The little incident of the rose however brought everything concerning her to his recollection again, and he bitterly repented his neglect. He returned to the house immediately and agitated by Greif, Apprehension and Shame wrote the following Letter to Rosa.

July 14th——.Evelyn

My dearest Sister

As it is now four months since I left Carlisle, during which period I have not once written to you, You will perhaps unjustly accuse me of Neglect and Forgetfulness. Alas! I blush when I own the truth of your accusation.—Yet if you are still alive, do not think too harshly of me, or suppose that I could for a moment forget the situation of my Rose. Beleive me I will forget you no longer, but will hasten as soon as possible to——Castle if I find by your answer that you are still alive. Maria joins me in every dutiful and affectionate wish, and I am yours sincerely

F. Gower.

He waited in the most anxious expectation for an answer to his Letter, which arrived as soon as the great distance from Carlisle would admit of.—But alas, it came not from Rosa.

Carlisle July 17th——

Dear Brother

My Mother has taken the liberty of opening your Letter to poor Rose, as she has been dead these six weeks. Your long absence and continued Silence gave us all great uneasiness and hastened her to her Grave. Your Journey to——Castle therefore may be spared. You do not tell us where you have been since the time of your quitting Carlisle, nor in any way account for your tedious absence, which gives us some surprise. We all unite in Comp^ts to Maria, and beg to know who she is—.

Y^r affec^te Sister
M. Gower.

This Letter, by which Mr Gower was obliged to attribute to his own conduct, his Sister's death, was so violent a shock to his feelings, that in spite of his living at Evelyn where Illness was scarcely ever heard of, he was attacked by a fit of the gout, which confining him to his own room afforded an opportunity to Maria of shining in that favourite character of Sir Charles Grandison's, a nurse. No woman could ever appear more amiable than Maria did under such circumstances, and at last by her unremitting attentions had the pleasure of seeing him gradually recover the use of his feet. It was a blessing by no means lost on him, for he was no sooner in a condition to leave the house, than he mounted his horse, and rode to——Castle, wishing to find whether his Lordship softened by his Son's death, might have been brought to consent to the match, had both *he* and Rosa been alive. His amiable Maria followed him with her Eyes till she could see him no longer, and then sinking into her chair overwhelmed with Greif, found that in his absence she could enjoy no comfort.

Mr Gower arrived late in the evening at the castle, which was situated on a woody Eminence commanding a beautiful prospect of the Sea. Mr Gower did not dislike the situation, tho' it was certainly greatly inferior to that of his own house. There was an irregularity in the fall of the ground, and a profusion of old Timber which appeared to him illsuited to the stile of the Castle, for it being a building of a very ancient date, he thought it required the Paddock of Evelyn lodge to form a Contrast, and enliven the structure. The gloomy appearance of the old Castle frowning on him as he followed its' winding approach, struck him with terror. Nor did he think himself safe, till he was introduced into the Drawing room where the Family were assembled to tea. Mr

Gower was a perfect stranger to every one in the Circle but tho' he was always timid in the Dark and easily terrified when alone, he did not want that more necessary and more noble courage which enabled him without a Blush to enter a large party of superior Rank, whom he had never seen before, and to take his Seat amongst them with perfect Indifference. The name of Gower was not unknown to Lord——. He felt distressed and astonished; yet rose and received him with all the politeness of a well-bred Man. Lady—— who felt a deeper sorrow at the loss of her son, than his Lordships harder heart was capable of, could hardly keep her Seat when she found that he was the Brother of her lamented Henry's Rosa. "My Lord said Mr Gower as soon as he was seated, You are perhaps surprised at receiving a visit from a Man whom you could not have the least expectation of seeing here. But my Sister my unfortunate Sister is the real cause of my thus troubling you: That luckless Girl is now no more—and tho' *she* can receive no pleasure from the intelligence, yet for the satisfaction of her Family I wish to know whether the Death of this unhappy Pair has made an impression on your heart sufficiently strong to obtain that consent to their Marriage which in happier circumstances you would not be persuaded to give supposing that they now were both alive." His Lordship seemed lossed in astonishment. Lady—— could not support the mention of her Son, and left the room in tears; the rest of the Family remained attentively listening, almost persuaded that Mr Gower was distracted. "Mr Gower, replied his Lordship This is a very odd question—It appears to me that you are supposing an impossibility—No one can more sincerely regret the death of my Son than I have always done, and it gives me great concern to know that Miss Gower's was hastened by his—. Yet to suppose them alive is destroying at once the Motive for a change in my sentiments concerning the affair." "My Lord, replied Mr Gower in anger, I see that you are a most inflexible Man, and that not even the death of your Son can make you wish his future Life happy. I will no longer detain your Lordship. I see, I plainly see that you are a very vile Man—And now I have the honour of wishing all your Lordships, and Ladyships a good Night." He immediately left the room, forgetting in the heat of his Anger the lateness of the hour, which at any other time would have made him tremble, and leaving the whole Company unanimous in their opinion of his being Mad. When however he had mounted his horse and the great Gates of the Castle had shut him out, he felt an universal tremor through out his whole frame. If we consider his Situation indeed, alone, on horseback, as late in the year as August, and in the day, as nine o'clock, with no light to direct him but that of the Moon almost full, and the Stars which alarmed him by their twinkling, who can refrain from pitying him?—No house within a quarter of a mile, and a Gloomy Castle blackened by the deep shade of Walnuts and Pines, behind him.—He felt indeed almost distracted with his fears, and shutting his Eyes till he arrived at the Village to prevent his seeing either Gipsies or Ghosts, he rode on a full gallop all the way.

CATHARINE, OR THE BOWER

To Miss Austen

Madam
 Encouraged by your warm patronage of The beautiful Cassandra, and The History of England, which through your generous support, have obtained a place in every library in the Kingdom, and run through threescore Editions, I take the liberty of begging the same Exertions in favour of the following Novel, which I humbly flatter myself, possesses Merit beyond any already published, or any that will ever in future appear, except such as may proceed from the pen of Your Most Grateful Humble Servt
The Author

Steventon August 1792—

CATHARINE HAD the misfortune, as many heroines have had before her, of losing her Parents when she was very young, and of being brought up under the care of a Maiden Aunt, who while she tenderly loved her, watched over her conduct with so scrutinizing a severity, as to make it very doubtful to many people, and to Catharine amongst the rest, whether she loved her or not. She had frequently been deprived of a real pleasure through this jealous Caution, had been sometimes obliged to relinquish a Ball because an Officer was to be there, or to dance with a Partner of her Aunt's introduction in preference to one of her own Choice. But her Spirits were naturally good, and not easily depressed, and she possessed such a fund of vivacity and good humour as could only be damped by some very serious vexation.—Besides these antidotes against every disappointment, and consolations under them, she had another, which afforded her constant releif in all her misfortunes, and that was a fine shady Bower, the work of her own infantine Labours assisted by those of two young Companions who had resided in the same village—. To this Bower, which terminated a very pleasant and retired walk in her Aunt's Garden, she always wandered whenever anything disturbed her, and it possessed such a charm over her senses, as constantly to tranquillize her mind and quiet her spirits—Solitude and reflection might perhaps have had the same effect in her Bed Chamber, yet Habit had so strengthened the idea which Fancy had first suggested, that such a thought never occurred to Kitty who was firmly persuaded that her Bower alone could restore her to herself. Her imagination was warm, and in her Freindships, as well as in the whole tenure of her Mind, she was enthousiastic. This beloved Bower had been the united work of herself and two amiable Girls, for whom since her earliest Years, she had felt the tenderest regard. They were the daughters of the Clergyman of the Parish with whose Family, while it had continued there, her Aunt had been on the most intimate terms, and the little Girls tho' separated for the greatest part of the Year by the different Modes of their Education, were constantly together during the holidays of the Miss Wynnes. In those days of happy Childhood, now so often regretted by Kitty this arbour had been formed, and separated perhaps for ever from these dear freinds, it encouraged more than any other place the tender and Melancholly recollections, of hours rendered pleasant by *them*, at once so sorrowful, yet so soothing! It was now two years since the death of Mr Wynne, and the consequent dispersion of his Family who had been left by it in great distress. They had been reduced to a state of absolute dependance on some relations, who though very opulent, and very nearly connected with them, had with difficulty been prevailed on to contribute anything towards their Support. Mrs Wynne was fortunately spared the knowledge and participation of their distress, by her release from a painful illness a few months before the death of her husband.—. The eldest daughter had been obliged to accept the offer of one of her cousins to equip her for the East Indies, and tho' infinitely against her inclinations had been necessitated to embrace the only possibility that was offered to her, of a Maintenance; Yet it was *one*, so opposite to all her ideas of Propriety, so contrary to her Wishes, so repugnant to her feelings, that she would almost have preferred Servitude to it, had Choice been allowed her—. Her personal Attractions had gained her a husband as soon as she had arrived at Bengal and she had now been married nearly a twelvemonth. Splendidly, yet unhappily married. United to a Man of double her own age, whose disposition was not amiable, and whose Manners were unpleasing, though his Character was respectable. Kitty had heard twice from her freind since her marriage, but her Letters were always unsatisfactory, and though she did not openly avow her feelings, yet every line proved her to be Unhappy. She spoke with pleasure of nothing, but of those Amusements which they had shared together and which could return no more, and seemed to have no happiness in veiw but that of returning to England again. Her sister had been taken by another relation the Dowager Lady Halifax as a companion to her Daughters, and had accompanied her family into Scotland about the same time of Cecilia's leaving England. From Mary therefore Kitty had the power of hearing more frequently, but her Letters were scarcely more comfortable—. There was not indeed that hopelessness of sorrow in her situation as in her sisters; she was not married, and could yet look forward to a change in her circumstances; but situated for the present without any immediate hope of it, in a family where, tho' all were her relations she had no freind, she wrote usually in depressed Spirits, which her separation from her Sister and her Sister's Marriage had greatly contributed to make so.—Divided thus from the two she loved best on Earth, while Cecilia and Mary were still more endeared to her by their loss, everything that brought a remembrance of them was doubly cherished, and the Shrubs they had planted, and the keepsakes they had given were rendered sacred—. The living of Chetwynde was now in the possession of a Mr Dudley, whose Family unlike the Wynnes, were productive only of vexation and trouble to Mrs Percival, and her Neice. Mr Dudley, who was the younger Son of a very noble Family, of a Family more famed for their Pride than their opulence, tenacious of his Dignity, and jealous of his rights, was forever quarrelling, if not with Mrs P herself, with her Steward and Tenants concerning tythes, and with the principal Neighbours themselves concerning the respect and parade, he exacted. His Wife, an ill-educated, untaught Woman of ancient family, was proud of that family almost without knowing why, and like him too was haughty and quarrelsome, without considering for what. Their only daughter, who inherited the ignorance, the insolence, and pride of her parents, was from that Beauty of which she was unreasonably vain, considered by them as an irresistable Creature, and looked up to as the future restorer, by a Splendid Marriage, of the dignity which their reduced Situation and Mr Dudley's being obliged to take orders for a Country Living had so much lessened. They at once despised the Percivals as people of mean family, and envied them as people of fortune. They were jealous of their being more respected than themselves and while they affected to consider them as of no Consequence, were continually seeking to lessen them in the opinion of the Neighbourhood by Scandalous and Malicious reports. Such a family as this, was ill calculated to console Kitty for the loss of the Wynnes, or to fill up by their society, those occasionally irksome hours which in so retired a Situation would sometimes occur for want of a Companion. Her aunt was most excessively fond of her, and miserable if she saw her for a moment out of spirits; Yet she lived in such constant apprehension of her marrying imprudently if she were allowed the opportunity of Choosing, and was so dissatisfied with her behaviour when she saw her with Young Men, for it was, from her natural disposition remarkably open and unreserved, that though she frequently wished for her Neice's sake, that the Neighbourhood were larger, and that She had used herself to mix more with it, yet the recollection of there being young Men in almost every Family in it, always conquered the Wish. The same fears that prevented Mrs Peterson's joining much in the Society of her Neighbours, led her equally to avoid inviting her relations to spend any time in her House—She had therefore constantly repelled the Annual attempt of a distant relation to visit her at Chetwynde, as there was a young Man in the Family of whom she had heard many traits that alarmed her. This Son was however now on his travels, and the repeated solicitations of Kitty, joined to a consciousness of having declined with too little Ceremony the frequent overtures, of her Freinds to be admitted, and a real wish to see them herself, easily prevailed on her to press with great Earnestness the pleasure of a visit from them during the Summer. Mr and Mrs Stanley were accordingly to come, and Catharine, in having an object to look forward to, a something to expect that must inevitably releive the dullness of a constant tete-a tete with her Aunt, was so delighted, and her spirits so elevated, that for the three or four days immediately preceding their Arrival, she could scarcely fix herself to any employment. In this point Mrs Percival always thought her defective, and frequently complained of a want of Steadiness and perseverance in her occupations, which were by no means congenial to the eagerness of Kitty's Disposition, and perhaps not often met with in any young person. The tediousness too of her Aunt's conversation and the want of agreable Companions greatly encreased this desire of Change in her Employments, for Kitty found herself much sooner tired of Reading, Working, or Drawing, in Mrs Peterson's parlour than in her own Arbour, where Mrs Peterson for fear of its being damp never accompanied her.

As her Aunt prided herself on the exact propriety and Neatness with which everything in her Family was conducted, and had no higher Satisfaction than that of knowing her house to be always in complete Order, as her fortune was good, and her Establishment Ample, few were the preparations Necessary for the reception of her Visitors. The day of their arrival so long expected, at length came, and the Noise of the Coach and 4 as it drove round the sweep, was to Catherine a more interesting sound, than the Music of an Italian Opera, which to most Heroines is the hight of Enjoyment. Mr and Mrs Stanley were people of Large Fortune and high Fashion. He was a Member of the house of Commons, and they were therefore most agreably necessitated to reside half the Year in Town; where Miss Stanley had been attended by the most capital Masters from the time of her being six years old to the last Spring, which comprehending a period of twelve Years had been dedicated to the acquirement of Accomplishments which were now to be displayed and in a few Years entirely neglected. She was elegant in her appearance, rather handsome, and naturally not deficient in Abilities; but those Years which ought to have been spent in the attainment of useful knowledge and Mental Improvement, had been all bestowed in learning Drawing, Italian and Music, more especially the latter, and she now united to these Accomplishments, an Understanding unimproved by reading and a Mind totally devoid either of Taste or Judgement. Her temper was by Nature good, but unassisted by reflection, she had neither patience under Disappointment, nor could sacrifice her own inclinations to promote the happiness of others. All her Ideas were towards the Elegance of her appearance, the fashion of her dress, and the Admiration she wished them to excite. She professed a love of Books without Reading, was Lively without Wit, and generally Good humoured without Merit. Such was Camilla Stanley; and Catherine, who was prejudiced by her appearance, and who from her solitary Situation was ready to like anyone, tho' her Understanding and Judgement would not otherwise have been easily satisfied, felt almost convinced when she saw her, that Miss Stanley would be the very companion She wanted, and in some degree make amends for the loss of Cecilia and Mary Wynne. She therefore attached herself to Camilla from the first day of her arrival, and from being the only young People in the house, they were by inclination constant Companions. Kitty was herself a great reader, tho' perhaps not a very deep one, and felt therefore highly delighted to find that Miss Stanley was equally fond of it. Eager to know that their sentiments as to Books were similar, she very soon began questioning her new Acquaintance on the subject; but though She was well read in Modern history herself, she Chose rather to speak first of Books of a lighter kind, of Books universally read and Admired.

"You have read Mrs Smith's Novels, I suppose?" said she to her Companion—. "Oh! Yes, replied the other, and I am quite delighted with them—They are the sweetest things in the world—" "And which do you prefer of them?" "Oh! dear, I think there is no comparison between them—Emmeline is *so much* better than any of the others—"

"Many people think so, I know; but there does not appear so great a disproportion in their Merits to *me*; do you think it is better written?"

"Oh! I do not know anything about *that*—but it is better in *everything*—Besides, Ethelinde is so long—" "That is a very common Objection I beleive, said Kitty, but for my own part, if a book is well written, I always find it too short."

"So do I, only I get tired of it before it is finished." "But did not you find the story of Ethelinde very interesting? And the Descriptions of Grasmere, are not they Beautiful?" "Oh! I missed them all, because I was in such a hurry to know the end of it—Then from an easy transition she added, We are going to the Lakes this Autumn, and I am quite Mad with Joy; Sir Henry Devereux has promised to go with us, and that will make it so pleasant, you know—"

"I dare say it will; but I think it is a pity that Sir Henry's powers of pleasing were not reserved for an occasion where they might be more wanted.—However I quite envy you the pleasure of such a Scheme." "Oh! I am quite delighted with the thoughts of it; I can think of nothing else. I assure you I have done nothing for this last Month but plan what Cloathes I should take with me, and I have at last determined to take very few indeed besides my travelling Dress, and so I advise you to do, when ever you go; for I intend in case we should fall in with any races, or stop at Matlock or Scarborough, to have some Things made for the occasion."

"You intend then to go into Yorkshire?"

"I beleive not—indeed I know nothing of the Route, for I never trouble myself about such things—. I only know that we are to go from Derbyshire to Matlock and Scarborough, but to which of them first, I neither know nor care—I am in hopes of meeting some particular freinds of mine at Scarborough—Augusta told me in her last Letter that Sir Peter talked of going; but then you know that is so uncertain. I cannot bear Sir Peter, he is such a horrid Creature—"

"He *is*, is he?" said Kitty, not knowing what else to say. "Oh! he is quite Shocking." Here the Conversation was interrupted, and Kitty was left in a painful Uncertainty, as to the particulars of Sir Peter's Character; She knew only that he was Horrid and Shocking, but why, and in what, yet remained to be discovered. She could scarcely resolve what to think of her new Acquaintance; She appeared to be shamefully ignorant as to the Geography of England, if she had understood her right, and equally devoid of Taste and Information. Kitty was however unwilling to decide hastily; she was at once desirous of doing Miss Stanley justice, and of having her own Wishes in her answered; she determined therefore to suspend all Judgement for some time. After Supper, the Conversation turning on the State of Affairs in the political World, Mrs P, who was firmly of opinion that the whole race of Mankind were degenerating, said that for her part, Everything she beleived was going to rack and ruin, all order was destroyed over the face of the World, The house of Commons she heard did not break up sometimes till five in the Morning, and Depravity never was so general before; concluding with a wish that she might live to see the Manners of the People in Queen Elizabeth's reign, restored again. "Well Ma'am, said her Neice, but I hope you do not mean with the times to restore Queen Elizth. herself."

"Queen Eliz[th], said Mrs Stanley who never hazarded a remark on History that was not well founded, lived to a good old Age, and was a very Clever Woman."

"True Ma'am, said Kitty; but I do not consider either of those Circumstances as meritorious in herself, and they are very far from making me wish her return, for if she were to come again with the same Abilities and the same good Constitution She might do as much Mischeif and last as long as she did before—then turning to Camilla who had been sitting very silent for some time, she added What do *you* think of Elizabeth Miss Stanley? I hope you will not defend her."

"Oh! dear, said Miss Stanley, I know nothing of Politics, and cannot bear to hear them mentioned." Kitty started at this repulse, but made no answer; that Miss Stanley must be ignorant of what she could not distinguish from Politics, she felt perfectly convinced.— She retired to her own room, perplexed in her opinion about her new Acquaintance, and fearful of her being very unlike Cecilia and Mary. She arose the next morning to experience a fuller conviction of this, and every future day encreased it—. She found no variety in her conversation; She received no information from her but in fashions, and no Amusement but in her performance on the Harpsichord; and after repeated endeavours to find her what she wished, she was obliged to give up the attempt and to consider it as fruitless. There had occasionally appeared a something like humour in Camilla which had inspired her with hopes, that she might at least have a natural Genius, tho' not an improved one, but these Sparklings of Wit happened so seldom, and were so ill-supported that she was at last convinced of their being merely accidental. All her stock of knowledge was exhausted in a very few Days, and when Kitty had learnt from her, how large their house in Town was, when the fashionable Amusements began, who were the celebrated Beauties and who the best Millener, Camilla had nothing further to teach, except the Characters of any of her Acquaintance as they occurred in Conversation, which was done with equal Ease and Brevity, by saying that the person was either the sweetest Creature in the world, and one of whom she was doatingly fond, or horrid, Shocking and not fit to be seen.

As Catherine was very desirous of gaining every possible information as to the Characters of the Halifax Family, and concluded that Miss Stanley must be acquainted with them, as she seemed to be so with every one of any Consequence, she took an opportunity as Camilla was one day enumerating all the people of rank that her Mother visited, of asking her whether Lady Halifax were among the number.

"Oh! Thank you for reminding me of her, She is the sweetest Woman in the world, and one of our most intimate Acquaintance; I do not suppose there is a day passes during the six Months that we are in Town, but what we see each other in the course of it—. And I correspond with all the Girls."

"They *are* then a very pleasant Family? said Kitty. They ought to be so indeed, to allow of such frequent Meetings, or all Conversation must be at end."

"Oh! dear, not at all, said Miss Stanley, for sometimes we do not speak to each other for a month together. We meet perhaps only in Public, and then you know we are often not able to get near enough; but in that case we always nod and smile."

"Which does just as well—. But I was going to ask you whether you have ever seen a Miss Wynne with them?"

"I know who you mean perfectly—she wears a blue hat—. I have frequently seen her in Brook Street, when I have been at Lady Halifax's Balls—She gives one every Month during the Winter—. But only think how good it is in her to take care of Miss Wynne, for she is a very distant relation, and so poor that, as Miss Halifax told me, her Mother was obliged to find her in Cloathes. Is not it shameful?"

"That she should be so poor;? it is indeed, with such wealthy connexions as the Family have."

"Oh! no; I mean, was not it shameful in Mr Wynne to leave his Children so distressed, when he had actually the Living of Chetwynde and two or three Curacies, and only four Children to provide for—. What would he have done if he had had ten, as many people have?"

"He would have given them all a good Education and have left them all equally poor."

"Well I do think there never was so lucky a Family. Sir George Fitzgibbon you know sent the eldest Girl to India entirely at his own Expence, where they say she is most nobly married and the happiest Creature in the World—Lady Halifax you see has taken care of the youngest and treats her as if she were her Daughter; She does not go out into Public with her to be sure; but then she is always present when her Ladyship gives her Balls, and nothing can be kinder to her than Lady Halifax is; she would have taken her to Cheltenham last year, if there had been room enough at the

Lodgings, and therefore I dont think that *she* can have anything to complain of. Then there are the two Sons; one of them the Bishop of M——has got into the Army as a Leiutenant I suppose; and the other is extremely well off I know, for I have a notion that somebody puts him to School somewhere in Wales. Perhaps you knew them when they lived here?"

"Very well, We met as often as your Family and the Halifaxes do in Town, but as we seldom had any difficulty in getting near enough to speak, we seldom parted with merely a Nod and a Smile. They were indeed a most charming Family, and I beleive have scarcely their Equals in the World; The Neighbours we now have at the Parsonage, appear to more disadvantage in coming after them."

"Oh! horrid Wretches! I wonder You can endure them."

"Why, what would you have one do?"

"Oh! Lord, If I were in your place, I should abuse them all day long."

"So I do, but it does no good."

"Well, I declare it is quite a pity that they should be suffered to live. I wish my Father would propose knocking all their Brains out, some day or other when he is in the House. So abominably proud of their Family! And I dare say after all, that there is nothing particular in it."

"Why Yes, I beleive they *have* reason to value themselves on it, if any body has; for you know he is Lord Amyatt's Brother."

"Oh! I know all that very well, but it is no reason for their being so horrid. I remember I met Miss Dudley last Spring with Lady Amyatt at Ranelagh, and she had such a frightful Cap on, that I have never been able to bear any of them since.—And so you used to think the Wynnes very pleasant?"

"You speak as if their being so were doubtful! Pleasant! Oh! they were every thing that could interest and Attach. It is not in my power to do Justice to their Merits, tho' not to feel them, I think must be impossible. They have unfitted me for any Society but their own!"

"Well, That is just what I think of the Miss Halifaxes; by the bye, I must write to Caroline tomorrow, and I do not know what to say to her. The Barlows too are just such other sweet Girls; but I wish Augusta's hair was not so dark. I cannot bear Sir Peter—Horrid Wretch! He is *always* laid up with the Gout, which is exceedingly disagreable to the Family."

"And perhaps not very pleasant to *himself*—. But as to the Wynnes; do you really think them very fortunate?"

"Do I? Why, does not every body? Miss Halifax and Caroline and Maria all say that they are the luckiest Creatures in the World. So does Sir George Fitzgibbon and so do Every-body."

"That is, Every body who have themselves conferred an obligation on them. But do you call it lucky, for a Girl of Genius and Feeling to be sent in quest of a Husband to Bengal, to be married there to a Man of whose Disposition she has no opportunity of judging till her Judgement is of no use to her, who may be a Tyrant, or a Fool or both for what she knows to the Contrary. Do you call *that* fortunate?"

"I know nothing of all that; I only know that it was extremely good in Sir George to fit her out and pay for her Passage, and that she would not have found Many who would have done the same."

"I wish she had not found *one*, said Kitty with great Eagerness, she might then have remained in England and been happy."

"Well, I cannot conceive the hardship of going out in a very agreable Manner with two or three sweet Girls for Companions, having a delightful voyage to Bengal or Barbadoes or wherever it is, and being married soon after one's arrival to a very charming Man immensely rich—. I see no hardship in all that."

"Your representation of the Affair, said Kitty laughing, certainly gives a very different idea of it from Mine. But supposing all this to be true, still, as it was by no means certain that she would be so fortunate either in her voyage, her Companions, or her husband; in being obliged to run the risk of their proving very different, she undoubtedly experienced a great hardship—. Besides, to a Girl of any Delicacy, the voyage in itself, since the object of it is so universally known, is a punishment that needs no other to make it very severe."

"I do not see that at all. She is not the first Girl who has gone to the East Indies for a Husband, and I declare I should think it very good fun if I were as poor."

"I beleive you would think very differently *then*. But at least you will not defend her Sister's situation? Dependant even for her Cloathes on the bounty of others, who of course do not pity her, as by your own account, they consider her as very fortunate."

"You are extremely nice upon my word; Lady Halifax is a delightful Woman, and one of the sweetest tempered Creatures in the World; I am sure I have every reason to speak well of her, for we are under most amazing Obligations to her. She has frequently chaperoned me when my Mother has been indisposed, and last Spring she lent me her own horse three times, which was a prodigious favour, for it is the most beautiful Creature that ever was seen, and I am the only person she ever lent it to.

And then, continued she, the Miss Halifaxes are quite delightful—. Maria is one of the cleverest Girls that ever were known—Draws in Oils, and plays anything by sight. She promised me one of her Drawings before I left Town, but I entirely forgot to ask her for it—. I would give any thing to have one."

"But was not it very odd, said Kitty, that the Bishop should send Charles Wynne to sea, when he must have had a much better chance of providing for him in the Church, which was the profession that Charles liked best, and the one for which his Father had intended him? The Bishop I know had often promised Mr Wynne a living, and as he never gave him one, I think it was incumbant on him to transfer the promise to his Son."

"I beleive you think he ought to have resigned his Bishopric to him; you seem determined to be dissatisfied with every thing that has been done for them."

"Well, said Kitty, this is a subject on which we shall never agree, and therefore it will be useless to continue it farther, or to mention it again—" She then left the room, and running out of the House was soon in her dear Bower where she could indulge in peace all her affectionate Anger against the relations of the Wynnes, which was greatly heightened by finding from Camilla that they were in general considered as having acted particularly well by them—. She amused herself for some time in Abusing, and Hating them all, with great Spirit, and when this tribute to her regard for the Wynnes, was paid, and the Bower began to have its usual influence over her Spirits, she contributed towards settling them, by taking out a book, for she had always one about her, and reading—. She had been so employed for nearly an hour, when Camilla came running towards her with great Eagerness, and apparently great Pleasure—. "Oh! my Dear Catherine, said she, half out of Breath—I have such delightful News for You—But you shall guess what it is—We are all the happiest Creatures in the World; would you beleive it, the Dudleys have sent us an invitation to a Ball at their own House—. What Charming People they are! I had no idea of there being so much Sense in the whole Family—I declare I quite doat upon them—. And it happens so fortunately too, for I expect a new Cap from Town tomorrow which will just do for a Ball—Gold Net.—It will be a most angelic thing—Every Body will be longing for the pattern—" The expectation of a Ball was indeed very agreable intelligence to Kitty, who fond of Dancing and seldom able to enjoy it, had reason to feel even greater pleasure in it than her Freind; for to *her*, it was now no novelty—. Camilla's delight however was by no means inferior to Kitty's, and she rather expressed the most of the two. The Cap came and every other preparation was soon completed; while these were in agitation the Days passed gaily away, but when Directions were no longer necessary, Taste could no longer be displayed, and Difficulties no longer overcome, the short period that intervened before the day of the Ball hung heavily on their hands, and every hour was too long. The very few Times that Kitty had ever enjoyed the Amusement of Dancing was an excuse for *her* impatience, and an apology for the Idleness it occasioned to a Mind naturally very Active; but her Freind without such a plea was infinitely worse than herself. She could do nothing but wander from the house to the Garden, and from the Garden to the avenue, wondering when Thursday would come, which she might easily have ascertained, and counting the hours as they passed which served only to lengthen them.—.

They retired to their rooms in high Spirits on Wednesday night, but Kitty awoke the next Morning with a violent Toothake. It was in vain that she endeavoured at first to deceive herself; her feelings were witnesses too acute of it's reality; with as little success did she try to sleep it off, for the pain she suffered prevented her closing her Eyes—. She then summoned her Maid and with the Assistance of the Housekeeper, every remedy that the receipt book or the head of the latter contained, was tried, but ineffectually; for though for a short time releived by them, the pain still returned. She was now obliged to give up the endeavour, and to reconcile herself not only to the pain of a Toothake, but to the loss of a Ball; and though she had with so much eagerness looked forward to the day of its arrival, had received such pleasure in the necessary preparations, and promised herself so much delight in it, Yet she was not so totally void of philosophy as many Girls of her age, might have been in her situation. She considered that there were Misfortunes of a much greater magnitude than the loss of a Ball, experienced every day by some part of Mortality, and that the time might come when She would herself look back with Wonder and perhaps with Envy on her having known no greater vexation. By such reflections as these, she soon reasoned herself into as much Resignation and Patience as the pain she suffered, would allow of, which after all was the greatest Misfortune of the two, and told the sad Story when she entered the Breakfast room, with tolerable Composure. Mrs Percival more greived for her toothake than her Disappointment, as she feared that it would not be possible to prevent her Dancing with a *Man* if she went, was eager to try everything that had already been applied to alleviate the pain, while at the same time She declared it was impossible for her to leave the House. Miss Stanley who joined to her concern for her Freind, felt a mixture of Dread lest her Mother's proposal that they should all remain at home, might be accepted, was very violent in her sorrow on the occasion, and though her apprehensions on the subject were soon quieted by Kitty's protesting that sooner than allow any one to stay with her, she would herself go, she continued to lament it with such unceasing vehemence as at last drove Kitty to her own room. Her Fears for herself being now entirely dissipated left her more than ever at leisure to pity and persecute her Freind who tho' safe when in her own room, was frequently removing from it to some other in hopes of being more free from pain, and then had no opportunity of escaping her—.

"To be sure, there never was anything so shocking, said Camilla; To come on such a day too! For one would not have minded it you know had it been at *any other* time. But it always is so. I never was at a Ball in my Life, but what something happened to prevent somebody from going! I wish there were no such things as Teeth in the World; they are nothing but plagues to one, and I dare say that People might easily invent something to eat with instead of them; Poor Thing! what pain you are in! I declare it is quite Shocking to look at you. But you w'ont have it out, will you? For Heaven's sake do'nt; for there is nothing I dread so much. I declare I had rather undergo the greatest Tortures in the World than have a tooth drawn. Well! how patiently you do bear it! how can you be so quiet? Lord, if I were in your place I should make such a fuss, there would be no bearing me. I should torment you to Death."

"So you do, as it is." thought Kitty.

"For my own part, Catherine said Mrs Percival I have not a doubt but that you caught this toothake by sitting so much in that Arbour, for it is always damp. I know it has ruined your Constitution entirely; and indeed I do not beleive it has been of much service to mine; I sate down in it last May to rest myself, and I have never been quite well since—. I shall order John to pull it all down I assure you."

"I know you will not do that Ma'am, said Kitty, as you must be convinced how unhappy it would make me."

"You talk very ridiculously Child; it is all whim and Nonsense. Why cannot you fancy this room an Arbour?"

"Had this room been built by Cecilia and Mary, I should have valued it equally Ma'am, for it is not merely the name of an Arbour, which charms me."

"Why indeed Mrs Percival, said Mrs Stanley, I must think that Catherine's affection for her Bower is the effect of a Sensibility that does her Credit. I love to see a Freindship between young Persons and always consider it as a sure mark of an amiable affectionate disposition. I have from Camilla's infancy taught her to think the same, and have taken great pains to introduce her to young people of her own age who were likely to be worthy of her regard. nothing forms the taste more than sensible and Elegant Letters—. Lady Halifax thinks just like me—. Camilla corresponds with her Daughters, and I believe I may venture to say that they are none of them *the worse* for it." These ideas were too modern to suit Mrs Percival who considered a correspondence between Girls as productive of no good, and as the frequent origin of imprudence and Error by the effect of pernicious advice and bad Example. She could not therefore refrain from saying that for her part, she had lived fifty Years in the world without having ever had a correspondent, and did not find herself at all the less respectable for it—. Mrs Stanley could say nothing in answer to this, but her Daughter who was less governed by Propriety said in her thoughtless way, "But who knows what you might have been Ma'am, if you *had* had a Correspondent; perhaps it would have made you quite a different Creature. I declare I would not be without those I have for all the World. It is the greatest delight of my Life, and you cannot think how much their Letters have formed my taste as Mama says, for I hear from them generally every week."

"You received a Letter from Augusta Barlow to day, did not you my Love? said her Mother—. She writes remarkably well I know."

"Oh! Yes Ma'am, the most delightful Letter you ever heard of. She sends me a long account of the new Regency walking dress Lady Susan has given her, and it is so beautiful that I am quite dieing with envy for it."

"Well, I am prodigiously happy to hear such pleasing news of my young freind; I have a high regard for Augusta, and most sincerely partake in the general Joy on the occasion. But does she say nothing else? it seemed to be a long Letter—Are they to be at Scarborough?"

"Oh! Lord, she never once mentions it, now I recollect it; and I entirely forgot to ask her when I wrote last. She says nothing indeed except about the Regency." "She *must* write well thought Kitty, to make a long Letter upon a Bonnet and Pelisse." She then left the room tired of listening to a conversation which tho' it might have diverted her had she been well, served only to fatigue and depress her, while in pain. Happy was it for *her*, when the hour of dressing came, for Camilla satisfied with being surrounded by her Mother and half the Maids in the House did not want her assistance, and was too agreably employed to want her Society. She remained therefore alone in the parlour, till joined by Mr Stanley and her Aunt, who however after a few enquiries, allowed her to continue undisturbed and began their usual conversation on Politics. This was a Subject on which they could never agree, for Mr Stanley who considered himself as perfectly qualified by his Seat in the House, to decide on it without hesitation, resolutely maintained that the Kingdom had not for ages been in so flourishing and prosperous a state, and Mrs Percival with equal warmth, tho' perhaps less argument, as vehemently asserted that the whole Nation would speedily be ruined, and everything as she expressed herself be at sixes and sevens. It was not however unamusing to Kitty to listen to the Dispute, especially as she began then to be more free from pain, and without taking any share in it herself, she found it very entertaining to observe the eagerness with which they both defended their opinions, and could not help thinking that Mr Stanley would not feel more disappointed if her Aunt's expectations were fulfilled, than her Aunt would be mortified by their failure. After waiting a considerable time Mrs Stanley and her daughter appeared, and Camilla in high Spirits, and perfect good humour with her own looks, was more violent than ever in her lamentations over her Freind as she practised her scotch Steps about the room—. At length they departed, and Kitty better able to amuse herself than she had been the whole Day before, wrote a long account of her Misfortunes to Mary Wynne. When her Letter was concluded she had an opportunity of witnessing the truth of that assertion which says that Sorrows are lightened by Communication, for her toothake was then so much releived that she began to entertain an idea of following her Freinds to Mr Dudley's. They had been gone an hour, and as every thing relative to her Dress was in complete readiness, She considered that in another hour since there was so little a way to go, She might be there—. They were gone in Mr Stanley's Carriage and therefore She might follow in her Aunt's. . As the plan seemed so very easy to be executed, and promising so much pleasure, it was after a few Minutes deliberation finally adopted, and running up stairs, She rang in great haste for her Maid. The Bustle and Hurry which then ensued for nearly an hour was at last happily concluded by her finding herself very well-dressed and in high Beauty. Anne was then dispatched in the same haste to order the Carriage, while her Mistress was putting on her gloves, and arranging the folds of her dress. In a few Minutes she heard the Carriage drive up to the Door, and tho' at first surprised at the expedition with which it had been got ready, she concluded after a little reflection that the Men had received some hint of her intentions beforehand, and was hastening out of the room, when Anne came running into it in the greatest hurry and agitation, exclaiming "Lord Ma'am! Here's a Gentleman in a Chaise and four come, and I cannot for my Life conceive who it is! I happened to be crossing the hall when the Carriage drove up, and I knew nobody would be in the way to let him in but Tom, and he looks so awkward you know Ma'am, now his hair is just done up, that I was not willing the gentleman should see him, and so I went to the door myself. And he is one of the handsomest young Men you would wish to see; I was almost ashamed of being seen in my Apron Ma'am, but however he is vastly handsome and did not seem to mind it at all.—And he asked me whether the Family were at home; and so I said everybody was gone out but you Ma'am, for I would not deny you because I was sure you would like to see him. And then he asked me whether Mr and Mrs Stanley were not here, and so I said Yes, and then—

"Good Heavens! said Kitty, what can all this mean! And who can it possibly be! Did you never see him before? And Did not he tell you his Name?"

"No Ma'am, he never said anything about it—So then I asked him to walk into the parlour, and he was prodigious agreable, and—"

"Whoever he is, said her Mistress, he has made a great impression upon you Nanny—But where did he come from? and what does he want here?"

"Oh! Ma'am, I was going to tell you, that I fancy his business is with You; for he asked me whether you were at leisure to see anybody, and desired I would give his Compliments to you, and say he should be very happy to wait on you— However I thought he had better not come up into your Dressing room, especially as everything is in such a litter, so I told him if he would be so obliging as to stay in the parlour, I would run up Stairs and tell you he was come, and I dared to say that you would wait upon *him*. Lord Ma'am, I'd lay anything that he is come to ask you to dance with him tonight, and has got his Chaise ready to take you to Mr Dudley's."

Kitty could not help laughing at this idea, and only wished it might be true, as it was very likely that she would be too late for any other partner—"But what in the name of wonder, can he have to say to me? Perhaps he is come to rob the house—. he comes in stile at least; and it will be some consolation for our losses to be robbed by a Gentleman in a Chaise and 4—. What Livery has his Servants?"

"Why that is the most wonderful thing about him Ma'am, for he has not a single servant with him, and came with hack horses; But he is as handsome as a Prince for all that, and has quite the look of one—. Do dear Ma'am, go down, for I am sure you will be delighted with him—"

"Well, I beleive I must go; but it is very odd! What can he have to say to me." Then giving one look at herself in the Glass, she walked with great impatience, tho' trembling all the while from not knowing what to expect, down Stairs, and after pausing a moment at the door to gather Courage for opening it, she resolutely entered the room.

The Stranger, whose appearance did not disgrace the account she had received of it from her Maid, rose up on her entrance, and laying aside the Newspaper he had been reading, advanced towards her with an air of the most perfect Ease and Vivacity, and said to her, "It is certainly a very awkward circumstance to be thus obliged to introduce myself, but I trust that the necessity of the case will plead my Excuse, and prevent your being prejudiced by it against me—. *Your* name, I need not ask Ma'am—. Miss Percival is too well known to me by description to need any information of that." Kitty, who had been expecting him to tell his own name, instead of hers, and who from having been little in company, and never before in such a situation, felt herself unable to ask it, tho' she had been planning her speech all the way down stairs, was so confused and distressed by this unexpected address that she could only return a slight curtesy to it and accepted the chair he reached her, without knowing what she did. The gentleman then continued. "You are, I dare say, surprised to see me returned from France so soon, and nothing indeed but business would have brought me to England; a very Melancholy affair has now occasioned it, and I was unwilling to leave it without paying my respects to the Family in Devonshire whom I have so long wished to be acquainted with—."

Kitty, who felt much more surprised at his supposing her *to be so*, than at seeing a person in England, whose having ever left it was perfectly unknown to her, still continued silent from Wonder and Perplexity, and her visitor still continued to talk. "You will suppose Madam that I was not the *less* desirous of waiting on you, from your having Mr and Mrs Stanley with You—. I hope they are well? And Mrs Percival how does *she* do?" Then without waiting for an answer he gaily added, "But my dear Miss Percival you are going out I am sure; and I am detaining you from your appointment. How can I ever expect to be forgiven for such injustice! Yet how can I, so circumstanced, forbear to offend! You seem dressed for a Ball? But this is the Land of gaiety I know; I have for many years been desirous of visiting it. You have Dances I suppose at least every week—But where are the rest of your party gone, and what kind Angel in compassion to me, has excluded *you* from it?"

"Perhaps Sir, said Kitty extremely confused by his manner of speaking to her, and highly displeased with the freedom of his Conversation towards one who had never seen him before and did not *now* know his name, perhaps Sir, you are acquainted with Mr and Mrs Stanley; and your business may be with *them*?"

"You do me too much honour Ma'am, replied he laughing, in supposing me to be acquainted with Mr and Mrs Stanley; I merely know them by sight; very distant relations; only my Father and Mother; Nothing more. I assure you."

"Gracious Heaven! said Kitty, are *you* Mr Stanley then?—I beg a thousand pardons—Though really upon recollection I do not know for what—for you never told me your name—"

"I beg your pardon—I made a very fine Speech when you entered the room, all about introducing myself; I assure you it was very great for *me*."

"The speech had certainly great Merit, said Kitty smiling; I thought so at the time; but since you never mentioned your name in it, as an *introductory one* it might have been better."

There was such an air of good humour and Gaiety in Stanley, that Kitty, tho' perhaps not authorized to address him with so much familiarity on so short an acquaintance, could not forbear indulging the natural Unreserve and Vivacity of her own Disposition, in speaking to him, as he spoke to her. She was intimately acquainted too with his Family who were her relations, and she chose to consider herself entitled by the connexion to forget how little a while they had known each other. "Mr and Mrs Stanley and your Sister are extremely well, said She, and will I dare say be very much surprised to see you—But I am sorry to hear that your return to England has been occasioned by any unpleasant circumstance."

"Oh! Do'nt talk of it, said he, it is a most confounded shocking affair, and makes me miserable to think of it; But where are my Father and Mother, and your Aunt gone? Oh! Do you know that I met the prettiest little waiting maid in the World, when I came here; she let me into the house; I took her for you at first."

"You did me a great deal of honour, and give me more credit for good nature than I deserve, for I *never* go to the door when any one comes."

"Nay do not be angry; I mean no offence. But tell me, where are you going to so smart? Your carriage is just coming round."

"I am going to a Dance at a Neighbour's, where your Family and my Aunt are already gone."

"Gone, without you! what's the meaning of *that?* But I suppose you are like myself, rather long in dressing."

"I must have been so indeed, if that were the case for they have been gone nearly these two hours; The reason however was not what you suppose—I was prevented going by a pain—"

"By a pain! interrupted Stanley, Oh! heavens, that is dreadful indeed! No Matter where the pain was. But my dear Miss Percival, what do you say to my accompanying you? And suppose you were to dance with me too? *I* think it would be very pleasant."

"I can have no objection to either I am sure, said Kitty laughing to find how near the truth her Maid's conjecture had been; on the contrary I shall be highly honoured by both, and I can answer for Your being extremely welcome to the Family who give the Ball."

"Oh! hang them; who cares for that; they cannot turn me out of the house. But I am afraid I shall cut a sad figure among all your Devonshire Beaux in this dusty, travelling apparel, and I have not wherewithal to change it. You can procure me some powder perhaps, and I must get a pair of Shoes from one of the Men, for I was in such a devil of a hurry to leave Lyons that I had not time to have anything pack'd up but some linen." Kitty very readily undertook to procure for him everything he wanted, and telling the footman to shew him into Mr Stanley's dressing room, gave Nanny orders to send in some powder and pomatum, which orders Nanny chose to execute in person. As Stanley's preparations in dressing were confined to such very trifling articles, Kitty of course expected him in about ten minutes; but she found that it had not been merely a boast of vanity in saying that he was dilatory in that respect, as he kept her waiting for him above half an hour, so that the Clock had struck ten before he entered the room and the rest of the party had gone by eight.

"Well, said he as he came in, have not I been very quick? I never hurried so much in my Life before."

"In that case you certainly have, replied Kitty, for all Merit you know is comparative."

"Oh! I knew you would be delighted with me for making so much haste—. But come, the Carriage is ready; so, do not keep

CATHARINE, OR THE BOWER

me waiting." And so saying he took her by the hand, and led her out of the room. "Why, my dear Cousin, said he when they were seated, this will be a most agreable surprize to every body to see you enter the room with such a smart Young Fellow as I am—I hope your Aunt w'ont be alarmed."

"To tell you the truth, replied Kitty, I think the best way to prevent it, will be to send for her, or your Mother before we go into the room, especially as you are a perfect stranger, and must of course be introduced to Mr and Mrs Dudley—"

"Oh! Nonsense, said he; I did not expect *you* to stand upon such Ceremony; Our acquaintance with each other renders all such Prudery, ridiculous; Besides, if we go in together, we shall be the whole talk of the Country—"

"To *me* replied Kitty, that would certainly be a most powerful inducement; but I scarcely know whether my Aunt would consider it as such—. Women at her time of life, have odd ideas of propriety you know."

"Which is the very thing that you ought to break them of; and why should you object to entering a room with me where all our relations are, when you have done me the honour to admit me without any chaprone into your Carriage? Do not you think your Aunt will be as much offended with you for one, as for the other of these mighty crimes."

"Why really said Catherine, I do not know but that she may; however, it is no reason that I should offend against Decorum a second time, because I have already done it once."

"On the contrary, that is the very reason which makes it impossible for you to prevent it, since you cannot offend for the *first time* again."

"You are very ridiculous, said she laughing, but I am afraid your arguments divert me too much to convince me."

"At least they will convince you that I am very agreable, which after all, is the happiest conviction for me, and as to the affair of Propriety we will let that rest till we arrive at our Journey's end—. This is a monthly Ball I suppose. Nothing but Dancing here—."

"I thought I had told you that it was given by a Mr Dudley—"

"Oh! aye so you did; but why should not Mr Dudley give one every month? By the bye who *is that* Man? Every body gives Balls now I think; I beleive I must give one myself soon—. Well, but how do you like my Father and Mother? And poor little Camilla too, has not she plagued you to death with the Halifaxes?" Here the Carriage fortunately stopped at Mr Dudley's, and Stanley was too much engaged in handing her out of it, to wait for an answer, or to remember that what he had said required one. They entered the small vestibule which Mr Dudley had raised to the Dignity of a Hall, and Kitty immediately desired the footman who was leading the way upstairs, to inform either Mrs Peterson, or Mrs Stanley of her arrival, and beg them to come to her, but Stanley unused to any contradiction and impatient to be amongst them, would neither allow her to wait, or listen to what she said, and forcibly seizing her arm within his, overpowered her voice with the rapidity of his own, and Kitty half angry, and half laughing was obliged to go with him up stairs, and could even with difficulty prevail on him to relinquish her hand before they entered the room. Mrs Percival was at that very moment engaged in conversation with a Lady at the upper end of the room, to whom she had been giving a long account of her Neice's unlucky disappointment, and the dreadful pain that she had with so much fortitude, endured the whole Day—"I left her however, said She, thank heaven!, a little better, and I hope she has been able to amuse herself with a book, poor thing! for she must otherwise be very dull. She is probably in bed by this time, which while she is so poorly, is the best place for her you know Ma'am." The Lady was going to give her assent to this opinion, when the Noise of voices on the stairs, and the footman's opening the door as if for the entrance of Company, attracted the attention of every body in the room; and as it was in one of those Intervals between the Dances when every one seemed glad to sit down, Mrs Peterson had a most unfortunate opportunity of seeing her Neice whom she had supposed in bed, or amusing herself as the height of gaity with a book, enter the room most elegantly dressed, with a smile on her Countenance, and a glow of mingled Chearfulness and Confusion on her Cheeks, attended by a young Man uncommonly handsome, and who without any of her Confusion, appeared to have all her vivacity. Mrs Percival, colouring with anger and Astonishment, rose from her Seat, and Kitty walked eagerly towards her, impatient to account for what she saw appeared wonderful to every body, and extremely offensive to *her*, while Camilla on seeing her Brother ran instantly towards him, and very soon explained who he was by her words and her actions. Mr Stanley, who so fondly doated on his Son, that the pleasure of seeing him again after an absence of three Months prevented his feeling for the time any anger against him for returning to England without his knowledge, received him with equal surprise and delight; and soon comprehending the cause of his Journey, forbore any further conversation with him, as he was eager to see his Mother, and it was necessary that he should be introduced to Mr Dudley's family. This introduction to any one but Stanley would have been highly unpleasant, for they considered their dignity injured by his coming uninvited to their house, and received him with more than their usual haughtiness; But Stanley who with a vivacity of temper seldom subdued, and a contempt of censure not to be overcome, possessed an opinion of his own Consequence, and a perseverance in his own schemes which were not to be damped by the conduct of others, appeared not to perceive it. The Civilities therefore which they coldly offered, he received with a gaiety and ease peculiar to himself, and then attended by his Father and Sister walked into another room where his Mother was playing at Cards, to experience another Meeting, and undergo a repetition of pleasure, Surprise, and Explanations. While these were passing, Camilla eager to communicate all she felt to some one who would attend to her, returned to Catherine, and seating herself by her, immediately began—"Well, did you ever know anything so delightful as this? But it always is so; I never go to a Ball in my Life but what something or other happens unexpectedly that is quite charming!"

"A Ball replied Kitty, seems to be a most eventful thing to You—".

"Oh! Lord, it is indeed—But only think of my brother's returning so suddenly—And how shocking a thing it is that has brought him over! I never heard anything so dreadful—!"

"What is it pray that has occasioned his leaving France? I am sorry to find that it is a melancholy event."

"Oh! it is beyond anything you can conceive! His favourite Hunter who was turned out in the park on his going abroad, somehow or other fell ill—No, I beleive it was an accident, but however it was something or other, or else it was something else, and so they sent an Express immediately to Lyons where my Brother was, for they knew that he valued this Mare more than anything else in the World besides; and so my Brother set off directly for England, and without packing up another Coat; I am quite angry with him about it; it was so shocking you know to come away without a change of Cloathes—"

"Why indeed said Kitty, it seems to have been a very shocking affair from beginning to end."

"Oh! it is beyond anything You can conceive! I would rather have had *anything* happen than that he should have lossed that mare."

"Except his coming away without an other coat."

"Oh! yes, that has vexed me more than you can imagine—. Well, and so Edward got to Brampton just as the poor Thing was dead,—but as he could not bear to remain there *then*, he came off directly to Chetwynde on purpose to see us—. I hope he may not go abroad again."

"Do you think he will not?"

"Oh! dear, to be sure he must, but I wish he may not with all my heart—. You cannot think how fond I am of him! By the bye are not you in love with him yourself?"

"To be sure I am replied Kitty laughing, I am in love with every handsome Man I see."

"That is just like me—*I* am always in love with every handsome Man in the World."

"There you outdo me replied Catherine for I am only in love with those I *do* see." Mrs Percival who was sitting on the other side of her, and who began now to distinguish the words, *Love* and *handsome Man*, turned hastily towards them, and said "What are you talking of Catherine?" To which Catherine immediately answered with the simple artifice of a Child, "Nothing Ma'am." She had already

CATHARINE, OR THE BOWER

received a very severe lecture from her Aunt on the imprudence of her behaviour during the whole evening; She blamed her for coming to the Ball, for coming in the same Carriage with Edward Stanley, and still more for entering the room with him. For the last-mentioned offence Catherine knew not what apology to give, and tho' she longed in answer to the second to say that she had not thought it would be civil to make Mr Stanley *walk*, she dared not so to trifle with her aunt, who would have been but the more offended by it. The first accusation however she considered as very unreasonable, as she thought herself perfectly justified in coming. This conversation continued till Edward Stanley entering the room came instantly towards her, and telling her that every one waited for *her* to begin the next Dance led her to the top of the room, for Kitty impatient to escape from so unpleasant a Companion, without the least hesitation, or one civil scruple at being so distinguished, immediately gave him her hand, and joyfully left her Seat. This Conduct however was highly resented by several young Ladies present, and among the rest by Miss Stanley whose regard for her brother tho' *excessive*, and whose affection for Kitty tho' *prodigious*, were not proof against such an injury to her importance and her peace. Edward had however only consulted his own inclinations in desiring Miss Peterson to begin the Dance, nor had he any reason to know that it was either wished or expected by anyone else in the Party. As an heiress she was certainly of consequence, but her Birth gave her no other claim to it, for her Father had been a Merchant. It was this very circumstance which rendered this unfortunate affair so offensive to Camilla, for tho' she would sometimes boast in the pride of her heart, and her eagerness to be admired that she did not know who her grandfather had been, and was as ignorant of everything relative to Genealogy as to Astronomy, (and she might have added, Geography) yet she was really proud of her family and Connexions, and easily offended if they were treated with Neglect. "I should not have minded it, said she to her Mother, if she had been *anybody* else's daughter; but to see her pretend to be above *me*, when her Father was only a tradesman, is too bad! It is such an affront to our whole Family! I declare I think Papa ought to interfere in it, but he never cares about anything but Politics. If I were Mr Pitt or the Lord Chancellor, he would take care I should not be insulted, but he never thinks about *me*; And it is so provoking that *Edward* should let her stand there. I wish with all my heart that he had never come to England! I hope she may fall down and break her neck, or sprain her Ancle." Mrs Stanley perfectly agreed with her daughter concerning the affair, and tho' with less violence, expressed almost equal resentment at the indignity. Kitty in the meantime remained insensible of having given any one Offence, and therefore unable either to offer an apology, or make a reparation; her whole attention was occupied by the happiness she enjoyed in dancing with the most elegant young Man in the room, and every one else was equally unregarded. The Evening indeed to *her*, passed off delightfully; he was her partner during the greatest part of it, and the united attractions that he possessed of Person, Address and vivacity, had easily gained that preference from Kitty which they seldom fail of obtaining from every one. She was too happy to care either for her Aunt's illhumour which she could not help remarking, or for the Alteration in Camilla's behaviour which forced itself at last on her observation. Her Spirits were elevated above the influence of Displeasure in any one, and she was equally indifferent as to the Cause of Camilla's, or the continuance of her Aunt's. Though Mr Stanley could never be really offended by any imprudence or folly in his Son that had given him the pleasure of seeing him, he was yet perfectly convinced that Edward ought not to remain in England, and was resolved to hasten his leaving it as soon as possible; but when he talked to Edward about it, he found him much less disposed towards returning to France, than to accompany them in their projected tour, which he assured his Father would be infinitely more pleasant to him, and that as to the affair of travelling he considered it of no importance, and what might be pursued at any little odd time, when he had nothing better to do. He advanced these objections in a manner which plainly shewed that he had scarcely a doubt of their being complied with, and appeared to consider his father's arguments in opposition to them, as merely given with a veiw to keep up his authority, and such as he should find little difficulty in combating. He concluded at last by saying, as the chaise in which they returned together from Mr Dudley's reached Mrs Percivals, "Well Sir, we will settle this point some other time, and fortunately it is of so little consequence, that an immediate discussion of it is unnecessary." He then got out of the chaise and entered the house without waiting for his Father's reply. It was not till their return that Kitty could account for that coldness in Camilla's behaviour to her, which had been so pointed as to render it impossible to be entirely unnoticed. When however they were seated in the Coach with the two other Ladies, Miss Stanley's indignation was no longer to be suppressed from breaking out into words, and found the following vent.

"Well, I must say *this*, that I never was at a stupider Ball in my Life! But it always is so; I am always disappointed in them for some reason or other. I wish there were no such things."

"I am sorry Miss Stanley, said Mrs Percival drawing herself up, that you have not been amused; every thing was meant for the best I am sure, and it is a poor encouragement for your Mama to take you to another if you are so hard to be satisfied."

"I do not know what you mean Ma'am about Mama's *taking* me to another. You know I am come out."

"Oh! dear Mrs Percival, said Mrs Stanley, you must not beleive every thing that my lively Camilla says, for her Spirits are prodigiously high sometimes, and she frequently speaks without thinking. I am sure it is impossible for *any one* to have been at a more elegant or agreable dance, and so she wishes to express herself I am certain."

"To be sure I do, said Camilla very sulkily, only I must say that it is not very pleasant to have any body behave so rude to one as to be quite shocking! I am sure I am not at all offended, and should not care if all the World were to stand above me, but still it is extremely abominable, and what I cannot put up with. It is not that I mind it in the least, for I had just as soon stand at the bottom as at the top all night long, if it was not so very disagreeable—. But to have a person come in the middle of the Evening and take everybody's place is what I am not used to, and tho' I do not care a pin about it myself, I assure you I shall not easily forgive or forget it."

This speech which perfectly explained the whole affair to Kitty, was shortly followed on her side by a very submissive apology, for she had too much good Sense to be proud of her family, and too much good Nature to live at variance with any one. The Excuses she made, were delivered with so much real concern for the Offence, and such unaffected Sweetness, that it was almost impossible for Camilla to retain that anger which had occasioned them; She felt indeed most highly gratified to find that no insult had been intended and that Catherine was very far from forgetting the difference in their birth for which she could *now* only pity her, and her good humour being restored with the same Ease in which it had been affected, she spoke with the highest delight of the Evening, and declared that she had never before been at so pleasant a Ball. The same endeavours that had procured the forgiveness of Miss Stanley ensured to her the cordiality of her Mother, and nothing was wanting but Mrs P's good humour to render the happiness of the others complete; but She, offended with Camilla for her affected Superiority, Still more so with her brother for coming to Chetwynde, and dissatisfied with the whole Evening, continued silent and Gloomy and was a restraint on the vivacity of her Companions. She eagerly seized the very first opportunity which the next Morning offered to her of speaking to Mr Stanley on the subject of his Son's return, and after having expressed her opinion of its being a very silly affair that he came at all, concluded with desiring him to inform Mr Edward Stanley that it was a rule with her never to admit a young Man into her house as a visitor for any length of time.

"I do not speak Sir, she continued, out of any disrespect to You, but I could not answer it to myself to allow of his stay; there is no knowing what might be the consequence of it, if he were to continue here, for girls nowadays will always give a handsome young Man the preference before any other, tho' for why, I never could discover, for what after all is Youth and Beauty?—It is but a poor substitute for real worth and Merit; Beleive me Cousin that, what ever people may say to the contrary, there is certainly nothing like Virtue for making us what we ought to be, and as to a young Man's, being Young and handsome and having an agreable person, it is nothing at all to the purpose for he had much better be respectable. I always *did* think so, and I always *shall*, and therefore you will oblige me very much by desiring your Son to leave Chetwynde, or I cannot be answerable for what may happen between him and my Neice. You will be surprised to hear *me* say it, she continued, lowering her voice, but truth will out, and I must own that Kitty is one of the most impudent Girls that ever existed. I assure you Sir, that I have seen her sit and laugh and whisper with a young Man whom she has not seen above half a dozen times. Her behaviour indeed is scandalous, and therefore I beg you will send your Son away immediately, or everything will be at sixes and sevens." Mr Stanley who from one part of her Speech had scarcely known to what length her insinuations of Kitty's impudence were meant to extend, now endeavoured to quiet her fears on the occasion, by assuring her, that on every account he meant to allow only of his Son's continuing that day with them, and that she might depend on his being more earnest in the affair from a wish of obliging her. He added also that he knew Edward to be very desirous himself of returning to France, as he wisely considered all time lost that did not forward the plans in which he was at present engaged, tho' he was but too well convinced of the contrary himself. His assurance in some degree quieted Mrs P, and left her tolerably releived of her Cares and Alarms, and better disposed to behave with civility towards his Son during the short remainder of his Stay at Chetwynde. Mr Stanley went immediately to Edward, to whom he repeated the Conversation that had passed between Mrs P and himself, and strongly pointed out the necessity of his leaving Chetwynde the next day, since his word was already engaged for it. His son however appeared struck only by the ridiculous apprehensions of Mrs Peterson; and highly delighted at having occasioned them himself, seemed engrossed alone in thinking how he might encrease them, without attending to any other part of his Father's Conversation. Mr Stanley could get no determinate Answer from him, and tho' he still hoped for the best, they parted almost in anger on his side.

His Son though by no means disposed to marry, or any otherwise attached to Miss Percival than as a good-natured lively Girl who seemed pleased with him, took infinite pleasure in alarming the jealous fears of her Aunt by his attentions to her, without considering what effect they might have on the Lady herself. He would always sit by her when she was in the room, appeared dissatisfied if she left it, and was the first to enquire whether she meant soon to return. He was delighted with her Drawings, and enchanted with her performance on the Harpsichord; Everything that she said, appeared to interest him; his Conversation was addressed to her alone, and she seemed to be the sole object of his attention. That such efforts should succeed with one so tremblingly alive to every alarm of the kind as Mrs Percival, is by no means unnatural, and that they should have equal influence with her Neice whose imagination was lively, and whose Disposition romantic, who was already extremely pleased with him, and of course desirous that he might be so with her, is as little to be wondered at. Every moment as it added to the conviction of his liking her, made him still more pleasing, and strengthened in her Mind a wish of knowing him better. As for Mrs Percival, she was in tortures the whole Day; Nothing that she had ever felt before on a similar occasion was to be compared to the sensations which then distracted her; her fears had never been so strongly, or indeed so reasonably excited.—Her dislike of Stanly, her anger at her Neice, her impatience to have them separated conquered every idea of propriety and Goodbreeding, and though he had never mentioned any intention of leaving them the next day, she could not help asking him after Dinner, in her eagerness to have him gone, at what time he meant to set out.

"Oh! Ma'am, replied he, if I am off by twelve at night, you may think yourself lucky; and if I am not, you can only blame yourself for having left so much as the *hour* of my departure to my own disposal." Mrs Percival coloured very highly at this speech, and without addressing herself to any one in particular, immediately began a long harangue on the shocking behaviour of modern

Young Men, and the wonderful Alteration that had taken place in them, since her time, which she illustrated with many instructive anecdotes of the Decorum and Modesty which had marked the Characters of those whom she had known, when she had been young. This however did not prevent his walking in the Garden with her Neice, without any other companion for nearly an hour in the course of the Evening. They had left the room for that purpose with Camilla at a time when Mrs Peterson had been out of it, nor was it for some time after her return to it, that she could discover where they were. Camilla had taken two or three turns with them in the walk which led to the Arbour, but soon growing tired of listening to a Conversation in which she was seldom invited to join, and from its turning occasionally on Books, very little able to do it, she left them together in the arbour, to wander alone to some other part of the Garden, to eat the fruit, and examine Mrs Peterson's Greenhouse. Her absence was so far from being regretted, that it was scarcely noticed by them, and they continued conversing together on almost every subject, for Stanley seldom dwelt long on any, and had something to say on all, till they were interrupted by her Aunt.

Kitty was by this time perfectly convinced that both in Natural Abilities, and acquired information, Edward Stanley was infinitely superior to his Sister. Her desire of knowing that he was so, had induced her to take every opportunity of turning the Conversation on History and they were very soon engaged in an historical dispute, for which no one was more calculated than Stanley who was so far from being really of any party, that he had scarcely a fixed opinion on the Subject. He could therefore always take either side, and always argue with temper. In his indifference on all such topics he was very unlike his Companion, whose judgement being guided by her feelings which were eager and warm, was easily decided, and though it was not always infallible, she defended it with a Spirit and Enthouisasm which marked her own reliance on it. They had continued therefore for sometime conversing in this manner on the character of Richard the 3^d, which he was warmly defending when he suddenly seized hold of her hand, and exclaiming with great emotion, "Upon my honour you are entirely mistaken," pressed it passionately to his lips, and ran out of the arbour. Astonished at this behaviour, for which she was wholly unable to account, she continued for a few Moments motionless on the Seat where he had left her, and was then on the point of following him up the narrow walk through which he had passed, when on looking up the one that lay immediately before the arbour, she saw her Aunt walking towards her with more than her usual quickness. This explained at once the reason of his leaving her, but his leaving her in such Manner was rendered still more inexplicable by it. She felt a considerable degree of confusion at having been seen by her in such a place with Edward, and at having that part of his conduct, for which she could not herself account, witnessed by one to whom all gallantry was odious. She remained therefore confused distressed and irresolute, and suffered her Aunt to approach her, without leaving the Arbour. Mrs Percival's looks were by no means calculated to animate the spirits of her Neice, who in silence awaited her accusation, and in silence meditated her Defence. After a few Moments suspence, for Mrs Peterson was too much fatigued to speak immediately, she began with great Anger and Asperity, the following harangue. "Well; *this* is beyond anything I could have supposed. *Profligate* as I *knew* you to be, I was not prepared for such a sight. This is beyond any thing you ever did *before*; beyond any thing I ever heard of in my Life! Such Impudence, I never witnessed before in such a Girl! And this is the reward for all the cares I have taken in your Education; for all my troubles and Anxieties, and Heaven knows how many they have been! All I wished for, was to breed you up virtuously; I never wanted you to play upon the Harpsichord, or draw better than any one else; but I had hoped to see you respectable and good; to see you able and willing to give an example of Modesty and Virtue to the Young people here abouts. I bought you Blair's Sermons, and Coelebs in Search of a Wife, I gave you the key to my own Library, and borrowed a great many good books of my Neighbours for you, all to this purpose. But I might have spared myself the trouble—Oh! Catherine, you are an abandoned Creature, and I do not know what will become of you. I am glad however, she continued softening into some degree of Mildness, to see that you have some shame for what you have done, and if you are really sorry for it, and your future life is a life of penitence and reformation perhaps you may be forgiven. But I plainly see that every thing is going to sixes and sevens and all order will soon be at an end throughout the Kingdom."

"Not however Ma'am the sooner, I hope, from any conduct of mine, said Catherine in a tone of great humility, for upon my honour I have done nothing this evening that can contribute to overthrow the establishment of the kingdom."

"You are mistaken Child, replied she; the welfare of every Nation depends upon the virtue of it's individuals, and any one who offends in so gross a manner against decorum and propriety, is certainly hastening it's ruin. You have been giving a bad example to the World, and the World is but too well disposed to receive such."

"Pardon me Madam, said her Neice; but I *can* have given an Example only to *You*, for You alone have seen the offence. Upon my word however, there is no danger to fear from what I have done; Mr Stanley's behaviour has given me as much surprise, as it has done to You, and I can only suppose that it was the effect of his high spirits, authorized in his opinion by our relationship. But do you consider Madam that it is growing very late? Indeed You had better return to the house." This speech as she well knew, would be unanswerable with her Aunt, who instantly rose, and hurried away under so many apprehensions for her health, as banished for the time all anxiety about her Neice, who walked quietly by her side, revolving within her own Mind the occurrence that had given her Aunt so much alarm. "I am astonished at my own imprudence, said Mrs Percival; How could I be so forgetful as to sit down out of doors at such a time of night? I shall certainly have a return of my rheumatism after it—I begin to feel very chill already. I must have caught a dreadful cold by this time—I am sure of being lain-up all the winter after it—" Then reckoning with her fingers, "Let me see; This is July; the cold Weather will soon be coming in—August—September—October—November—December—January—February—March—April—Very likely

I may not be tolerable again before May. I must and will have that arbour pulled down—it will be the death of me; who knows *now*, but what I may never recover—Such things *have* happened—My particular freind Miss Sarah Hutchinson's death was occasioned by nothing more—She staid out late one Evening in April, and got wet through for it rained very hard, and never changed her Cloathes when she came home—It is unknown how many people have died in consequence of catching Cold! I do not beleive there is a disorder in the World except the Smallpox which does not spring from it." It was in vain that Kitty endeavoured to convince her that her fears on the occasion were groundless; that it was not yet late enough to catch cold, and that even if it were, she might hope to escape any other complaint, and to recover in less than ten Months. Mrs Percival only replied that she hoped she knew more of Ill health than to be convinced in such a point by a Girl who had always been perfectly well, and hurried up stairs leaving Kitty to make her apologies to Mr and Mrs Stanley for going to bed—. Tho' Mrs Percival seemed perfectly satisfied with the goodness of the Apology herself, Yet Kitty felt somewhat embarrassed to find that the only one she could offer to their Visitors was that her Aunt had *perhaps* caught cold, for Mrs Peterson charged her to make light of it, for fear of alarming them. Mr and Mrs Stanley however who well knew that their Cousin was easily terrified on that Score, received the account of it with very little surprise, and all proper concern. Edward and his Sister soon came in, and Kitty had no difficulty in gaining an explanation of his Conduct from him, for he was too warm on the subject himself, and too eager to learn its success, to refrain from making immediate Enquiries about it; and She could not help feeling both surprised and offended at the ease and Indifference with which he owned that all his intentions had been to frighten her Aunt by pretending an affection for *her*; a design so very incompatible with that partiality which she had at one time been almost convinced of his feeling for her. It is true that she had not yet seen enough of him to be actually in love with him, yet she felt greatly disappointed that so handsome, so elegant, so lively a young Man should be so perfectly free from any such Sentiment as to make it his principal Sport. There was a Novelty in his character which to *her* was extremely pleasing; his person was uncommonly fine, his Spirits and Vivacity suited to her own, and his Manners at once so animated and insinuating, that she thought it must be impossible for him to be otherwise than amiable, and was ready to give him Credit for being perfectly so. He knew the powers of them himself; to them he had often been endebted for his father's forgiveness of faults which had he been awkward and inelegant would have appeared very serious; to them, even more than to his person or his fortune, he owed the regard which almost every one was disposed to feel for him, and which Young Women in particular were inclined to entertain. Their influence was acknowledged on the present occasion by Kitty, whose Anger they entirely dispelled, and whose Chearfulness they had power not only to restore, but to raise—. The Evening passed off as agreably as the one that had preceded it; they continued talking to each other, during the cheif part of it, And such was the power of his Address, and the Brilliancy of his Eyes, that when they parted for the Night, tho' Catherine had but a few hours before totally given up the idea, yet she felt almost convinced again that he was really in love with her. She reflected on their past Conversation, and tho' it had been on various and indifferent subjects, and she could not exactly recollect any Speech on his side expressive of such a partiality, she was still however nearly certain of it's being so; But fearful of being vain enough to suppose such a thing without sufficient reason, she resolved to suspend her final determination on it, till the next day, and more especially till their parting which she thought would infallibly explain his regard if any he had—. The more she had seen of him, the more inclined was she to like him, and the more desirous that he should like *her*. She was convinced of his being naturally very clever and very well disposed, and that his thoughtlessness and negligence, which tho' they appeared to *her* as very becoming in *him*, she was aware would by many people be considered as defects in his Character, merely proceeded from a vivacity always pleasing in Young Men, and were far from testifying a weak or vacant Understanding. Having settled this point within herself, and being perfectly convinced by her own arguments of it's truth, she went to bed in high Spirits, determined to study his Character, and watch his Behaviour still more the next day. She got up with the same good resolutions and would probably have put them in execution, had not Anne informed her as soon as she entered the room that Mr Edward Stanley was already gone. At first she refused to credit the information, but when her Maid assured her that he had ordered a Carriage the evening before to be there at seven o'clock in the Morning and that she herself had actually seen him depart in it a little after eight, she could no longer deny her beleif to it. "And this, thought she to herself blushing with anger at her own folly, this is the affection for me of which I was so certain. Oh! what a silly Thing is Woman! How vain, how unreasonable! To suppose that a young Man would be seriously attached in the course of four and twenty hours, to a Girl who has nothing to recommend her but a good pair of eyes! And he is really gone! Gone perhaps without bestowing a thought on me! Oh! why was not I up by eight o'clock? But it is a proper punishment for my Lazyness and Folly, and I am heartily glad of it. I deserve it all, and ten times more for such insufferable vanity. It will at least be of service to me in that respect; it will teach me in future *not* to think Every Body is in love with me. Yet I *should* like to have seen him before he went, for perhaps it may be many Years before we meet again. By his Manner of leaving us however, he seems to have been perfectly indifferent about it. How very odd, that he should go without giving us notice of it, or taking leave of any one! But it is just like a Young Man, governed by the whim of the Moment, or actuated merely by the love of doing anything oddly! Unaccountable Beings indeed! And Young Women are equally ridiculous! I shall soon begin to think like my Aunt that everything is going to Sixes and Sevens, and that the whole race of Mankind are degenerating." She was just dressed, and on the point of leaving her room to make her personal enquiries after Mrs Peterson, when Miss Stanley knocked at her door, and on her being admitted began in her Usual Strain a long harangue upon her Father's being so shocking as to make Edward go at all, and upon Edward's being so horrid as to leave them at such an hour in the Morning. "You have no idea, said she, how surprised I was, when he came into my Room to bid me good bye—"

"Have you seen him then, this Morning?" said Kitty.

"Oh Yes! And I was so sleepy that I could not open my eyes. And so he said, Camilla, goodbye to you for I am going away—. I have not time to take leave of any body else, and I dare not trust myself to see Kitty, for then you know I should never get away—"

"Nonsense, said Kitty; he did not say that, or he was in joke if he did."

"Oh! no I assure You he was as much in earnest as he ever was in his life; he was too much out of Spirits to joke *then*. And he desired me when we all met at Breakfast to give his Compts. to your Aunt, and his Love to You, for you was a nice Girl he said, and he only wished it were in his power to be more with You. You were just the Girl to suit him, because you were so lively and good-natured, and he wished with all his heart that you might not be married before he came back, for there was nothing he liked better than being here. Oh! You have no idea what fine things he said about You, till at last I fell a sleep and he went away. But he certainly is in love with you—I am sure he is—I have thought so a great while I assure You."

"How can You be so ridiculous? said Kitty smiling with pleasure; I do not beleive him to be so easily affected. But he *did* desire his Love to me then? And wished I might not be married before his return? And said I was a nice Girl, did he?"

"Oh! dear, Yes, And I assure You it is the greatest praise in his opinion, that he can bestow on any body; I can hardly ever persuade him to call *me* one, tho' I beg him sometimes for an hour together."

"And do You really think that he was sorry to go?"

"Oh! You can have no idea how wretched it made him. He would not have gone this Month, if my Father had not insisted on it; Edward told me so himself yesterday. He said that he wished with all his heart he had never promised to go abroad, for that he repented it more and more every day; that it interfered with all his other schemes, and that since Papa had spoke to him about it, he was more unwilling to leave Chetwynde than ever."

"Did he really say all this? And why would your father insist upon his going? 'His leaving England interfered with all his other plans, and his Conversation with Mr Stanley had made him still more averse to it.' What can this Mean?"

"Why that he is excessively in love with You to be sure; what other plans can he have? And I suppose my father said that if he had not been going abroad, he should have wished him to marry you immediately.—But I must go and see your Aunt's plants—There is one of them that I quite doat on— and two or three more besides—"

"Can Camilla's explanation be true? said Catherine to herself, when her freind had left the room. And after all my doubts and Uncertainties, can Stanley really be averse to leaving England for *my sake* only? 'His plans interrupted.' And what indeed can his plans be, but towards Marriage? Yet *so soon* to be in love with me!—But it is the effect perhaps only of a warmth of heart which to *me* is the highest recommendation in any one. A Heart disposed to love—And such under the appearance of so much Gaiety and Inattention, is Stanley's! Oh! how much does it endear him to me! But he is gone—Gone perhaps for Years—Obliged to tear himself from what he most loves, his happiness is sacrificed to the vanity of his Father! In what anguish he must have left the house! Unable to see me, or to bid me adeiu, while I, senseless wretch, was daring to sleep. This, then explains his leaving us at such a time of day—. He could not trust himself to see me—. Charming Young Man! How much must you have suffered! I *knew* that it was impossible for one so elegant, and so well bred, to leave any Family in such a Manner, but for a Motive like this unanswerable." Satisfied, beyond the power of Change, of this, She went in high spirits to her Aunt's apartment, without giving a Moment's recollection on the vanity of Young Women, or the unaccountable conduct of Young Men.——

GENERAL NOTES

The items in this volume follow the arrangement of Jane Austen's three notebooks, in which there are later revisions and corrections by Jane Austen (and other family members). She gave specific dates for several works, and these have been included here.

DEDICATIONS

These are to Jane Austen's family and freinds. Jane's elder sister **Cassandra** is the dedicatee of 'The Beautiful Cassandra', 'The History of England' and 'Catharine, or the Bower'. The epistolary 'Amelia Webster' is dedicated to Jane's mother **Cassandra Leigh Austen**, 'The Visit' to her eldest brother **James** and 'The three sisters' to brother **Edward**, already by this time adopted by the wealthy Knights of Godmersham in Kent. **Fanny**, Edward's eldest daughter, is the dedicatee of 'The female philosopher'.

Francis, Jane's fifth brother, served as midshipman on HMS *Perseverance* mentioned in the dedications to him of 'Jack and Alice' and 'The adventures of Mr Harley'. Her fourth brother **Henry**, a student at Oxford while Jane was writing her childhood works, is the dedicatee of 'Lesley Castle', while the naming of 'Henry and Eliza' nods to Henry and their cousin (later his wife) **Eliza de Feuillide**, to whom 'Love and Freindship' in Volume the Second is dedicated. **Jane Cooper**, another of Jane Austen's cousins, is the dedicatee both of 'Henry and Eliza' and of 'A Collection of Letters'.

Some dedications are wildly inappropriate, such as 'Sir William Mountague' and 'Memoirs of Mr Clifford' to Jane's very young brother **Charles** and 'A fragment' to her baby niece **Anna** (Jane Anna Elizabeth), daughter of brother James.

GENERAL NOTES

Outside the family the Lloyd sisters, lifelong freinds of the Austen family, receive dedications: **Martha Lloyd** of 'Frederic and Elfrida' and **Mary Lloyd** of 'Evelyn'.

At least one detail in a dedication must have been added later: the hundred guineas supposedly offered by brother Henry for 'Lesley Castle'. Henry became a banker long after the tale was written.

In the dedication to 'Catharine, or the Bower', Jane Austen makes comically exaggerated (though prescient) claims for the popularity of her work: it will go through sixty editions.

CARRIAGES

Vehicles varied widely in cost, speed and class of travellers they attracted as owners and passengers. The private **chaise** was a light, closed, often family carriage drawn by two or four horses and holding two or three passengers; the grand **landau** with folding top held two couples facing each other, the preferred seats looking forwards. The fashionable **landaulette** carried between one and three passengers and was sometimes regarded as a ladies' vehicle; Anne Elliot is seen in one at the end of *Persuasion*.

High carriages were expensive and provided the best view, but low carriages were more stable. The **phaeton** had four large wheels and is used by Henry Tilney in *Northanger Abbey* and Miss de Bourgh in *Pride and Prejudice*; in 'Love and Freindship', its height helps cause the accident in which two young men are sent 'sprawling in the Dust'. The light one-horse **gig** and the more expensive two-horse **curricle** were used by the single gentleman; see John Thorpe in *Northanger Abbey*, a character much obsessed with horses and carriages. An **Italian chair** was a light one-horse carriage with no top used for short rides and a **buggy** was a small carriage seating one passenger. Coaches could be drawn ostentatiously by six horses but, as they became lighter, this was less common and between one to four horses was the norm.

The **hackney-coach** with two horses was for hire by the mile; the commercial **post-chaise** was used for conveying mail and passengers as speedily as possible. The less affluent took the **stage-coach,** a public transport carriage carrying paying passengers and packages for distances that required a change of horses. For the poorer, there was the **stage wagon,** a slow public coach in which people sat on benches. The **wheelbarrow** was any cheap one-horse carriage; the **whisky** was a speedy version, which could 'whisk' past larger vehicles.

Austen makes absurd demands on her carriages, for example seating nine children and two adults in one vehicle in 'Edgar and Emma'; in 'Love and Freindship' she puts passengers in the **basket**, the back compartment for baggage on the outside of a stage-coach.

CLOTHES

In the 1780s and early 1790s fashionable clothes for both men and women were expensive and elaborate. Common material included **muslin,** which originally came from India through the East India Company but by the later eighteenth century faced competition from a cheaper British-manufactured variety initially produced only in white. Young Jane Austen owned a 'muslin Cloak', mentioned in the dedication of 'Frederic & Elfrida'. **Book-muslin** was fine muslin folded rather like a book for sale. **Cambric** was fine white linen imported from Chambray in France. **Lace** was costly and much prized.

Women's clothes included the **pelisse**, a long cloak often of satin or silk, worn over a dress, and the **bedgown**, a dress worn by day or night. In the 1770s, the woman's **cap** became a **bonnet**, a hat with a small brim often tied with a ribbon beneath the chin and usually of a pale colour. A **net nightcap** was a large cap worn indoors, popular in the earlier 1790s.

Men's clothes, especially **waistcoats** and **breeches**, were patterned and colourful, with stress on modish dark blue and green. **Shoes** were adorned with silver buckles. Shoes of both sexes could be 'capped and heelpeiced', that is, provided with new toe coverings and heels for extended life.

Occasionally Jane Austen added later sartorial details to a tale to bring it up to date, for example the **Regency walking dress** inserted into 'Catharine'; this detail must have been added after the Regency began in 1811.

COSMETICS

These were much used in the mid to late eighteenth century. The desired female complexion was pale and would be enhanced with white lead, which also covered pox marks. **Red paint** (rouge) was applied to give a youthful contrast, but was less fashionable from the 1780s onwards. Patches provided beauty spots. Some cosmetics used plant products, but many included lead and mercury which, when used over time, could become toxic.

Hair powder (made from starch or flour mixed with ground-up bones) was employed by men and women of the higher ranks; it became less common after 1795 when fashions changed and users had to pay an annual tax of a guinea, but the habit was continued by some professional men, especially lawyers (see *The Watsons* in *Later Manuscripts*), and for manservants in wealthier houses. **Pomatum** (ointment) was used to control hair and wigs.

COUNTRY HOUSES

Larger country houses had **deer parks** both for hunting and for display. Many had expensive **hothouses** or heated greenhouses for cultivating delicate plants and dessert fruit; in *Northanger Abbey* and *Sense and Sensibility* they are used as markers of extravagance. The **horsepond** was used for watering and washing horses and also for ducking parish offenders. Along with the **pigsty**, it was smelly and would usually be placed far from the mansion.

See **Gilpin** below for description of the picturesque movement that affected landscape gardeners employed to improve the grounds of country houses in the eighteenth century. Newly fashioned **grounds** should eschew the symmetry and formality of earlier times, as described in the madly ordered estate in 'Evelyn'; instead they should provide vistas for picturesque viewing. In 'The History of England' Austen comically suggests that Henry VIII may have abolished the monasteries primarily to cause **ruins** and so foster the picturesque in the English landscape, so admired by Gilpin. Landowners lacking such ruins often created fake ones to enhance their grounds and view, like the owner of Blaize Castle, the object of desire for deluded Catherine Morland in *Northanger Abbey*.

Inside the house, the **drawing room**, once close to the bedroom, tended to be where ladies congregated to gossip and drink tea, while the **dining room** was a more masculine space, associated after dinner with men drinking alcohol. A **closet** was a small room usually adjoining a bedroom where ladies could be private. In the later eighteenth century, among the upper ranks **dressing rooms** were increasingly used as sitting rooms, primarily by ladies spending their mornings indoors, often in informal loose clothing or 'dishabille'. Some country houses had private **theatres** for amateur theatricals, but most made do with modifying barns and rooms in the house, as happens in *Mansfield Park*, to Sir Thomas's horror.

Two movable items popular in the mid eighteenth century were the **sofa**, supposedly originating in the east and often covered by a fine carpet, and the **harpsichord** (see also the beginning of *The Watsons* in *Later Manuscripts*), but by the 1790s the pianoforte was largely superseding it.

GILPIN

William Gilpin (1724–1804) was the main theorist of the **picturesque** as a way of looking at landscape as if it were a picture. Such looking and the touring of the wilder parts of Britain associated with it were a craze in late eighteenth-century England. Henry Austen wrote that 'at a very early age' his sister was 'enamoured of Gilpin on the Picturesque', and in 'The History of England' Jane Austen called Gilpin 'one of the first of Men'. His popular theories of the picturesque are behind many of her comic scenes and are referenced repeatedly in the published novels, especially the ones begun in Steventon, *Northanger Abbey*, *Sense and Sensibility* and *Pride and Prejudice*.

Gilpin published many books of tours including the popular *Observations, Relative Chiefly to Picturesque Beauty, Made in the Year 1788, On Several Parts of Great Britain, Particularly the High-Lands of Scotland* (1789). His *Observations on the River Wye and Several Parts of South Wales* (1782) forms the background to Austen's skit, 'A Tour through Wales'.

Touring with Gilpin as guide was primarily associated with the middle ranks. Austen may be mocking rather than admiring the supposed democratic aspect of picturesque looking when in 'Jack and Alice' she describes Lord Harcourt stopping his carriage to allow the lowly postilion to admire a prospect.

HISTORY

Jane Austen's comically 'prejudiced' **'History of England'** mocks serious works by such historians as **David Hume** and **William Robertson**. It is primarily a riposte to **Oliver Goldsmith's** four-volume *The History of England, from the Earliest Times to the Death of George II* (1771) aimed at educating young readers. Goldsmith boasts of his 'impartiality', which Jane Austen disputes; she displays his Protestant prejudices by gleefully declaring her own Stuart Catholic ones. She also highlights Goldsmith's apparent relish for torture and ghastly deaths. The Austens owned a copy of Goldsmith's *History*, in which young Jane Austen wrote scornful marginalia: these are reproduced in the Cambridge edition of *Juvenilia* (2006).

Jane Austen suggests that anyone disagreeing with her ardently expressed opinions had better stop reading her 'History of England', for she admits she writes 'to vent my Spleen *against*, and shew my Hatred *to* all those people whose parties or principles do not suit with mine, and not to give information'. Her 'facts' are primarily anecdotal and taken from fiction, her main source being **Shakespeare's history plays**. These begin with the struggle between Richard II and Henry IV, where Jane Austen also begins her 'History'. In addition to Shakespeare, she uses **Richard Brinsley Sheridan**'s *The Critic* (1779), in which a play-within-a-play dramatises the Elizabethan courtiers Sir Walter Raleigh and Sir Christopher Hatton, and **Nicholas Rowe**'s *The Tragedy of Jane Shore, Written in Imitation of Shakespeare's Style* (1714), still often staged in the 1780s and 1790s. Jane Austen dismisses Rowe's play as a tragedy, so not worth reading. Delamere is a much-admired character in **Charlotte Smith's** novel *Emmeline, or The Orphan of the Castle* (1788); in the 'History', he becomes as 'real' as the

Elizabethan courtier, the Earl of Essex, and the eighteenth-century author, William Gilpin.

Jane Austen was a staunch supporter of the Stuart dynasty and the history is designed to vindicate the bloodline. Regarding the Lancastrians as forerunners of the hated Tudor monarchs, she sides with the Yorkists against them in her depiction of the fifteenth-century civil conflict, the Wars of the Roses. Following the same prejudice, she blames the first Tudor monarch **Henry VII** rather than the Yorkist **Richard III** for killing Richard's nephews, the **Princes in the Tower** – the culprit was (and still is) much debated. Jane Austen sympathises with the executed queens of Henry VIII, Catherine Howard and Anne Boleyn, despite the latter being the mother of 'that pest of society', the Tudor monarch Elizabeth I. Primarily, however, she demands sympathy and justice for the heroine of her 'History', the Stuart **Mary Queen of Scots**, 'one of the first Characters in the World' whom she links to most of the admirable people she describes. Mary was executed in 1587 for plotting against Elizabeth. Jane Austen returns to the contrast between amiable Mary and villainous Elizabeth in 'Catharine, or the Bower'.

In the seventeenth-century Civil Wars, Jane Austen continues with her Stuart bias, robustly supporting the 'martyred' Stuart king, Charles I, grandson of Mary, as well as praising the Cavalier followers of his son Charles II. Inevitably she denigrates the opponents of monarchy, the Parliamentarians and Puritans under Oliver Cromwell, blaming them alone for the 'distresses' of the wars.

LITERARY AND THEATRICAL ALLUSIONS

Passing references to the poets **John Milton** and **Alexander Pope** appear in the three volumes, while **Edmund Spencer**'s Bower of Bliss from his long allegorical poem *The Faerie Queene* comically shadows 'Catharine, or the Bower'. In her own 'Ode to Pity', Austen burlesques **William Collins**'s very popular 'Ode to Pity' (1746) with its stock Gothic images and melancholy tone. The eighteenth-century nursery song 'Malbrouck s'en va-t-en guerre' commemorated the **Duke of Marlborough**'s exploits in the War of the Spanish Succession. 'Yes, I'm in love…' alludes to the first line of a rather misogynous light poem, 'The Je ne scai Quoi, A Song' by **William Whitehead** (1715–1785). Henry Crawford also refers to it in *Mansfield Park*.

Novels are the frequent butt of jokes. **Samuel Richardson**'s long epistolary novel *Sir Charles Grandison* (1753) presents the perfect gentleman in domestic and romantic settings. Austen much appreciated the novel and learnt from its skill at intermingling conversations, but she burlesqued its presentation of fastidious sentimental manners and, in the depiction of the amazing Charles Adams in 'Jack and Alice', laughed at the admiration lavished on its idealised hero, the 'best of Men'.

Proper appreciation of **Goethe**'s sentimental novel of hopeless passion, *The Sorrows of Young Werther* (1774), became a touchstone of sensibility in the late eighteenth century: in 'Love and Freindship' a sentimental character wears blue in imitation of Werther. **Laurence Sterne**'s comic masterpiece of procrastination, **Tristram Shandy** (1760–67), lies behind the scene in 'Love and Freindship' where characters long to hear who is knocking but fail to open the door.

The clichés and commonplaces of popular sentimental and Gothic romances used by writers such as **Sarah Fielding**, **Sophia Lee**, **Frances Burney** and **Charlotte Smith** are repeatedly mocked by Jane Austen in exaggerated language and adventures; 'Catharine, or the Bower' refers to the opening chapters of Smith's five-volume *Ethelinde, or the Recluse of the Lake* (1789) set in picturesque Grasmere in the Lake District, while **Hannah More**'s didactic novel *Coelebs in Search of a Wife* (1809), especially disliked by Austen, was a later addition.

Shakespeare is alluded to throughout the volumes, especially the tragedies and *Henry VIII*, then thought to be entirely by Shakespeare. **Hannah Cowley**'s *Which is the Man* (1783) is mentioned in 'The Three Sisters': Austen's stylish cousin Eliza de Feuillide proposed the comedy for acting in the Austens' converted barn at Christmas 1787, herself playing the spirited heroine Lady Bell Bloomer.

Plays referred to in 'Love and Freindship' include **Richard Steele's** *The Tender Husband* (1705) in which the heroine Bridget dislikes her common name and favours a more polysyllabic one, and *The Clandestine Marriage* (1766) by **George Colman the Elder** and **David Garrick. William Thomas Lewis** (c. 1746–1811) and **John Quick** (1748–1831), mentioned at the end of the tale, were comic actors in London's Covent Garden theatre.

Some plays referred to such as 'The travelled Man', now unknown, might be lost comedies written by Jane or her brother James; if so, the reference underlines the collective family context in which all the items in the notebooks were composed.

MARRIAGE

Between the ages of sixteen and eighteen a girl in the upper ranks endured the ritual of **coming out**, in which her family, in the feminist Mary Wollstonecraft's disapproving words, 'bring to market a Marriageable miss'. In *Pride and Prejudice* Lady Catherine de Bourgh is appalled to discover all five Bennet girls are 'out' with none yet married.

Marriages were often arranged among families although with the consent of the young people. Unions between cousins were common; the notion initially worried Sir Thomas Bertram in *Mansfield Park* when taking a poor niece into his family. After a gentleman had offered for a lady's hand and been accepted, financial **settlements** had to be made, including arrangements for **pin money**, a small allowance given to a wife for her use during her husband's life, and a **jointure**, an annuity paid after his death and based on property or money brought into a marriage by the wife.

To marry well a girl needed a substantial **portion** or dowry from her family. Without it, one expedient was for the young woman to find a husband in **India**, especially in the north-east province of Bengal where many single Englishmen, often rather older than the young women, were working for the East India Company and in want of English wives.

Marriage was regulated by the **Marriage Act** of 1753, instituted to prevent runaway weddings, especially with heiresses. The act excluded Scotland; hence the Scottish border town of **Gretna Green** became useful for eloping couples escaping parents and wishing to avoid the usual requirement of having banns read out in the local church on three successive Sundays. It is of course absurd for people already in Scotland to be rushing to Gretna Green, as happens in 'Love and Freindship'. A **Licence** from a bishop allowed a couple to marry in their parish church after a week, without banns being read. The rare **Special Licence** from the Archbishop of Canterbury allowed a wedding to be held anywhere, without banns. The method was largely confined to the titled and politically powerful; hence in *Pride and Prejudice* Mrs Bennet's desire for Elizabeth and Darcy to be married in this way.

As a clergyman's daughter, Austen was well aware of Church regulations. Many of the unions described in these childhood writings are illegal, without licence or banns. In 'Lesley Castle', Lesley becomes a Roman Catholic and so is able to annul his marriage through a papal bull or edict and marry again, although not in England.

A married woman had status over a spinster, as Mrs Elton points out in *Emma*. A new stepmother as a wife would take precedence at the dining table over her husband's daughter, whatever their respective ages.

MONEY

Jane Austen enjoyed imagining huge sums of money. In 'Henry and Eliza' the young people spend £12,000, an amount exceeding Mr Darcy's supposed large income in *Pride and Prejudice*. The 'eight Million' mentioned in 'A letter from a Young Lady' would make the owner the richest man in England while the large sum of £5,000 a year is called a 'Small pittance'. At the other end of the financial scale, 14 shillings is a ludicrously small sum to compensate for a murder.

Occasionally more realistic sums are mentioned: Mr Watts in 'The Three Sisters' is aware that his £3,000 a year could not support the desires of his greedy betrothed and a man with a few hundred a year in 'A Collection of Letters' should not aspire to an heiress. In *Sense and Sensibility* the Dashwood ladies have an income of £500 between them and it is considered insufficient for living or entertaining in any style.

State lotteries were established in the late seventeenth century by the Bank of England to raise revenue and fund military projects; they were popular throughout the eighteenth century. Tickets were expensive but could bring rich rewards to the lucky winner.

An **annuity** could be given to a relative, retired employee or freind and would consist of the annual return on capital, which ceased with the death of the recipient. In *Sense and Sensibility*, Mrs John Dashwood laments that people in receipt of an annuity always live 'for ever'.

If a person fell into **debt** and could not pay creditors, goods from the house would be seized and sold; the execution would be enforced by Officers of Justice. London's King's Bench prison was primarily used for debtors.

A **bad guinea** (21 shillings) was a forged one.

NAMES OF PLACES AND PEOPLE

Many place names such as Pammydiddle are invented for comic effect; others like **Buckinghamshire, Berkshire, Bedfordshire, Overton, Devizes** and the **Vale of Usk** are real towns, villages, counties and regions. Far-flung places are yoked together or given unlikely attributes. **Perth** in Scotland and **Sussex** in the south of England are united in 'Lesley Castle'. **The Isle of Wight** is off the Hampshire coast near **Calshot Castle** on the mainland, one of Henry VIII's defensive artillery forts; the narrow nearby channel is unlikely to experience a storm big enough to wreck a ship as suggested in 'Evelyn'.

Portland Place, Portman Square, Queen's Square, Brook Street, Grosvenor Street and **Sackville Street** refer to actual **London** locations, often with absurd embellishments – no one in Portland Place could have extensive grounds. **Bond Street** was known for its fashionable shops, including milliners which sold caps, hats, trimmings and other accessories. **Vauxhall Gardens** was the oldest of London's commercial pleasure gardens, with walks, concerts and refreshments on offer. Newer **Ranelagh** was more expensive; it boasted a rotunda, lighting effects and fireworks.

By the later eighteenth century, the spa of **Tunbridge Wells** was giving way to rivals **Bath, Bristol Hot Wells** and **Cheltenham**. Like London, these **spas** had their popular seasons. The Bath season lasted from autumn to early spring and would be at its height in February; Bristol was more appreciated in the summer, from early April to the end of September. Meanwhile **seaside resorts** were becoming more and more attractive to rich invalids as well as the idle and leisured. **Scarborough** in Yorkshire was one of the earliest to be developed; **Brighthelmstone** (Brighton) on the south coast was increasingly fashionable after the Prince of Wales patronised it in the 1780s.

Beyond the historical characters in 'The History of England', real people are mentioned in 'Catharine, or the Bower': **William Pitt the Younger** (1759–1806), Prime Minister from 1783 to 1801, then again from 1804 to 1806, and the **Lord Chancellor**, who presided over the House of Lords and judiciary.

For names of fictional characters such as Strephon, Chloe and Corydon, Austen mined the **pastoral romance** tradition. When using common female names, she oscillated between the original and its **variants and diminutives**: Matilda/Maud, Sarah/Sally, Margaret/Peggy, Catharine or Catherine/Kitty ('Catharine, or the Bower' could as well be called 'Kitty, or the Bower'), Arabella/Belle, Susan/Sukey and Sophia/Sophy. Likewise for men: Ned for Edward, Sam for Samuel and Jem for James. As with places, so with characters, Jane Austen enjoyed **eccentric or unusual names** such as Wilhelminus, Robertus, Godfrey, Elfrida and Jezalinda. In this volume we have preserved Austen's idiosyncrasies of naming. In 'Catharine, or the Bower', the heroine is sometimes 'Catharine', sometimes 'Catherine' and often 'Kitty'. The name of Percival alternates with 'Peterson' and 'P'.

PROFESSIONS

The acceptable professions for younger sons of the gentry were the Church, the army or navy, and the law. A **living** in the Church of England included a residence – vicarage or rectory – and an income from parish tithes (a tenth of landowners' annual production, usually converted into money) and the farming of glebe land. Much discussion of the burden of tithes occurred during Austen's time (see 'Plan of a Novel' in *Later Manuscripts*). Livings varied in value, some providing an income of over £1,000 and others nearer £100 (see the very different values for livings mentioned in *Sense and Sensibility* and *Mansfield Park*). **Curates** who deputed for regular clergymen were notoriously low paid, sometimes receiving as little as £40–50 a year.

Boys intending to become officers entered the **navy**, usually by attending the Royal Naval Academy at Portsmouth, as Jane's naval brothers Francis and Charles did. Tuition was free for sons of naval officers but otherwise cost about £75 per annum for tuition and expenses. Naval **chaplains** ranked lower than commissioned officers.

Although the **Law** is comically involved in the childhood writings, no lawyers are presented in the finished novels.

SOCIAL CLASS

Jane Austen delights in mocking the rigidities of class, the distinctions in behaviour, marriage, style of living and possessions. **Aristocrats** disapproved of alliances with commoners and the **gentry** disapproved of those with merchants and tradesmen or other social inferiors. Here Austen describes romantic couplings that are wildly improbable in class terms: one gentlewoman elopes with a coachman and another with a butler. Meanwhile her ladies make confidantes and freinds of cooks and other servants. Sometimes her gentry live in vast houses but just as often in accommodation more suited to poor workers. They stay in tents made of old blankets and travel by means usually confined to the lowest orders. They eat coarse peasant food like crow, hashes and toasted cheese and make their own pies. In *Pride and Prejudice* Mrs Bennet, originally middle class but now a gentleman's wife, is keen to stress her daughters have nothing to do in the kitchen.

Some of Austen's characters seek to humiliate inferiors. The gentry sneer at **tradesmen and merchants** who live above their shops and rent out upper storeys to poor lodgers. They are eager to keep sartorial distinctions between themselves and servants who should dress humbly, as the housekeeper of Sotherton insists in *Mansfield Park*. In Letter the Third of a 'A Collection of Letters', an upper-class lady humiliates an inferior as the daughter supposedly of a grocer or bookbinder, considered tradesmen, where the inferior insists her father was actually a wine merchant, ranked slightly above. Neither merchants nor tradesmen were part of polite society.

Outside the gentry and merchant classes are an array of **servants** and **outsiders**: cooks, butlers, coachmen and ostlers, teachers at Dame schools charging two pence a week, charwomen hired for odd work in the kitchen and paid and fed badly, **poachers** and **gipsies**. Poachers on landowners' estates were deterred from taking game by steel man-traps laid in the grounds. Regarded as threatening outsiders, gipsies were treated harshly; recall Harriet Smith's fright at meeting some on the road in *Emma*.

SOCIAL CUSTOMS

Genteel life consisted of established rituals of visiting, dining and tea-drinking. The main meal of the day, **dinner**, was usually eaten around 3 or 4 o'clock with the host couple at head and foot of the table; in fashionable and metropolitan circles dinner was often served much later. **Tea** was often drunk several hours after dinner in the late afternoon or evening, although it could also be drunk following the meal. When dinner was early, **supper** could be a substantial meal, but when dinner was fashionably late, it became a light late-night snack.

To **stew soup** was to make soup by simmering meat and bones in water. **Jellies** were leftover meat preserved in jelly. A **whipped syllabub** was a cold dessert made with milk or cream, sherry, sugar and lemons, whisked together. Pullets or young hens would need to be **drawn** or eviscerated in preparation for cooking. Partridges and other **game** were **hung** for a time to give additional flavour. If hung too long, they became 'stinking', like the fish of Southampton in 'Love and Freindship'.

Men and women joined together for **dancing** and meeting at public **assemblies** held at a local hall or inn or at **private balls** in grand country and town houses where the genteel and chaperoned young could **dance** while their elders **played cards or gossiped**. A **rout** was a reception or evening party. **Masquerades** or **masked balls** allowed people of different ranks to socialise, especially if wearing a **domino**, a gown, usually black, which enveloped and hid the body; hence moralists deplored them as unruly and erotically dangerous.

Duelling was much less common in the later than in the earlier eighteenth century, when a gentleman was supposed to fight a duel if his honour were impugned. A middle-aged father would not usually be expected to challenge a daughter's recalcitrant lover – hence the comedy of Mrs Bennet's imagining her husband duelling in *Pride and Prejudice*. An actual duel occurs between Colonel Brandon and Willoughby in *Sense and Sensibility*, but it is inconclusive and not described.